W9-AHC-740

Crafting Authentic Voice

PROPERTY OF
CENTENNIAL DISTRICT #28JT

LYNCH MEADOWS SCHOOL

PROPERTY OF
CENTENNIAL DISTRICT #28JT

LYNCH MEADOWS SCHOOL

Tom Romano
Miami University

Crafting Authentic Voice

HEINEMANN
Portsmouth, NH

Heinemann
A division of Reed Elsevier Inc.
361 Hanover Street
Portsmouth, NH 03801–3912
www.heinemann.com

Offices and agents throughout the world

© 2004 by Tom Romano

All rights reserved. No part of this book may be reproduced in any form or by any electronic or mechanical means, including information storage and retrieval systems, without permission in writing from the publisher, except by a reviewer, who may quote brief passages in a review.

The author and publisher wish to thank those who have generously given permission to reprint borrowed material:

"A Minor Bird" and excerpt from "Stopping by Woods on a Snowy Evening" from *The Poetry of Robert Frost* edited by Edward Connery Lathem. Copyright 1923, 1928, © 1969 by Henry Holt and Company. Copyright 1951, 1956 by Robert Frost. Reprinted by permission of Henry Holt and Company, LLC.

"Poems" from *Blue Like the Heavens: New and Selected Poems* by Gary Gildner. Copyright © 1984. Reprinted by permission of the University of Pittsburgh Press.

"The Day School Gives Out" by Tom Romano from *English Journal* 79(9), November 1990. Copyright © 1990 by the National Council of Teachers of English. Reprinted with permission.

"I Am What I Am" by Rosario Morales from *Getting Home Alive* by Aurora Levins Morales and Rosario Morales. Copyright © 1986 by Aurora Levins Morales and Rosario Morales. Published by Firebrand Books.

"Saturday Night" from *Blending Genre, Altering Style* by Tom Romano. Copyright © 2000 by Tom Romano. Published by Boynton/Cook, a subsidiary of Reed Elsevier, Inc., Portsmouth, NH. Reprinted with permission.

Excerpts of "Crafting Authentic Voice" by Tom Romano in *Voices from the Middle* 3(2), April 1996. Copyright © 1982 by the National Council of Teachers of English. Reprinted with permission.

"The Teacher" by Tom Romano from *English Journal* 71(3), March 1982. Copyright © 1982 by the National Council of Teachers of English. Reprinted with permission.

Library of Congress Cataloging-in-Publication Data
Romano, Tom.
Crafting authentic voice / Tom Romano.
p. cm.
Includes bibliographical references.
ISBN 0-325-00597-4 (pbk.)
1. English language—Rhetoric. 2. Exposition (Rhetoric). I. Title.
PE1429.R47 2004
808'.042—dc22 2003018516

Editor: Lisa Luedeke
Production: Lynne Reed
Cover design: Judy Arisman
Typesetter: Argosy
Manufacturing: Steve Bernier

Printed in the United States of America on acid-free paper
11 12 13 14 RRD 6 7 8 9 10

For
Nancy McDonald
my sister
who has crossed chasms

A Minor Bird

I have wished a bird would fly away,
And not sing by my house all day;

Have clapped my hands at him from the door
When it seemed as if I could bear no more.

The fault must partly have been in me.
The bird was not to blame for his key.

And of course there must be something wrong
In wanting to silence any song.

—Robert Frost

Contents

Part I

The Delight and Dilemma of Voice

Antipasto

Stopping By Woods After a Bronchoscopy

Three rounds of antibiotics had failed to stop the cough that had been my companion more than a month. Our family doctor referred me to a pulmonologist, who suspected pneumonia and ordered a bronchoscopy. I wasn't keen on missing a day's teaching this close to semester's end, but the cough had worsened. I checked into the hospital as an outpatient.

A bronchoscopy is a painless procedure, the pulmonologist said. I would be made sleepy through an intravenous anesthetic, then he would insert a bronchoscope down my throat into my lungs. Through this flexible tube with a light source at its end, the doctor would squirt liquid into my lungs, give it time to mingle with the tissue, then draw it out. This "washing," as it was called, would be sent away for biopsy.

That word exploded in my mind. Biopsy? Suddenly the persistent cough wasn't just annoying, the fluctuating body temperature not merely uncomfortable. My brother had died of cancer a year and a half earlier. His first wife had died of cancer. My wife was surviving breast cancer. My sister had undergone lung cancer surgery. The word *biopsy* spooked me.

"You know," said Kathy, my registered-nurse wife, "they biopsy tissue for things other than cancer."

The bronchoscopy went smoothly, the procedure itself lasting a mere fifteen minutes. The biopsy later revealed that yes, indeed, I had pneumonia—interstitial pneumonitis, to be exact.

Minutes after the bronchoscopy, I lay in the recovery area, slowly gaining consciousness, sensing both stillness and busy efficiency about me. The only sound was the occasional voice of a nurse. The anesthetic hadn't quite released me. I surfaced and submerged, surfaced and submerged. Kathy stood beside me. I heard my voice begin to speak. I was disembodied, watching myself lying on the gurney. The voice was mine, but also somehow the voice of a stranger. It said, "Whose woods these are I think I know."

There was no stopping me. The entirety of Robert Frost's "Stopping By Woods on a Snowy Evening" rolled forth in my raspy, whispering voice, an expressive raspy, whispering voice, not the monotone I'd once heard Frost use on a recording. When I speak poetry aloud, I try to get the most out of the words, seek to give them meaning through inflection, pauses, and pitch, just the way a good speaker or conversationalist does. I teach students to do the same. Written words represent voice. Breath and sound animate them. I heard my voice rendering the voice of Frost's persona in this most unclassroomlike setting. I drove to the final lines:

> The woods are lovely, dark and deep.
> But I have promises to keep.
> And miles to go before I sleep.
> And miles to go before I sleep.

Since I was a boy I have memorized a number of poems, some inadvertently once I began teaching them. "Stopping By Woods on a Snowy Evening" has been in my head since my first year of teaching in 1971. So after the bronchoscopy, there I lay amid busy nurses and drowsing patients, using my lungs to give voice and meaning to written words, calling forth the little horse, the frozen lake, the snow falling in the dark woods.

Anxiety and fear had rooted deep in me. My sense of much left undone was strong. There were people to love, students to teach, poems and stories and essays to write—miles to go before I slept. My voice had much saying left to do. The voice of Robert Frost had risen from memory to remind me.

1

Reasons to Read

This book is about developing voice in our writing, particularly our expository writing. The best discussion of voice I've ever read occurs in Ralph Fletcher's *What a Writer Needs* (1993). He writes,

> When I talk about voice, I mean written words that carry with them the sense that someone has actually written them. Not a committee, not a computer: a single human being. Writing with voice has the same quirky cadence that makes human speech so impossible to resist listening to. (68)

Voice is the writer's presence on the page, the writer's DNA, as one of my students put it. Sometimes that presence might be indiscernible, like a clean windowpane. Sometimes that presence is raucous and spirited, like a roaring fire—I think of Tom Wolfe's voice in *The Electric Kool-Aid Acid Test* (1968). Sometimes that presence is subdued and sincere, like breakfast in a coffee shop after morning rush. Some writers' presence is aloof and distant, so abstractly intellectual and fraught with jargon that their words are impenetrable, like an unyielding brick wall. I've read voices that are windy and cluttered with wordiness and qualifications. I've read voices riddled with spelling aberrations, nonstandard usage, and incorrect punctuation, yet the meaning of the words was unmistakable, the presence of the writer undeniable.

I've used the word *presence* for *voice*. This bespeaks the unease in some of academia about the term *voice*. Darsie Bowden, in *The Mythology of Voice* (1999), writes that voice is a worn-out metaphor, that it was useful once "in the movement away from current-traditional rhetoric," but its "particular historical moment" has passed (viii). She suggests that women's studies offers alternatives to voice, like "web" or "fluid" or "embrace" or "the dance" (105–17). Peter Elbow has used the word *juice* in place of *voice* (1981, 286). A writer friend of mine has of late been using the word *stance*. He refers to a writer's stance in a piece of writing.

Voice, juice, presence. Web, embrace, stance. Call it what you will. In this book I'm sticking with *voice*, except when I think other words will better fit the spirit of what I'm writing.

Style used to be the word to describe the particular ways that writers wrote. Don Murray, that venerable writing teacher-memoirist-poet-columnist-fiction writer, prefers the word *voice* to the word *style*. *Style*, he says, "implies something can be bought off the rack, something that can be easily imitated" (1998, 152). I'm sympathetic to this view, especially when I think of the style of the five-paragraph you-know-what and how that style has skewed voice, blocked energy, drained juice. So numbing and disappointing is it to read such essays that some teachers have called them "voiceless." Oh, I think such writing has voice, all right, just as legal documents, insurance forms, and educational pronouncements have voice. The voice, though, is not one most of us can read for long without our eyelids drooping.

I'll use the word *voice*—the sense we have while reading that someone occupies the middle of our mind, filling the space with the sound of a voice, the sense we have while writing that something is whispering in our ear. There is a human quality to writing, related to its sibling, the spoken word, which survived thousands of years before some distant ancestor made marks on sand or dirt or rock, marks that represented what came out of the mouth when the brain formulated thought, the voice box vibrated, and breath pushed out the vibrations.

Voice does not arise from nothing. It's influenced by much. Our voices are shaped by the places where we learned language—in our parents' arms, at our school desks, in the neighborhood, on playgrounds and streets. In my case, my dad's barroom and bowling alleys had me experimenting with spicy vocabulary by third grade. People we play, work, and socialize with influence our voices.

Reading shapes our written voices, too. Reading can determine how we come to think words should sound on the page. In the register and vocabulary of early British literature that we read in high school? In the staccato cadences of Hemingway? The reasoned, conversational structures of Barbara Kingsolver's nonfiction? Lack of reading can cause us to miss picking up useful words like *vanish, visage, beneath, stealth, chagrin*—any words we more likely encounter in written texts than speech. There are other features of written text we might not pick up without reading, like the skill of sustaining, developing, and elaborating an idea in a monolog that isn't prompted and interrupted by a speaking partner.

Our very personalities shape our voices and determine how and what we put on the page. Are we timid, reticent, circumspect? Verbal, brash, arrogant? Devious, disdainful, suspicious? Any personality traits can work their way into our written language. Or not. Sometimes outward personality works in reverse: the brash, verbal person has trouble eking out a line of writing, or the timid, reticent person uses the safety of writing to romp on the page.

When others talk to me about my writing, they often talk about voice. "Your book was easy to read," they tell me. "It sounds as if you are right there in front of me, explaining and demonstrating what heights my writing can go to." These readers attribute that effect to my voice, which they see as accessible, clear, and companionable.

That's my bias in *Crafting Authentic Voice*. I won't be showing you how to cultivate an erudite, distanced voice, one that is complex, convoluted, unassailable. I'll show you what I know about being vivid on the page. I'll show you what I know about pulling readers in and keeping them reading. I want the writing of my students to be direct, accessible, and clear, capable of connecting emotionally and intellectually with readers. I want that for anyone who writes.

In more than three decades of working with writers of all ages, I've learned to emphasize information in teaching writing. Writers must learn to choose topics that matter to them. They must learn to find places within assignments that activate their passions. I've learned to take students through writing processes, too, not simply make an assignment and designate a due date. I've sought to help students write clearly, succinctly, and vividly with detail, drama, and verve. They know when they've written this way. Sometimes a quiet sureness comes over them. Sometimes they light right up, so transforming is the experience of writing with voice. Maybe the brightest moment for me as a writing teacher occurs when I see students quicken to the power of their voices.

I am a writer but I am not a writer first. I am a teacher first, a teacher who writes and teaches the craft of writing to others. I've done this since 1970. Even before then I was lured by words on paper. Though I don't remember being read to as a child, I loved reading novels as a schoolboy. It naturally followed that in seventh grade during back-to-back, forty-five-minute study halls at the end of the day, a schoolmate and I began writing stories for each other's reading pleasure.

We wrote what we knew about. The material we worked with was right out of reruns of old movies on television. When we were done writing stories about soldiers and war and heroism in which we were the main characters slogging through jungles, flying P-140s, or operating submarines, we traded our writing across the aisle. In the brown atmosphere of those afternoon study halls, above the worn wooden floor, beside the long bank of windows, I found out what it was like for my voice to travel beyond me without speaking. I saw my voice take hold of someone's attention amid the enforced silence of study hall.

That self-sponsored writing and sharing between twelve-year-olds hooked me. In high school in the mid-1960s I continued to enjoy writing, even though the diet there was strictly essays, book reports, and show-me-what-you-know short answers to questions. I saw these writing tasks, however, as chances to show off with language, flaunting the new words I was learning like *demise, implacable*, and *repose*. But despite my pompous diction, the writing itself caused me to lean into the page, discover insight, create logical, connected thought, and come to understanding.

Writing processes were not broken down and taught during my schooling, but all the writing caused me to discover a magic way to be smarter. After I wrote an essay or book report and read it a day later, I found I had more to say. Sometimes I merely added clarifying words, sometimes I thought of a more accurate way to say something, sometimes a new idea announced itself and I rushed to write it down. I was discovering the power and pleasure of revision. I was, as William Stafford put it, "closing with the material" (1986, 65). I used a green-ink pen to revise my blue words written on college-ruled paper. I loved the mixed color and the margins busy with words, phrases, and sentences. After one such fulfilling immersion in revision, I pronounced to friends, "I'm Edgar Allan Romano!"

Oh, the hubris!

Just what a young writer needs.

This book is about voice and about habits of writing that can help you and your students identify, develop, and shape your voices so readers sit up in their chairs, perhaps even read a little faster, so pleasurable is the language rhythm, so interesting and provocative is the meaning, so companionable is the sound of your voice in their heads.

Crafting Authentic Voice is divided into five parts:

Part I: The Delight and Dilemma of Voice
Part II: Qualities of Voice
Part III: Trust the Gush
Part IV: Crafting Authentic Voice
Part V: Voice and Identity

At the beginning of each section is an antipasto, which translates literally from the Italian as "before the meal." Antipasto is the first course that serves as an appetizer. "It is designed to stay hunger pains, whet the appetite, and fill the pause while the pasta water or broth is coming to a boil" (Romagnoli and Romagnoli 1974, 1). Chef Jeff Smith maintains that antipasto "is no light little bit of nibbly but rather a serious display of fine food items that help you prepare for the rest of the meal" (1993, 63). That's what I am shooting for with the stories and poem that serve as antipasti to the five sections of *Crafting Authentic Voice*. A good antipasto is delicious and fulfilling in its own right. It's a serious part of the meal. So don't offend the cook. Read the antipasto before you begin each section.

I often like to read books with short chapters. It makes me feel productive as I fly along, knocking off one chapter after another. *Crafting Authentic Voice* has seventeen chapters under a thousand words. I couldn't make all the chapters short, though. Sometimes I had a lot to say about a topic. But sometimes I could make a point or tell a pertinent story with a few hundred words. And often in such cases, a short chapter is connected by theme or topic to the chapter that comes after or before it.

I take philosophical stances throughout the book, stances about language and grammar and teaching and learning. You'll agree with some. Others you'll oppose. Use my stances to affirm and extend your thinking. Use them to stimulate counterstances. There are practical ideas here, too, ideas about spontaneous written expression and ideas about crafting your writing. I'm hoping that these strategies and techniques will be of immediate use to you in your teaching and writing. You might use the "I Am What I Am" prompt found in Chapters 20 and 22 to launch your students' voices. You might ask students to create parallel language structures to enhance both the rhythm and meaning of their words, as I do in Chapter 23. You might direct students to revise their writing with an eye toward creating a reader-friendly visage on the page (Chapter 38).

I've puzzled about who my audience is in *Crafting Authentic Voice*. In the previous paragraph I addressed teachers. But I also have in mind readers who look at themselves as writers. I have in mind students, too. I look at myself as a mixture of those identities: teacher, writer, student. I write for my job and my pleasure. I teach for my job and my pleasure. And I am ever a student. I learn from what I read and watch and write and listen to. I learn from my students, whom I accompany on their writing journeys. I hope that however you see yourself—as teacher, writer, student, or blend of all three—you take away from my book ideas, teaching strategies, and examples of strong voice that move you and others along in writing.

I've sought to write this book in a voice that keeps you with me until the final word, which matters just as much as the first word and all the words in between. I've tried to create a voice so compelling that it might keep you awake some night longer than you intend. You can decide whether I've succeeded. I've enjoyed the work of writing. And it has been work, no question about it. But it was the sweet work of creating—work that both empties and replenishes mind and spirit. May *Crafting Authentic Voice* quicken your voice and the voices of your students.

2

Voice Lessons

A writer with no voice is no writer at all.

BONNIE NICKLES, College Junior

In 1973 I attended my first professional conference—a creative writing conference at Miami University. I was twenty-four and had just completed my second year teaching high school students. The organizer of the conference was Milton White, my writing teacher two years earlier at Miami. Milton's humanity, linguistic intelligence, sense of humor, and deep knowledge of literature and writing craft made him the best teacher I'd ever had. Milton had published three slim novels and numerous short pieces. Each class we talked about our peers' short stories that we had read on reserve at the King Library. Although I don't remember Milton ever using the word *voice*, he spoke frequently of style. He preferred one of simplicity, directness, and understatement. "Don't hit me over the head, Romano."

One of the conference speakers was Dotson Rader, a hot freelance magazine writer, who had recently published a profile of Josephine Baker, expatriate dancer and singer in France in the 1920s.

Someone asked Rader when he felt confident about something he was writing.

Rader leaned forward, elbows on his knees. Almost reverently, he said, "When I get the voice of the piece."

> Voice is the magical heard quality in writing. Voice is what allows the reader's eyes to move over silent print and hear the writer speaking. Voice is the quality in writing, more than any other, that makes the reader read on, that makes the reader interested in what is being said and makes the reader trust the person who is saying it. We return to the columns, articles, poems, books we like because of the writer's individual voice. Voice is the music of language. (1998, 151)
>
> *Don Murray, Writer, Teacher*

According to Walker Gibson (1969), "voice" made its debut as a metaphor used to refer to something other than passive and active verbs at the Dartmouth Conference in 1966. (1999, 49)

Darsie Bowden, Teacher, Researcher

Voice livens things up. When I read a textbook for a science class, it seems like a machine shooting out facts on the page—it's hard to even imagine a person behind it. I believe that it's OK to think about the writer behind the voice. Crafting voice is necessary in order to write, and for me at least, to make it more interesting.

Annie Masters, College Junior

[Voice] underlies every part of the [writing] process. To ignore voice is to present the process as a lifeless, mechanical act. Divorcing voice from process is like omitting salt from stew, love from sex, or sun from gardening. . . . Voice is the imprint of ourselves on our writing. It is that part of the self that pushes the writing ahead, the dynamo in the process. . . . The voice shows how I choose information, organize it, select the words, all in relation to what I want to say and how I want to say it. The reader says, "Someone is here. I know that person. I've been there, too." (1983, 227)

Don Graves, Teacher, Writer, Researcher

Voice is crucial to me. More so than the actual writing, as without voice, what are you conveying? Your reader won't know anything about you anything about what you're writing you convey nothing. Voice is atmosphere voice is vocabulary voice is form voice is what gives our work its LIFE. Without voice, there is no context no meaning no depth to what we write. Voice is the shadow we leave on the page.

Melissa Asbrock, College Freshman

In the mid-1980s, our high school English department of six was charged with the responsibility of assessing the writing of sophomores. Instead of administering a timed writing prompt to obtain what we thought would be a bogus, one-shot writing sample from each student, we argued successfully to the administration that the most accurate indicator of students' writing ability would come from their writing folders, which they had kept first semester in an intensive, untracked writing workshop. Students chose their best piece of writing, recopied it into a blue book, and submitted it anonymously.

We holistically scored each paper twice. None of us scored papers written by our own students. We designed a rubric of five categories. One category was voice. We had read Murray and Elbow and Macrorie. Four of us had been to the Ohio Writing Project. We heard each other's voices regularly in a writing group we had started. We couldn't conceive of judging the effectiveness of a piece of writing without considering its voice.

I remember Saraliz, a genteel, older colleague from Tennessee, ever open to new learning. Saraliz scored the voice of one paper a 6, the highest rating possible. Her other scores for that paper were 1s and 2s. I recognized the author as one of my students, a young man with Appalachian roots who suffered school against his wishes. Two of Mike's great pleasures were dipping Skoal and listening to Hank Williams Jr. Mike's writing was full of slang, subject-verb disagreements, and nonstandard usage. I understood Saraliz's scoring the paper's voice a 6. If it had anything, the writing had voice, although Mike's "briar" dialect, as it was called in the area, wasn't what we had in mind when we identified voice as a category we wanted to honor and value.

Mike needed much growth and development in his writing, much more immersion in standard, edited English. It was hard to imagine him a 6 in anything. Voice put us in a dilemma. The writing did sound like Mike. His presence in the piece was unmistakable. So a 6 it was. We valued voice so much that we didn't want to let go of it on our rubric. We could live with this occasional dilemma.

> The moment I fell in love with writing was when I realized that I could be myself and write like I was talking to the reader.
>
> *Lisa Hollins, College Junior*

I took our department's holistic scoring rubric for student writing to a workshop with English teachers at a large high school in another state. When they saw voice as a category to holistically score, discontent spread among the participants. Voice is too hard to explain, one teacher argued, too slippery, too messy, too elusive. Others agreed. It's impossible to score voice, ludicrous.

What does voice involve, anyway? they asked.

Others answered: Sentence rhythm.

OK, they said, score that.

Organization.

Score that.

Diction.

Score that. But don't score voice. It's impossible to pin down.

The workshop was rough going. Some teachers remained upset. I had lost credibility by merely suggesting we could score voice as a feature of effective writing. The teachers all valued voice, they said, but they didn't want to include voice as a category on the rubric.

To my mind, what is unnamed is unrecognized, what is unrecognized is unvalued. Voice is made up of many things, but there is a gestalt at work, too. Voice emerges as greater than the sum of its parts.

I returned to graduate school in 1989 to finish my doctorate in reading and writing instruction. In the fall of that year, nine of us graduate students in the program met in a Monday morning seminar at Don Graves' house, three miles outside Durham, New Hampshire. Each Monday I picked up my fellow student, Danling Fu. A native of China, Danling had an incisive mind, a natural inclination for making metaphors, and a penchant for saying words that cut to the bone. Danling had read my first book in addition to my weekly one-pagers, so she knew my writing voice well.

One autumn morning as we drove through New Hampshire woods to Don's house, we talked about graduate school, writing, and voice. "You be careful, Tom," Danling said, "You get this degree and end up sounding like Vygotsky!"

My first college teaching job was at Utah State University. In an orientation for new teachers, experienced professors emphasized the importance of the course syllabus. To avoid problems later, they said, be detailed about requirements, policies, and attendance. I labored over my syllabi. Each ran five to six pages. I spelled out everything I could think of and folded into the text my philosophies of teaching and learning. At forty-two years old, I was no rookie to writing. I wrote my syllabi in the conversational, storytelling voice I'd come to know as my own.

Months later, in her final learning portfolio, one student featured the class syllabus as an artifact. In her cover letter she explained,

> The reason I included this in my portfolio is because I remember being immediately intrigued the first day of class as I read, "I am a little crazy when it comes to class attendance . . . I become agitated. I don't exactly break out in hives, but I am personally affronted." I thought, "Wow, our class syllabus has a voice!"
>
> *Wendy Westra, College Junior*

In a graduate class I taught on site at a high school one hour from Miami University, we read Bill Strong's *Coaching Writing: The Power of Guided Practice* (2001). His chapter titled "Coaching Voice" had us talking at length about our own writing voices and those of authors and our students.

One teacher mentioned how important she thought journal writing was as a way for students to develop their voices. Her sophomores wrote daily in their journals in response to writing prompts about the literature they were reading. In marginal notes and end comments, Arlene wrote back to her students, affirming their thinking, asking questions, trying to nudge, spur, and inspire. "If there is no voice in the writing," Arlene said, "it doesn't make my pen move."

In a writing seminar with Don Murray at the University of New Hampshire, our major writing project was to investigate another means of creative expression and to relate what we learned to writing and the teaching of writing. I researched filmmaking. Each week we wrote one-page, single-spaced papers about our thinking and learning. One-pagers were part of the UNH writing culture in many English and literacy courses. We made copies of these informal, experimental, think pieces and distributed them to class members, so we could be in on each other's thinking.

One week Bruce Ballenger, an accomplished writer in class, said of my one-pagers, "I've never known anyone whose speaking voice so closely matched his writing voice."

No one asked Bruce to explain his comment. I didn't need him to. I was glowing with pride. Years later, though, I was suddenly struck: Speaking voice matching writing voice . . . was that a strength or a limitation?

> There is a chain reaction to what can happen if one person uses her voice and another person chooses to listen.
>
> *Jenny Hartman-Tripp, College Junior*

Near the end of my stay on Martha's Vineyard in the summer of 2001 while teaching in Northeastern University's Summer Institute, I received an email message from one of my graduate advisees in Ohio. Brooke had read a compelling young adult novel about the rape of an adolescent girl, her recovery, and her eventual triumphant return to self. Brooke's mentor teacher for the fall had read the novel, too, and they planned to teach the book in one class. I was delighted to learn of their summer planning. The match between mentor and student teacher was working even before the school year began.

The Martha's Vineyard institute attracted hungry teachers from across the country. My class met from 7:30 to 9:30 each morning; sometimes conferences with students followed. This schedule left me time for my own reading, writing, and Vineyarding. One afternoon my wife and I explored Edgartown, on the east side of the island. We came upon Bickerton and Ripley Books. I immediately thought of Brooke's recommendation, but was hazy about the exact title.

"The book I'm looking for," I told the clerk, "is titled *Voice*, I think. It's a young adult novel."

The clerk checked the database.

"No book titled *Voice*," he said. "You know the author?"

"Anderson," I answered. I wasn't sure that was right, either, but that's the name that offered itself.

"Young adult, you said?"

"Right."

"How about Laurie Anderson's *Speak*?"

Voice? Speak? I delighted at the surprise, and I understood completely. Right folder, wrong file. In my heart there's a close connection between speaking voice and writing voice.

> What we really want to help youngsters learn is how to express ideas of universal value in a personal voice. (1983, 170–71)
>
> *James Moffett, Teacher, Researcher*

3

Email Admissions

I made a number of close friends when I taught at Utah State University from 1991 to 1995. One was poet and essayist Ken Brewer. Ken's most recent book is *Sum of Accidents: New and Selected Poems* (2003). In 2003 Ken became poet laureate of Utah. At USU Ken headed the graduate program in English and a wonderful master's degree called the Theory and Practice of Writing. Graduate students were expected to take courses in writing fiction, poetry, and essays along with literature and composition theory.

When I arrived at USU, Ken had already taught there twenty years. He became a mentor to me in teaching, campus politics, and writing (five of us brought our poetry each Thursday to a luncheon group). When I was building steam to write this book, I wrote an email message to Ken about my topic. Here is our exchange—casual, passionate, sometimes playful words about voice:

> Date: Thur, 9 May 2002
> From: Tom Romano
> Subject: query
> To: Ken Brewer
>
> Ken, I'm embarking on a book about voice. I thought you might have suggestions for reading.
>
> There's an NCTE book titled *Voices on Voice*, which I just read. Made me think and connect a lot.
>
> Your voice in your poetry has become so clear, moving, and accessible over the years, you were a natural for me to think about.

Date: Fri, 10 May 2002
From: Ken Brewer
Subject: RE: query
To: Tom Romano

Tom—Good to hear from you. One of the best things I've ever read on "voice" was a piece by Bakhtin entitled "The Architectonics of the Self" (at least I think that was the title). It made me realize that "voice" is not a constant but a variable—always changing as it collides with everyone and everything around it. As writers, we don't really have a "voice" the way we often talk about it. We teach students to try to create their writing "voice," but what I believe happens is that each piece of writing has the potential for multiple voices based on who reads it. I'm not certain the writer necessarily "creates" the voice of the text willfully. I think as writers we often achieve a voice by accident, and we don't even know what "voice" the various readers will perceive. In a very real sense, the readers actually create a voice for whatever they're reading based more on their own history with language and reading than we writers care to admit. I'm a notoriously slow reader because I pronounce each word in my mind. What this does, though, is to make most texts sound very much like my own voice because I "hear" myself reading it. I impose my own rhythm and pace, my own definitions of words, my own connotations, my own history (not to mention the larger historical contexts in which I have learned language and reading). In short, when I write, everything that I have experienced to that moment makes up my "stance" (a term I've started to use in place of "voice"); and when someone reads what I have written, that person re-constructs the text based upon everything that person has experienced. So the writer and the reader "collide" in the text like plate architectonics and what we call a "voice" is the result of all that complex of variables.

Good grief! I'm obviously interested in this.

Date: Sat, 11 May 2002
From: Tom Romano
Subject: RE: query
To: Ken Brewer

While I was at USU, we should have had a nonrace in slow reading. I'm a tedious reader too, saying, as you do, every word in my mind. This slows me down terribly when I'm reading the work of others—or the "reports" of others, for God's sake. But I do think the practice for some time now—

40 years?—has made me conscious of creating an identity on the page. Sometimes, however, with all the reading demanded of me, I think I am in the wrong profession. I am acutely aware, however, when some paper, report, or meeting minutes are poorly written, since I'm slogging through it a word at a time, trying to make music out of first blurt verbiage.

You bring up a good point, though: the reader. I have colleagues who love reading what I write. I have other colleagues who dismiss out of hand what I write.

I'm concerned about my reader having a pleasurable experience on the page when they read my writing. Maybe it is because I want a pleasurable experience in the writing. Would it be terrible of me to say that I care more about the language than the ideas? That's not entirely true, I guess. Language and meaning are part and parcel. But sometimes I wonder when I read essays by ________, for example, if he was more concerned about the ideas that he abstractly had in his head than he was about the language in which he purported to communicate with others.

Date: Sat, 11 May 2002
From: Ken Brewer
Subject: RE: query
To: Tom Romano

Tom—I'm hoping that a new edition of the LAKE'S EDGE book will be available by the Advanced Utah Writing Project this summer at Bear Lake. The focus is on nature writing. LAKE'S EDGE has some poems in it that I would call "nature" poems, though I seldom write about "nature" exclusive of people—probably because I don't believe in such exclusivity (damn, I'm not sure I've ever used that word in my own writing before). See, I agree with you about the focus on language over idea and I think I often do that. I suppose the ideal would be a mix of the two that is so complete they become intrinsic (damn, "exclusivity" and "intrinsic" in the same email message—this is fun).

4

Two Bands

One evening during the 1995 NCTE convention in San Diego, friends and I went to Croce's in the Gas Lamp District. Croce's served food but most prominently featured two bars for music. In the first bar, adjoining the restaurant, near the entrance, a Latino jazz band played. Lead guitar, piano, maracas, drums, bongos. They played a driving, Latin-rhythmed jazz, urgent and upbeat. In no time, the music was bumping through your nervous system, and your feet were tapping, your shoulders rolling. I caught sight of my face in the mirror behind the bar. I was smiling broadly, my eyebrows raised in delight. The band made you feel that good. They created one sound—an energetic, nonstop, head-bobbing groove. The singular voices of drums, bongos, guitar, maracas, and piano sublimated themselves to one collective, irresistible musical voice.

One door down was the other Croce music bar, where a wonderfully raunchy, Chicago-style blues band played. Male lead singer and sometime lead guitarist, bass guitar, drums, harmonica, organ, saxophone, and two female backup singers who periodically took the lead. This band got you rocking slowly in your seat and smiling at the ornery humor of the lyrics. Customers packed the small dance floor. Like the Latino band, these musicians created one sound—this one a painfully sweet I-been-wronged-baby-and-it's-oh-so-bad. But within their collective sound, individual voices stood out. The lead singer passed the spotlight off to the sax player, whose expert fingering made you think of Charlie Parker and pain and strain about to burst from all the volume and velocity poured into his horn. The harmonica player took his turn. He curled his hands 'round the instrument, playing right up against the mike, his breath doing the ferocious work of making music, keeping it going both on the exhale and the inhale. He wore sunglasses, but you knew his eyes were closed.

We had a great evening, John, Renee, Katy, and I. We liked both bands, but I liked the blues band better. I liked the individual voices that broke from the group—always eventually coming back and fitting into their collective sound—

but for a few minutes each musician, alone, expressing musical ideas and personal passion within the tradition of American blues. Their voices were distinctive. Nobody blew a sax quite like that sax player. Nobody looked quite like that lead singer so clean-cut in a startling white shirt over his smooth brown skin and close-cropped curly hair. His voice rose and fell, sputtered and crooned. He rolled his eyes at a lyrical joke; he crunched together his eyebrows when he reached for something emotional or physically difficult.

It was a night for English teachers who appreciated all kinds of voices in many combinations.

Part II
Qualities of Voice

Antipasto

Poems

I sent my mother copies of my poems in print
to show her I was not a complete failure
and could do something besides
write dirty stories, and she was so happy
she replied with a poem of her own
about her heart waiting for spring and the beautiful
blue sky and some other lovelies
I don't remember, without calling it a poem
but you could tell that's what it was
because she lined it all out. The prettiest part
of her letter, however, was the end
where she said in her own true voice
"but mainly I can't wait for spring
because then my old man can get
to his garden and won't be bellyaching—
Oh he'll track in dirt and his hands
will never be clean and his breath
you can bet will be one big onion
once they get ripe, but it makes you
feel so good in your bones and it's all free!"

—*Gary Gildner*

5

Qualities of Voice

Information. Narrative. Perception. Surprise. Humor. They are balled into one when it comes to qualities of writing that make an accessible, distinctive voice, which in turn makes for good reading. In *Writing: Teachers and Children at Work*, Don Graves reports on a twelve-year-old boy in an urban school who wrote of his teacher: "When Mrs. Bell yelled, everyone's ass tightened a little bit" (1983, 205).

My mind lights right up. The information the boy delivers is a vital part of the classroom culture. He swiftly communicates the respect, fear, and awe that Mrs. Bell inspired. The boy's honesty is unflinching. His succinct, street-savvy sentence offers plot: Mrs. Bell yells; asses tighten. The tension promises conflict. The boy's perception surprises me, makes me more attentive, and creates humor as I continue reading with an inward smile.

In the next five chapters I will discuss these qualities of voice: information, narrative, perception, surprise, and humor.

6

Information Please

The best shot writers have to attain voice begins with information that absorbs them. "Find the material," says John Updike, "and the voice will take care of itself." Don Graves says that "[w]riters who do not learn to choose topics wisely lose out on the strong link between voice and subject" (1983, 21).

I resonate to the words of Updike and Graves. I know how passionate, committed, and driven I have become when I've chosen topics of burning interest: a letter to a high school girlfriend when I felt her slipping away from me, an article about teaching writing for *Voices from the Middle*, a poem about children and their metaphorical use of language.

After a recent workshop, a teacher came to me and said, "I need to get stirred up about writing." That isn't hard to do if the topic is important to you, if the information you have to explore and share is interesting.

In *The Right to Write* (1998), Julia Cameron has a chapter titled "Stakes." What's at stake, she asks, in the writing you do? Why should anyone care about the topic? Why should you care? If the stakes are not significant, chances are that your writing won't be compelling, the voice won't be strong and urgent. I think of things I've written when the stakes were high:

That letter to keep the girlfriend.

A proposal to gain a spot at a professional conference.

A personal statement of my professional accomplishments that accompanied my vita and was read by Promotion and Tenure Committee members.

My dissertation.

A eulogy for my mother.

A letter of recommendation for a former student.

A column for the local newspaper about Milton White, my beloved writing teacher at Miami University, a piece in which I sought to capture personal characteristics of his teaching that had been missing from the newspaper obituary.

The stakes were clear in these pieces. Love, prestige, professional advancement, money, education, grief and pride, responsibility and fondness. But how about the expressive writing I've done, the times I wrote about information for my eyes only that was not going out to another audience? What was at stake in that writing?

I wrote a poem when I was eighteen—my first—several months after the girlfriend I wrote the letter to broke up with me (sometimes the writing works, sometimes it doesn't). I didn't send the poem to her. I didn't turn it in for credit to a teacher. No one, in fact, but me ever laid eyes on it for twenty-one years. What was at stake in writing that poem?

Plenty, I think. At stake was the articulation of grief and longing and regret. I had to live with myself for the rest of my life. These feelings were mine. I couldn't reject them. I had been self-conscious and inward about the breakup, saying nothing, becoming stoic. The poem let me say those emotions, express that pain and melancholy. I lived them, I owned them.

In 1973 I began to keep a journal. For the next twelve years I was diligent about that writing, tried strategies and rhetorical moves in it that were suggested by Ken Macrorie, Donald Murray, and Peter Elbow. What was at stake in the information that went into those journals, that most egocentric of writing places? Again, I say plenty was at stake. Mainly, my intellectual self-respect. Into those journals went my perceptions about teaching, gardening, loving and learning to be a husband, politics and sports and relationships and fathering and films and books and people I'd just met and people I'd known years earlier. Often I simply wrote down events that had happened, wrote them in the fullness of their detail and drama. By being specific about those events, I came to better understand them.

Because I was trying to tell the truth about things that mattered to me, I found that it was "almost impossible to be honest and boring at the same time" (Cameron 1998, 139). It was my own integrity that was on the line in that journal writing. I tried to be precise and clear. I tried not to fool myself. And later—after I'd started to think about reaching others with my writing—the journal writing proved to be a seedbed where I first wrote arguments, scenes, passages, and metaphors I later used in poems and stories and books. These publications shaped my identity as a teacher and writer.

Bottom line, a lot was at stake in that journal, even more than I realized until this moment.

How about students? What stakes are they writing for? They write for a grade. They write to pass a proficiency test. They write to avoid embarrassment in front of peers. Important enough goals, I suppose. But I'm after more. One goal I have as a teacher is that students begin to see intellectual self-respect as high stakes in their writing lives.

Writing process pedagogy has been driven by the power of topic choice. Let students choose their own topics, and they will write from a core of knowledge that gives their writing authority and voice. How, though, do our students tap into the power of topic choice to propel their voices when they are assigned what to write about? With my students, that's sometimes 100 percent of their writing. Write about this novel or that economic theory or this historical incident or that scientific experiment. How do they create compelling writing about such topics? How do they write with voice?

Assigned topics aren't necessarily voice blockers. Teachers can make topics more malleable by leaving room for students to make topics personal and relevant within the framework of the assignment. For example, each year I ask my methods students to write about a piece of literature they have had a significant relationship with. That seems to be enough constraint to set them free. Students have written about children's books, classic novels, poems, plays, song lyrics, young adult novels, biblical verses. Almost without exception these literature relationship papers, as I call them, have been absorbing for students to write and interesting for me to read (Romano 1998). There is room in such an assignment for students to move around, to roll their shoulders, to meld narrative and analysis, to make the assignment their own, and to put their personal stamp on it.

Assigned topics and authentic voice are not mutually exclusive. William Zinsser maintains that those who write and expect to reach an audience should "convey a zest for what they are writing about" (1998, xi). That's the position students are in. They must reach an audience outside themselves, in most cases, the teacher.

I write plenty of pieces of my own choosing, but a fair amount of my writing is dictated by others. I can get passionate and voiceful about a wide variety of topics, some of them the damnedest things: (1) I'm railroaded into chairing a committee that explores the future of my department and makes recommendations. Eight colleagues and I meet biweekly for a year and a half. The responsibility of drafting the report falls to me. I work with our mutual ideas, many of them about parts of our work I have little to do with. But I care about the department. I care about our work. I care about language. So I am motivated to write the report in the most direct and vivid way I can. (2) I am on the department's Promotion and Tenure Committee. We have recommended a valued colleague for both. The dean agrees with us but is dissatisfied with our letter of evaluation and recommendation. She demands a new one. I take the lead and write with everything I've got, seeking clarity and urgency in marshalling the colleague's data that will make a convincing case for tenure and promotion. My department chair tweaks and adjusts the letter. Others on the committee see ways to strengthen it. The writing is pressured, time-constrained, and satisfying.

I urge you to make your writing assignments flexible so that students can make them their own and bring both personal and formal education together. And for you and your students—whether you choose the topic or it is chosen for you—immerse yourself in the information. Pay attention. Learn. Gather data. This will give you an investment in what you are writing. Then use your voice to write with zest, so readers quicken to the information you offer.

7

The Appeal of Narrative

That zest Zinsser writes about can often be added through narrative, which appeals to the storytelling bent in all of us. In *Coaching Writing*, Bill Strong writes, "A mind without stories is a mind awhirl, voiceless and frightened and alone" (2001, 102).

The quote is certainly true for me. I'm a narrative creature. Through telling stories I experience the power of my voice and come to understand what the stories mean. Give me your best abstract thinking and generalizations, and I do not comprehend them in a meaningful way until I hang a story on them.

Here is what I mean: Miami's much smaller regional, two-year campuses have open enrollment. Miami's main campus in Oxford does not. It admits about 30 percent of the students who apply. When students come to Oxford from the regional campuses to finish their degrees, they frequently feel that they don't fit in. These students are often older than the typical twenty-year-olds I teach. It is not uncommon in a classroom for regional campus students to sit apart from the Oxford students. When I came to Miami and was told about this situation, I understood the problem intellectually, but I didn't fully apprehend it until I interviewed one of my students about the climate for diversity in our division. When the topic of the interview turned to the fit of regional campus students on the Oxford campus, Cal said he knew a lot about that subject since he had spent two years on Miami's Middletown, Ohio, campus.

"I didn't know that," I said. "You fit in so well."

"Oh, I don't tell anyone," he said. "On the first day of a class when the professor asks everyone to say where they are from, I never tell. My lowest moment came when I was talking to some of my Oxford friends, and someone I'd known from Middletown was waving and shouting my name from across campus."

"What did you do?"

"That's the low part," Cal said. "I acted as though I didn't hear him."

That's when I understood the pressure felt by regional campus students, when I had a story with characters and plot and tension, when I had narrative to illustrate the point. Cal was decent, personable, witty, outgoing, and friendly. If he turned his back on a Middletown friend because of how he himself might be perceived, then the problem was significant.

Cal sat back in his chair, breathed in deeply and exhaled, "I'm actually glad to get this off my chest."

Even in my expository pieces—my articles, my persuasive letters, my reports—I try to weave in pertinent stories, try to give flesh and blood to my arguments by showing people in action.

In *Educating Esmé: Diary of a Teacher's First Year* (1999), Esmé Raji Codell uses story to illustrate how her inner-city fifth graders gained a degree of humanity and sympathy through discussing literature. Each day after lunch, Esmé read aloud to her students. She created an atmosphere of calm and coziness by pulling the window shades and softening the room's lighting. Her voice and a fine piece of children's literature filled the room. Through a story of her own, Esmé illustrates the power of story, conversation, and intellectual exchange:

> I was reading them *The Hundred Dresses* by Eleanor Estes, about a Polish immigrant girl who is so poor that she wears the same dress to school every day but insists that she has a hundred dresses lined up in her closet. The girls tease her mercilessly until she moves away. Her antagonists discover that she really did have a hundred dresses . . . a hundred beautiful *drawings* of dresses. Oh, God, it took everything not to cry when I closed the book! I especially like that the story is told from the teacher's point of view.
>
> Well, everything was quiet at the end, but then Ashworth asked if he could whisper something in my ear. He whispered, "I have to tell the class something," and discreetly showed me that he was missing half a finger. It was a very macabre moment, but I didn't flinch.
>
> I faced him toward the class and put my hands on his shoulders. He was trembling terribly. "Ashworth has something personal to share with you. I hope you will keep in mind *The Hundred Dresses* when he tells you."
>
> "I . . . I only have nine and a half fingers," he choked. "Please don't tease me about it." He held up his hands.
>
> The class hummed, impressed, then was silent as Ashworth shifted on his feet. Finally, Billy called out, "I'll kick the ass of anyone who makes fun of you!"
>
> "Yeah, me too!" said Kirk.
>
> "Yeah, Ash! You just tell us if anyone from another class messes with you, we'll beat their ass up and down!"
>
> Yeah, yeah, yeah! The class became united in the spirit of ass-kicking. Ashworth sighed and smiled at me. The power of literature! (33–34)

In that last paragraph, Esmé, with great craft and sensibility, enters authorial comment that plays off the children's ass-kicking language and interprets the story for the reader through a pedagogical lens.

Esmé also skillfully uses *narrative summary* and *narrative dramatization*. Both strategies do important work, but there is a chasm in how they are rendered. Summarized narrative is effective in giving readers background information and context so that we set up a scene for dramatization. Narrative summary plus exposition is what Esmé does in that first paragraph, but when Ashworth enters the scene, Esmé slows down the writing to dramatize what happens. We hear Ash whisper, we see him tremble. We see and hear his risky admission and the kids' raucous responses. The dramatized narrative creates a movie in our minds. It's life we're seeing played out, not merely commentary about it. Esmé hasn't just told us about the power of narrative; she's shown us. We have, in a word, been *storied*.

One of my students writes about the appeal of narrative in voice:

> When I write, I want a voice to emerge that is both reader-friendly and reader-challenging. I don't want people to necessarily agree with what I'm saying in my writing, but I want them to be able to approach my writing and really get a handle on it. The writing I admire is the writing that draws me in and tells stories to me; it's writing that makes me care about the message it is trying to convey.
>
> *Storey Christopherson, College Junior*

Here's another young woman writing about a two-week field experience she has had in a middle school. The assignment here was to write a paper that communicated a sense of their experience and learning during the two weeks. In this excerpt Jennifer uses dramatic narrative to show readers a character she encountered each day, the environment of the teacher's lounge, and something she has learned about perspective, attitude, and new adolescents:

> It's third period, and I find myself in the teachers' lounge again. Forty-five minutes to scribble notes and compose my thoughts (planning periods are a godsend!). Sitting on a crusty yellow couch, I watch as teachers sweat to make last-minute copies, praying that their classrooms don't self-destruct in their absences. In walks Mr. Marcum, a seasoned teacher of fifty-something, cup of coffee in hand and papers to grade in tote; he pushes the papers aside as he settles himself into a folding chair.
>
> "So, what bull shit have they handed you today?" he asks.
>
> I smile at his daily ritual. Mr. Marcum and I have formed a sort of friendship in our third period conversations; it has become his crusade to impart his years' worth of educational "insight" to me before my return to college life in less than two weeks.

"Not much—I actually am really enjoying my classes here," I say. I refuse to be reeled into openly bashing my students. Besides, I kind of like them!

"That's a bull shit answer," he says. I blush. "There's no room for idealism in the eighth grade. Too much stupid shit going on in these classrooms as there is."

What's this? No room for my idealism? I'm twenty years old—it's my job to be idealistic! And, honestly, could the language be toned down a bit? I hate the word shit, especially when used in an educational environment. I write LET ME DREAM! in my notebook, where Mr. Marcum can't see.

"Stupid shit," he continues when I fail to respond. "You just have to laugh sometimes, or else the job'll kill you."

I smile again—my idealistic smile that more than likely sends Mr. Marcum into fits of laughter as he returns to his classroom each day. He turns to his papers, red pen in hand, and I return to my scribbling. All of his shit-talk aside, I couldn't shake the truth behind his last statement. There's no doubt that two weeks in a middle school faced me with some situations that required the ability to laugh. Face it, adolescents (and adults) do (and say) some funny stuff. Without this gift of laughter, in the cynically sensitive and evocatively eloquent renditions of Mr. Marcum, "the job'll kill you."

Jennifer Herdeman, College Junior

8

Perception and Surprise

[Raymond Carver] denies the importance of talent, but says a writer needs "a unique and exact way of looking at things."

WILLIAM STAFFORD

I hadn't lived in Logan, Utah, many months when I encountered a quintessential story of optimism. I answered the doorbell one morning to find a Lutheran minister standing on the landing. He told me about the new parish he was starting and invited my wife and me to attend services. I was nonplussed. This was, after all, Utah, a state founded and governed by members of the Church of Jesus Christ of Latter-Day Saints. I asked the minister if there was presently a Lutheran parish in town. He said there was. I asked him if there were enough non-Mormons in the valley to make his new Lutheran parish viable.

"I think so," he said. "We did a study last spring and discovered that only 90 percent of Cache Valley is LDS."

That was optimism.

That was faith.

That was a unique and exact way of looking at things.

"Style," writes Martin Amis, "is absolutely embedded in the way you perceive" (quoted in Murray 1990, 129).

This relationship between voice and perception isn't talked about much. What we see and how we see is crucial to voice and vision. I once heard a magazine writer say that writers needed *sensibility*. Not the quality of being a sensible person, but the ability to feel or perceive. For writers, sensibility is related to all kinds of intelligences: verbal, emotional, musical, mathematical, spatial, interpsychological, intrapsychological. Any kind of acuteness of perception helps writers increase their overall sensibility.

Think of that twelve-year-old boy who wrote about the physical effect on students of Mrs. Bell's yell. Think of Esmé casting light on that classroom incident so we look at it through a lens of literature.

Perception is close kin to surprise, and both are essential qualities of voice. Not all of us notice the same things. Some of us see more, and some of us see more deeply, taking notice of detail that others miss. Some of us make astounding connections. Voiceful writers report these sightings, understandings, details, and connections. Writers respect their own amazement and know that readers will be surprised, delighted, and informed by reading what surprised, delighted, and informed the writer (Macrorie 1984, 29).

Writers can orchestrate their writing so that readers walk along, turn a corner, and voila!—there is an instructive surprise that propels them to read further. So the twelve-year-old boy surprises us by trusting the physical sensation he experiences when his teacher yells, believes the truth of it enough to write it down. Esmé loves children's literature. The image of the four-and-a-half-fingered hand and the raucous glory of the discussion surprised her. She has a sense of drama and she trusts the subject matter enough to report it to readers so they can be surprised just as she was.

Casey was a student of mine a few years ago who wrote a brave and uncompromising multigenre paper about her struggle with bulimia. A multigenre paper is about a single topic but is composed of many different genres that hang together. It isn't simply one expository or narrative monolog. In multigenre papers, writers put together information from many perspectives, angles, and voices. Casey began her paper in this unconventional way that was all too appropriate for her subject matter (see Figure 8–1). The genre surprised me, and the information taught me about symptoms of bulimia. As I sped into her paper, I was an absorbed, awakened reader, hungry for more unique perceptions and surprises.

People have varying degrees of sensibility, but everyone has some. We all perceive insight. When you write with voice, you put sensibility to work. When we report to readers what we perceive, they are often surprised. This sense of surprise keeps readers reading.

Teachers can heighten students' awareness of sensibility by talking about the perceptions and surprises embedded in the texts of authors they are reading. And all of us then can practice noticing, connecting, and looking closely. By writing with detail we perceive even more about our topic. Writing begets seeing, seeing begets writing.

Date: 3/17/94
Time: 11:00 am

Patient's Name: CASEY M. BROWN
Reported Problem: BULIMIA
Medication Prescribed: 20 mg Prozac/day

Notes:
- forces herself to vomit 2-3 times/day
- perfectionist, outgoing, well-liked
- low self-esteem, wears baggy sweats a lot
- hates mirrors + scales, yet obsesses over them
- biggest fear: being fat, gaining weight
- extremely active + works out at least 3-4 hrs/day
- began vomiting in 7th grade, gradually got worse
- last binge: yesterday - lunch + dinner, before dance class
- tries to smile, but tears keep falling down her face
- occassionally uses diet pills

Dr. Susan Taft, Psychiatrist 127 Rookwood Ln., Cincinnati, OH 45024

Figure 8–1

9

Surprise for Whom?

Surprise is a cherished quality of voice. I can't emphasize enough the crucial role that surprise and specific use of language play in sharpening our perception, which in turn makes our voices more interesting. So far I have discussed only how surprise affects readers. Surprise rewards them, keeps them interested and reading. But more elementally, writers themselves need to be alert for surprise, especially surprises that occur *during* the writing process. There are surprises of language, surprises of form, surprises of meaning.

When we use language systematically, we begin an exploratory journey. As we write, we happen upon a well-turned phrase. As we write, we learn that the piece is really about this and not about that. As we write, we discover an ending. We use this exploratory aspect of language even in mundane writing—when we compose a grocery list, we write down *pickles* and think of *buns* and *mustard*. Using language is generative. You won't find "surprise and discovery through language" in any state standards about writing. But anyone who writes and has thought about the act of writing knows that surprise and discovery are critical to writing well and that means writing with voice.

When writers put words on paper, they make connections. Let those connections come. When drafting, be wild and loose. The wild word, the outlandish metaphor, the ironic sentence. Let the wildness and looseness come. Welcome them into the writing. Follow their energy. You may end up cutting some (or all) of the wildness before putting the text before readers. But maybe not. The connections you make, the language you use, are what make you unique. Trust that uniqueness. Cultivate it. Be guided by it.

When you start to compose something, write with the most specific information you can conjure. Generalities be damned, concreteness is all. Specificity makes you think about details and details lead to greater awareness, increased sensibility, illuminating connections, and commonplace surprises. Language used in good faith is naturally exploratory. We seek to say what we mean, and language leads us to say more, see more, understand more than we intended. If you put your faith in specific language and concrete detail, perception and surprise follow fast.

Here is an entry from my journal, late winter 1987:

> I stood in the dim light of the bedroom having just hung up the telephone. Tears welled into my eyes. The inside of my nose stung. I'd just talked to Jenny, my seventeen-year-old daughter's good friend.
>
> Three weeks earlier Jenny and another friend snuck out of the house late at night, at one, on their way to a spontaneous half hour of sledriding. Both kids reached to adjust the radio. The car slammed into a parked dump truck. Jenny's friend broke her wrists on the steering wheel. Jenny was propelled into the windshield, face-first. Her body crunched up on the dash then dropped to the floor of the car.
>
> And now Jenny is out of hospitals—the emergency hospital, the hospital specializing in plastic surgery, the hospital with expert staff and physical and mental therapy.
>
> Three operations of plastic surgery behind her, she is home now. And one evening last week Jenny came down to visit. Her dad drove her the four blocks. She wasn't permitted to drive. Mariana wouldn't have been allowed to get her.
>
> I sat in the recliner, figuring grades when Jenny walked into the room. I'd last seen her six weeks ago, when an ice storm struck and the schools had already announced closings the next day. Mariana and Jenny were living it up and I arose from bed to come to the kitchen to calm their mirth. Jenny sat at the bar, smiling, eating a piece of my birthday cake. Mariana made chocolate chip cookies, all this at 12:30 A.M.
>
> Jenny smiled, "Hey, Mr. R, this cake is good."
>
> That moment was remote. I looked up from my gradebook. Jenny walked in carefully. Her aviator leather coat hung loosely about her, missing the pounds she had lost.
>
> She smiled bravely, revealing the complex wires restricting her jaw movement, the gaps where two front teeth had been. Her eyes were still black and yellow from the latest surgery which had added to her cheekbone.
>
> "I've still got staples in my head," she laughed faintly. That explained the hat.
>
> Her hair was a little dirty because she wasn't allowed to get the staples wet that secured her skin over the new bonework. To cover the hair, Jenny wore a bright red Atlanta Hawks cap, tilted on her head so it wouldn't rub the staples.
>
> "I didn't know you were a Hawks fan, Jenny."
>
> "I'm not. This is my brother's. He'd kill me if he knew I took it."

> No he wouldn't, I thought, he'd cradle you in his arms and say, "Wear it all you want, Jenny. Wear it all you want."

I knew that Jenny was hurting and slowly recovering, but I was shocked by her lost weight and fragility. Jenny had once been a swimmer, a volleyball player, a cheerleader. In the journal I noted what I perceived and wanted to report to my reader. I always write in my journal as though I will be reading it many years later as a stranger, which I will be then. I want to reexperience what I've written. By being specific about the surprising perceptions of my encounter with Jenny, I was led to that bright red Atlanta Hawks cap. I report my lame attempt to make small talk about Jenny being a Hawks fan. The cap is the crucial detail of the experience—more than the leather jacket over her thin torso, more than her wired jaw, more than the bruised skin around her eyes. The cap—that incongruous, out-of-place baseball cap—covered little but revealed much—the head staples, the dirty hair, the cap tilt. And I think I am most grateful to the mundane bit of dialog on my part that leads to Jenny's admission to cap theft. This leads to a final paragraph I couldn't have planned (blessed perceptual, linguistic surprise!): the ending in which I realize the depth of my feeling about Jenny's one wild and precious life. I didn't see it coming, but I'm so glad it came. Surprise and fulfillment and understanding.

"A good style in literature," writes Ford Maddox Ford, "if closely examined, will be seen to consist of a constant succession of tiny surprises" (quoted in Murray 1990, 132).

This cuts two ways: Surprises for the reader when reading. Surprises for the writer when writing.

Have your students take pieces of their writing and examine them for surprises that occurred during their composing: the detail unthought of before writing it, the argument expanded while making it, the ending they hadn't planned that appeared, seemingly, from nowhere.

Students need to understand how surprises for the writer are a boon to composition. This understanding can lift their confidence, teach them that they are creative and inventive, that the act of writing thrives on serendipity of language flow and meaning, even though we plan our writing the best we can.

10

Humor, Lightness, Play

In the mid-1970s, I taught Joy and Joy taught me. In four semester classes and her editorship of the creative arts magazine, I got to know Joy well. Her multiple intelligences ran high, but of most pleasure to me was her great linguistic intelligence. Poetry, fiction, persuasive essays, book reviews—you name the genre, Joy wrote it and wrote it well, or she could learn to do so in short order.

Her senior year a week before winter break, Joy came down with the flu. We had been working on poetry collections that were due the day before vacation. Joy sent in her collection of poems accompanied by the note in Figure 10–1.

Mr. Romano,
I have to apologize for how awful these poems are. Of course, it's hard to be poetic when you're deathly ill! Please don't throw up when you read these cause one of us throwing up is enough.

Joy

PS. Merry Christmas.

Figure 10–1

I carried myself a little lighter that day because of Joy. She was quiet in class, but articulate when required to speak. Joy's personality bloomed in her writing. IQ and wit combined beautifully in her. She was detailed, pointed, and, when her subject matter allowed it, playful, funny, and satirical. Gosh, I looked forward to reading her writing.

This chapter is not for everyone. Certainly humor and playfulness are not mandatory qualities of a distinctive, authentic voice (consider Poe, for example). In fact, sometimes humor or playfulness is inappropriate to topic and occasion, although sometimes, even in somber topics, there is room to admit lightness. In our eulogies about my mother, my daughter and I emphasized her sense of humor, her charming ingenuousness, and her love of a dry vodka martini, information the minister did not mention. In my journal entry about Jenny, there is much seriousness: the details of the accident, the head staples, the wired jaw, the weight loss. But there is also the mirthful camaraderie of Jenny's earlier visit to my daughter during the ice storm. And there is that jaunty Atlanta Hawks cap.

Ken Macrorie has pointed out that writers can be playful and serious at the same time (1984, 29). Lightness and seriousness often work well together. Look at Emily Dickinson being playful in making a serious statement about art, imagery, and imagination:

> To make a prairie it takes a clover and one bee,
> One clover, and a bee,
> And revery.
> The revery alone will do,
> If bees are few. (1890, 710)

Humor in writing has a lot to do with our personalities, our propensity to laugh and joke and be playful, and our wont of inserting those qualities into our writing. Again, humor and playfulness aren't for everybody. I can't imagine, for example, some of my past and present colleagues being playful in their writing. Some of us can manage only a grim smile amid hilarity and foolery. Still, many of us needlessly check our sense of humor at the door of invention when we sit down to write. One of my students explains why he thinks many of his peers do this:

> So often humor is absent from student writing. Students feel that everything must be serious, and the teacher is a robot who does not know how to laugh, and does not like to laugh. Well-placed humor is completely appropriate and does wonders for the voice of a piece. I found that placing humor somewhere in almost all my writing gives me a sense of freedom. When I'm writing and I think of something funny, I put it in.
>
> *Sean Elliot, College Junior*

A final examination, certainly, is not a place for humor to rear its buoyant head—or is it? One year, coming down to the final day, I was as eager to get out of school as my high school students. Yet I knew I had seventy-five final examinations to read by my sophomores. I needed something to keep me upright while sitting at my desk reading, so one of the writing questions read this way:

> Through the miraculous power of Romano, Atticus Finch of *To Kill a Mockingbird* and Brutus of *Julius Caesar* are no longer bound by their time. Brutus of ancient Rome suddenly finds himself in Depression-era Alabama right outside the law office of Atticus Finch. You take it from here. What would these two men have to say to each other? Create a dialog between them that reveals their characters and concerns.

I want to learn what students know about the literature we read, but the exam prompt invites playfulness, too. I want the voice of my first six words to reveal myself on the page, so my students will remember that I am a man who knows how to laugh. Few of those seventy-five sixteen-year-olds took the bait. Most wrote the dialog straight, trotting out pertinent information about Brutus and Atticus. There were two exceptions: Loretta and Rosanna.

Loretta was ebullient, outgoing, and heavily involved in the high school thespian troupe. Here is her first-draft-only-draft:

> A: (Taking off glasses) Well, now, how can I help you?
> B: Oh, I came not for legal help, but for a chat with a noble man such as yourself. Your will to help a man in a desperate case has arisen my curiosity. Do tell me of it.
> A: Not much to tell, I suppose.
> B: Ay, but there is.
> A: In a nutshell, I defended an innocent man. But there was more to just defending him. . . . I guess you might say I was defending my morals and ideals too.
> B: Same as when I killed my noble friend Caesar. I killed not for his blood, but for all of Rome's freedom.
> A: I guess you might say we were both fighting for freedom, only I lost.
> B: I too in my way. Tis true Rome was free, but many deaths before had happened. Tis sad that innocence must die for a worthy cause.
> A: I don't believe you have to have death for a cause. I wish folks would settle things peaceful. Understand the other's point of view, kinda walk in his shoes, ya know.
> B: Or sandals, as the case may be.
> (Both laugh)
>
> *Retta Hurlbert, High School Sophomore*

Rosanna was a contrast to Loretta in every way but intellect. She was inward, moody, and quiet, a reluctant student seeking to keep information about her substantial intellect under wraps. When she put pen to paper, though, her intelligence and wit would not be contained.

A: Sir, can I help you?
B: Hmmm, yes, you may help me. Where art I?
A: (Thinks "strange guy, must be a tourist") Well, ahh, you're in Maycomb County, and I'm Atticus Finch. Are you looking for someone?
B: Ay! So you're Atticus. Thank Gods! You seeth, Tom Romano has drug me Brutus from the era of Caesar to talk to you for his English class.
A: Hmm, well what do you wanna discuss? Hey, why did you kill Caesar? Did you have second thoughts?
B: Yea, I had "second thoughts." But I lovest Rome with all my heart and I tried to believe it was for the best.
A: I see. Well, I guess you've never heard of me.
B: I have not.
A: I have two beautiful children, Jem and Scout (hands Brut their pictures).
B: Ay! They are beautiful. Scout has eyes like my Portia.
A: So sorry, anyway, I'm this defense attorney for a black man convicted of rape, and it's really had me down lately. Could you go into the future maybe and see what happens?
B: No, not unless Romano would allow it.
A: Oh, well, that's O.K. Never mind. How's it been?
B: Well, it's tough being Brutus. I'm always being called to the future. I suppose I shall never rest in peace.
A: But you're in the history books as the noblest Roman of them all!
B: No, truly?! Well then, I will not mind being called forward any longer. Farewell, dear Atticus, good luck.
A: Yes, et tu, Bruté.

Rosanna O'Keefe, High School Sophomore

Playfulness and humor might not be for your authentic voice. Maybe you think writing and life are too serious to be playful. Or maybe not. Maybe you think writing and life are too serious *not* to be playful.

Part III

Trust the Gush

Antipasto
Olivia Leads the Way

The morning I visited Mindy Bauer's first graders in Mason, Ohio, my job was to demonstrate to the children how I write. They gathered on the carpet in front of me, and I listed on the board some topics I cared about. I chose one, brainstormed information that came to mind, and began to write. Through every step of my writing process, I talked about what I was thinking and why I was doing what I was doing. The children saw what my hand was writing; my talk let them see my thinking. They saw and heard me use information I had brainstormed and planned. They also saw and heard me discover surprises, think of new details, incorporate their participation into my thinking, and change direction in the writing. After I demonstrated a writing process, Mindy's students dived into their own topic choosing and writing.

They were fearless. As I moved about the classroom, conferring with the writers, I learned about a medal-winning goalie performance in soccer, a dog named Max that played basketball, a pet frog who ate a pet fish, a trip to a farm in Nebraska, and much more. With time to write, choice in topic, and understanding of what to do, these children charged forth with voice and information. Olivia was one of the children with a hot topic. Adjust your invented spelling lens and follow this little girl's superb mind. Work as hard decoding her words as she worked encoding them. When you see what Olivia has done with language (see page 46), the payoff will be even more rewarding:

I knelt beside Olivia's desk and asked her to read her piece to me. I copied her writing in Standard English:

> I know a lot about molecules. A molecule is a little thing that's made out of atoms. They are everywhere. Even you are made out of molecules. Everything you see is made out of molecules. Even the universe is made out of molecules.

Olivia had come into the classroom with her head full of science. When the students had opportunity to write, she launched into the information she had learned. She trusted the gush. Emily Dickinson said that she knew writing was good when it felt as though the top of her head had been taken off. Olivia's molecule piece had scalped me for sure.

Mar 31 1999

I DO

a lnt about Of mhleqwl a
mhleqwl is a lntl
feg this mheod aholt
Of Ahdms thex are
Hurewar evn you are
mad of
avehll you see mhleqwl
out of mhleqwl is mand
The unhrhs evhn
is mand
out of mh leqwl.

Olivia

Seven-year-old Olivia produced content area writing, a kind of exposition that students will be asked to produce often as they journey through formal education. Unlike most content area writing, though, Olivia's piece has verve. She uses direct, declarative sentences. You can tell that she is giddy and excited with the coolness of this molecule business. She uses humor: "Reader," I hear her thinking, "you think you're so smart? Well, let me tell you something—even you are made of molecules!" The most impressive linguistic feature for me in the writing is that Olivia builds meaning with sophisticated sentence rhythm:

> Even you are made out of molecules.
> Everything you see is made out of molecules.
> Even the universe is made out of molecules.

When I share Olivia's writing with teachers, some of them carp about the invented spelling and lack of punctuation and capitalization. Paramount for them is remediation of Olivia's mechanical skills. They minimize the rich content of Olivia's writing, the way she focused and developed an idea. They ignore Olivia's voice and what makes it so distinctive and compelling on the page: confidence, playfulness, rhythmic language, surprise, and a sense of urgency to share information she finds so fascinating.

Olivia will grow and develop and refine her skills of spelling and punctuation. You can see how hard she works. She closely attends to phonics skills as she bears down to match every sound she hears with letters. She uses a logical progression of greatness, going from you, the reader, to everything you see, to the very universe we live in. She is bold, too, using the words available in her oral vocabulary whether she knows how to spell them or not. She takes on a new word, captures it on paper the best she knows how with her developing phonics skills, and spells *mhleqwl* consistently throughout her forty-three-word text. She takes on *everywhere, everything*, and *universe*, too.

Olivia's writing isn't remedial.

It isn't below grade level.

It isn't developmentally immature.

And it definitely isn't cute. *Cute* is condescending, demeaning, and dismissive.

Know this: Olivia's writing is high-grade cognitive work. It is information and learning and spirit. It is a little girl synchronized with language. Olivia's writing is fearless, sophisticated, musical, and meaningful. Olivia's writing is voice.

And don't you forget it.

11

The Place of Passion

When Stephanie turned in her final portfolio, one of her artifacts was a piece of paper with one sentence written on it: "Trust the gush." In her portfolio cover letter, she explained why this was so important to her learning:

> I have jotted notes down in almost every notebook I own (which I doubt will help my geology grade) but it's worth it because I've morphed A LOT of my gushing into poems. Instead of simply praying for inspiration, I just started writing. By not trying to stop "the gush," I've really fallen in love with words again, even when they don't fall on the page in a perfectly crafted poem.
>
> *Stephanie Klare, College Sophomore*

"When the gush is upon you," I should have told Stephanie, "that's inspiration." But I think she knew that in her bones. With "trust the gush," Stephanie was alluding to Whitman, who had this to say about writing poems:

> And the secret of it all is to write in a gush, the throb, the flood, of the moment—to put things down without deliberation—without worrying about style—without waiting for a fit time and place. . . . You want to catch the first spirit—to tally its truth. By writing at the instant the very heartbeat of life is caught. (Quoted in Wallace 1982, 284–85)

Another of my students put it this way:

> I had no concept of my writing being particularly good or bad, it was simply something I did with the words tearing through my brain.
>
> *E. Brianna Doyal, College Junior*

Trusting the gush means moving on the heat quickening in you.
Trusting the gush means fearlessness with language.

Trusting the gush means writing about what you are emotionally moved by and perhaps don't even know why.

Trusting the gush means putting onto the page those thoughts, connections, and perceptions that stand ready to be uttered.

Trusting the gush means, as Emerson put it, speaking the rude truth.

Many of us censor that impulse to tell the rude truth. I say be brave. Tell truths from where you are right now—big truths, little truths, intellectual truths, emotional truths—your truths all. When you are sixteen, say what you think of your behavior that day after school when you were fourteen, and when you are fifty, say what you think of your behavior that same day. Each saying will be different, each will be true. Say what you understand about *Beowulf* and *Walden* and *The Bean Trees*. Say it when you are seventeen, say it when you are forty-five.

Ken Macrorie pointed out that nothing perks up readers' ears like truth telling on the part of the writer (1976). Not THE truth. But your truth. Use writing to tell what you saw and experienced and believe. Use writing to tell what you *come* to believe. Don't be circumspect. Don't be mealymouthed. Drive to the heart with detail.

When my college students and I talk about crafting authentic voice, it is often foreign territory for them. They live harried lives, sometimes working part-time jobs, juggling sixteen to eighteen semester hours in six, maybe seven, courses. At 9 A.M. it's nominative absolutes, at 10 the inclusion of learning disabled students, at 11 the transactional theory of reader response. That's just Monday, Wednesday, and Friday. They have many writing demands, most of them, they tell me, writing that is mechanical and formulaic. *Dry* and *boring* are two words they frequently use to describe their written assignments. Students often write these papers the day before they are due, sometimes the day they are due. They proofread and spellcheck, maybe, and then print that "sucker" (another word they often use to describe such a paper). They simply don't have time, they say, to stretch out their writing process so they can revise deeply and craft words on the page.

When they tell me these things, I am distressed, I who want them to love putting words on paper, tinkering with them, melding them to their personality, expressing themselves with clarity, power, and compelling voices.

When schedules are hectic, both for us and our students, heeding passion is a must. Students need to pay attention to their deep feeling and thinking. They will waste less time if they put aside the tangential, focus on what needs to be written, and respect the words tearing through the brain. They need to respond to their emotions. They need to move on the images flashing in their minds. This means writing immediately, trusting the gush. If they can't get to a computer, they need a notebook or journal at hand, something they can easily open and let words tumble forth on. When language and strong feeling are upon them, that is the time to write.

> Write while the heat is in you. When the farmer burns a hole in his yoke, he carries the hot iron quickly from the fire to the wood, for every moment it is less effectual to penetrate it. It must be used instantly, or it is useless. The writer who postpones the recording of his thoughts uses an iron which has cooled. (Quoted in Murray 1990, 145)
>
> *Henry David Thoreau*

On a recent Martin Luther King holiday, I went to the kitchen for breakfast. Airing on the radio was a tribute to Dr. King. The subject matter made me postpone breakfast and march back upstairs to my office to write a vivid memory from my senior year of high school, a memory I knew even then was a clear example of discrimination and exclusion (Romano 2003).

The heat was in me.

As I'm reading a book manuscript that Heinemann has sent, language rises in me, a sentence full of detail, stance, and urgency. I take the pen from my shirt pocket and scribble the words in the margin, starting at the top and trailing down the side of the page. Some of the words, I see, are illegible, so I print them over carefully, then add two more sentences that come in a rush. I bend down the corner of the page so I can locate the outburst later. The words will be part of a foreword I'll write for the book.

The heat was in me.

I awake with a dream fresh in my head, go to my office, boot up the computer, and begin writing down the particulars of it, knowing that once I start using language in this concerted way, more of the dream will unfold.

The heat was in me.

One morning I walk outside to place a letter in the mailbox. Out of the corner of one eye I notice a big brown chunk of something. I turn my head and see that the chunk is a fledgling red-tailed hawk standing in the grass close to the house, eyeing me without concern. It stands about a foot high with feathers raggedy brown and white. We watch each other for twenty-seven minutes, I immobile, hawk going about its bird business, cocking its head, digging about the yard with its beak, hunching its shoulders and striding to a new spot, spreading its wings now and then as though it is hiking up a skirt. After it flies off, I'm at my computer in two minutes, writing every detail and impression I remember, not postponing while the iron of astonishment is hot.

The heat was in me.

> Write. Write in the full flow of the inspiration that has taken hold of you. Don't stop to find the exact word or to correct the construction of a sentence; don't worry yourself over a point of grammar. If in need of a word, leave

> space, and when you read your work back to yourself later on you may find that the word comes to you then; but if it doesn't, you can take all the time you need to seek it out. The intensity that is yours when you first begin to write may not last too long, so use it. (Quoted in Murray 1990, 145)
>
> *Elizabeth Yates*

Students need to learn to take advantage of burning new thought, to write immediately upon the passion of seeing and feeling and thinking, especially when they cannot articulate where such writing might lead them. Oh, I believe in the rational mind. I believe in planning and organizing and setting about a writing task methodically, doing a little bit every day. It is the way this book was written. If I sat waiting to be inspired as I was with the MLK writing or the hawk encounter, days would pass before I put words on paper. I know that immersion in a topic enables me to write, even if I am not initially inspired or passionate. I can become passionate. Immersion stirs me and moves me to saying and shaping words.

But I don't turn my back on passion when it pulses. When an earlier flight is available, I say get a boarding pass.

And when you are moved to speak, when the passion is upon you, that's a likely time that you will forget about audience and protocol and correctness and procedures and get to your unfettered voice.

Peter Elbow believes that we all can write with passion, with power, with voice:

> [E]veryone, however inexperienced or unskilled, has real voice available; everyone can write with power. Even though it may take some people a long time before they can write well about certain complicated topics or write in certain formal styles, and even though it will take some people a long time before they can write without mistakes in spelling and usage, nevertheless, nothing stops anyone from writing words that will make readers listen and be affected. Nothing stops you from writing right now, today, words that people will want to read and even want to publish. Nothing stops you, that is, but your fear or unwillingness or lack of familiarity with what I am calling your real voice. (1981, 304)

Elbow is right. Voice will come. Voice will come when you heed passion, push forward with language, are brave on the page, everything else be damned. And voice will also come, later, when you take time to craft the words.

12

"Outcast"

BY LORIE BARNHART, HIGH SCHOOL SENIOR

The heavy, wooden ruler smacked across my desk. I jumped and turned around.

"Be quiet," Mrs. Jackson said, "Class, your first rule for school is to face front, mouths closed."

I squirmed in my seat. I could feel the heat rise and spread over my face. Everyone's eyes stared at me. The first day of school ever, and here I sat—the class example of *wrong*.

"Psst, Lorie," Dana's whisper broke in, "What did you bring for lunch?"

I turned slightly to face my new-found friend. "I think Mom made . . ."

Smack! Crash! Two raps with the ruler followed by an irritated, "What did I just get done telling you, young lady?"

I glanced to my teacher's angry face then back down to my fingers. "Not to talk," I mumbled, my embarrassment mounting again.

"Why are you?"

"She . . . . a . . . Dana asked me a question."

"Don't blame it on her. Go over to the principal's office. I'll tell him why you're there."

I stood and walked in front of the class. My fingers nervously gripped the door handle as I pushed it to go out. I stepped into the entry, letting the tears begin to fly, shutting the door behind me. The path to the office lay outside the next door. I shoved it open, and a wave of fresh summer air hit me immediately. I had a long walk ahead.

Dorothy-like and Toto-less, I skipped up the path, half scared and half filled with wonder.

The office door was more official-looking than the one in the kindergarten room. The knob was set higher.

The principal sat in a chair, his arms folded across his chest. "Are you Lorie?"

I nodded yes.

"Don't have much of a voice now, do you? Well, I'm Mr. Lawson. Mrs. Jackson tells me you were talking after she said not to. Correct?"

"But I . . . I mean."

"Yes or no!"

"Yes, sir."

"This is a bad way to start off your school career. Usually, I tell parents about problems, but since this is your first time here, I'll just warn you. If you're in here again, you'll get three swats . . . four if it's for talking. Now, go back to class!"

I ran back up the path to the kindergarten room.

"Lorie," Dana said, "what happened?"

I never answered.

13

How Voice Is Lost

The significance of the cough drop wrapper in my portfolio is to remind me not to lose my voice when I sit down to write.

MICHELLE FRANCOM, College Junior

Audience

"I have worked in many upper-grade classrooms populated by writers who have lost their voice," writes Ralph Fletcher in *What a Writer Needs*. "What kills it? I'd finger audience as the major murder suspect" (1993, 73).

Lorie Barnhart certainly understood the intimidation of audience. Although her new friend invited Lorie's voice and made speaking a pleasurable, rewarding act, Lorie's teacher and principal on this first day were against the free assertion of voice in the school setting. Lorie wrote "Outcast" a long time ago in a high school writing class I taught. For her, the memoir embodied social exclusion, embarrassment, and harsh discipline. I saw all that but also viewed "Outcast" as a classic story about the quelling of voice.

You've been among audiences, haven't you, that made you uneasy, guarded, self-conscious? Audiences in which you felt judged, disdained, belittled?

A few months after my father was killed in an automobile crash near the end of my freshman year of high school, I was promoted to the adult Sunday school class at the church my mother sent me to. In that class were high school students one and two years older than I, among them, a girl I had liked since seventh grade. Think of the pressures that came to bear on me: adolescent boyhood and its attendant problems, an environment of older, more sophisticated teenagers, a girl I was smitten with, and the hovering presence of my dead father. I just knew that whenever people saw me enter a room, they thought immediately of my fatherless state. I said little and kept a low profile.

One Sunday the teacher asked me to read aloud the pious little weekly lesson from our Sunday school manual, his attempt, I'm sure, to get me involved. I blushed, swallowed, and began to read. Throat dry, chest constricted, I croaked the words, barely able to finish each sentence. Several times I stopped the agonized reading to suck in breath at unnatural junctures. I died in the few minutes it took me to read the lesson. I felt the embarrassment of my friends for me. I knew the teacher was mortified that his effort to involve me had instead humiliated me. I was a better reader than I demonstrated that morning, much better. I liked to kid and joke, too. I enjoyed using my mind. None of that was apparent. Audience did me in. Any chance I had to infuse my reading with voice inflection, calculated pauses, and rhythms of meaning was dashed by my self-consciousness. Audience skewed my voice on that, the last day I attended Sunday school.

If you have student writers who are particularly jammed up and self-conscious in their writing, ask them to write rapidly about a time when a particular audience made speaking or writing difficult. Guarantee anonymity so that the thinking has a better chance of honesty. Such writing can lead to helpful classroom discussion or dialog with individual students.

Information

Information, too, can be a voice blocker—too little information, too much information. I write a great many letters for and to my students, maybe thirty letters each semester. I spend considerable time crafting these letters, explicating a student's skills, character traits, and accomplishments.

Despite the time these letters take, they are not difficult to write. That's because I write from a wealth of information. If the letter is an evaluation of the teaching a student has done in class, I write from the student's own self-assessment and the notes I have taken during her teaching. If I'm writing a letter of recommendation, I write from the notes I've taken during an interview I require of each student requesting a letter. In this interview the student jogs my memory further. I won't write a letter for a student I don't have substantial data on. If I try to write with little information, I find myself resorting to clichés and generalizations. It isn't a way I want to write.

When students have trouble getting their voices on the page, lack of information might be the problem. They might need to accumulate more, to become more of an expert on their topic by further reading, interviewing, observing, and note taking. They might need to brainstorm and reflect in order to bring information they already know to consciousness. The happier circumstance is to have so much rich and interesting information that the problem is deciding what to leave out. It is the opposite circumstance of facing gaps of information and knowledge that leave you frustrated and rudderless.

Which leads to another problem of information—too much of it can overwhelm writers and block their voices. They might try to pack so much information into sentences that the thinking becomes abstract, wordy, and convoluted. Or they might have so much information that they become overwhelmed and unable to write.

I don't suffer writing block much anymore, but the last time I did scared me thoroughly. I felt cowardly, worthless, unprofessional. It was 1985. I was two or three chapters into writing my first book. I was teaching high school full time and writing on weekends and holidays. I was trying to get the second chapter off the ground, the chapter I knew the most about: using writing for learning in the classroom. I had the most data for this chapter, the most examples from my students, the most quotations from professional literature.

Amid this plenty, I was stumped. I'd gotten words on paper, but they always took me in directions I wound up not wanting to go, directions that led me away from the good stuff I wanted to write about. I was panicked, wondering if what I feared deep inside might be true—that I really didn't have the intelligence, the skills, and the will to write a book.

That fall on a consulting trip to Halifax, Nova Scotia, I had breakfast with Don Graves, one of my teachers in graduate school the previous year. Don asked how my book was going. He was interested in my progress since he was the one who had suggested to his editor at Heinemann that I could write a book about teaching writing to high school students. I poured out my dilemma to Don, talked about the chapter topic, about the examples I had, about my stumbling first attempts, about staring at the monitor of my computer before dawn on Saturdays and Sundays, watching that blasted, impatient cursor steadily pulse.

Don listened and his expression grew pained like mine. This was a serious matter. He knew. I knew.

"Have you tried writing what the chapter isn't?" Don asked.

He read my befuddlement.

"Here's what I mean," he added. "The chapter isn't about conferencing with students."

I nodded.

"It isn't about writing and literature," he said. "You've already written chapters about that."

I understood those things well enough. Don's advice was not helping.

"It isn't about eating dinner on time, either," Don said. "It isn't about running or swimming or bicycling."

He didn't need to say more. I could see the playfulness that this tack invited, something I dearly needed in my suddenly grim writing process. I was willing to try whatever it took to make a successful inroad to the chapter.

First chance I got, I sat at the computer and let out all the stops. No, indeed, the chapter was not about swimming. Nor was it about the corn-silk beetles that had devastated my sweet corn that summer. It wasn't about my mother's unacknowledged hearing loss and her high-volume television that I feared were going to get her evicted from her apartment. It wasn't about our first schnauzer, Max, who got me started writing each weekend morning by waiting for me in the darkness of my writing room, lying under the computer desk, his eyes glowing demonically.

I wish I had that surreal piece of writing I batted out in desperate joy. Doing it got me to a better place. Writing about what the chapter wasn't helped me see what it was. The reckless writing led me to a story that embodied the topic, a story with characters, drama, mystery, and surprise, which served as the present-tense lead for the chapter:

> I sit on the sharing rug with twenty third graders and their teacher, Jan Roberts, of Mast Way School in Lee, New Hampshire. As part of Donald Graves and Jane Hansen's research team at the University of New Hampshire, I am gathering data on children's development as readers and writers. I've been visiting this classroom daily for more than three months. This day in our sharing circle Eddie sits upon the lone chair—the author's chair. He has just finished reading aloud his piece about fishing. Eddie calls upon the seven children who have their hands raised, and each, in turn, comments and asks questions about his writing.
>
> Eddie smiles, a fat cat in literacy learning. He relishes being in charge, hearing his words responded to, and divulging additional information about fishing. Eddie calls upon Melissa.
>
> She shifts her legs so that she is sitting on one of her sneakers. She bends her blond head forward, looking at Eddie's feet rather than his contented smile. She speaks hesitantly: "Did you ever notice . . . or, well . . . realize anything while you were writing?"
>
> "No," says Eddie, too quickly. He is puzzled by Melissa's inquiry. Many of the other children are too.
>
> "Melissa," I say, "has that happened to you? Have you realized something while you were actually writing?"
>
> "Yes," she answers softly. She seems embarrassed to reveal this. "Once when I was writing about an Encyclopedia Brown book, I realized one of the clues while I was writing."

"How does that happen?" I ask. "How do you realize something at the same time you're writing?"

"I just do," says Melissa. "Kaboom! And it's there." (1987, 17–18)

Kaboom, indeed! Language had led me to understanding—in this case, absurd, playful, wide-ranging language. Language had led me through the morass of information I had accumulated to the essence of my subject: Melissa's remarkable, articulated understanding that morning—the intuitive, experience-based knowledge of a child.

Students whose voices are jammed because of too much information might benefit from a little irreverent freewriting about what their topic isn't. Or they might benefit from sifting through their data and identifying hot spots, riveting information, significant details, and compelling points. If students start writing about those, it may break them free. It may lead them to words on the page they can work with. It may lead them to voice.

Form/Structure/Formula

Right behind audience in killing voice—and related to it—is rigid, often arbitrary form, strict rules about how something is said. In an earlier iteration of my present Department of Teacher Education, "Robert's Rules of Order" ran faculty meetings. Strictly. One false procedural move and one of several parliamentarians proclaimed, "Out of order! Out of order!" The form of the meeting often blocked the voices of new faculty and those less confident.

Precedence of form over content in writing can also smother voice. One of my students explains how rigid writing form affected her:

> What do I mean when I want my writing to be effective? I want the reader to feel what I feel as I write. The problem arises when I am not sure how I feel, when I have not taken a stand. This was often the case in high school. Writing was so formal and rigid that it was hard to develop emotions towards it. . . . When the writer is not passionate about his/her writing, the reader will surely not be passionate about it.
>
> *Meg McKinnon, College Junior*

I am not against form. I love elegant form—the striated eggplant developing in the garden, the muscular symmetry of two red-tailed hawks patrolling the neighborhood, the Olympic-sized swimming pool at the Miami University Recreation Center divided into eight lanes, each lane with a black line painted down the middle on the bottom of the pool. I especially like when form enhances meaning: the eggplant's shape and color pleasing to the eye and wonderful on the tongue in a pasta sauce of tomatoes, onions, olive oil, and basil; the red-tailed hawk lifting effortlessly into the air; the layout of the pool keeping swimmers out of each other's way and making the rhythm of breath, stroke, and kick easy to attain. I love writing that immediately engages me, illuminates me throughout the reading, plays off the very language it uses, and ends with a final compelling example that reminds me of the beginning or repeats a key word and makes a final, emphatic impression.

In writing, I'm against form for its own sake. I'm against the imposition of strict, unyielding writing forms that actually impede the writer's perception, honesty, and ability to report surprise, forms that short-circuit the exploratory use of language that leads to kabooms of insight, awareness, and further language. I'm against forms that seem to admit no chance for the telling of an interesting, pointed story, no possibility for humor.

Form should be a voice giver, not a voice taker.

14

The Five-Paragraph You-Know-What

All I ever wrote in high school was the five-paragraph essay. Start with the introduction and the thesis statement (make sure it is the last sentence in the paragraph and that it includes the three main points to be discussed). Fill each body paragraph with one main point and ONE MAIN POINT ONLY. The conclusion should restate the introduction and thesis and offer a final, universal, conclusive thought. Don't add your opinion. No place for fragments. The point is not to be effective or original, the point is to complete the assignment.

MEG MCKINNON, College Junior

I stopped teaching high school students in Ohio in 1988, was out of contact with Ohio schools until 1995, when I came to Miami University. Upon my return, I heard teachers referring to the five-paragraph you-know-what more than I had in my previous twenty-one years of teaching. The reason for this was the state's proficiency test in writing. Many teachers felt—with the encouragement of model essays from the state office of education—that students would do well on the tests if they used the form of the five-paragraph you-know-what. Narrative, descriptive, expository, persuasive. It didn't matter what writing task was solicited by this one-shot, antisocial, strictly monitored production of writing. Use the five-paragraph you-know-what, and assessors will see immediately that you know what you are doing and pass your essay.

Strict form can be a voice blocker, a voice stopper, a voice skewer. The five-paragraph you-know-what and the formal, sterile, abstract notion of academic writing that goes with it can be a killer and lead writers to all kinds of bad habits. Remember Holden Caulfield's immature, funny, feisty, adolescent, angst-ridden voice that kept you reading *The Catcher in the Rye* for 214 pages? How long would you have kept reading had the entire book been written in the voice of the examination essay Holden wrote for ol' Spencer's history class?

> The Egyptians were an ancient race of Caucasians residing in one of the northern sections of Africa. The latter as we all know is the largest continent in the Eastern Hemisphere. . . . The Egyptians are extremely interesting to us today for various reasons. Modern science would still like to know what the secret ingredients were that the Egyptians used when they wrapped up dead people so that their faces would not rot for innumerable centuries. This interesting riddle is still quite a challenge to modern science in the twentieth century. (Salinger 1964, 11)

I enjoy satire, but don't think I would have abided this kind of writing long. Reading the 214 pages would have seemed like innumerable centuries. That paragraph was written in the voice that Holden believes is what academia wants—a voice of serious-minded pretentiousness, statements of the obvious, and high-flown diction—a teenager's idea of a learned authority. Holden thought the writing was pretty crummy. To his credit, Mr. Spencer thought it was pretty crummy, too.

I urge teachers at all levels to stop what has happened to the essay, that flexible rhetorical form whose roots go back at least to Michel de Montaigne. To my mind, there is no greater threat to an interesting, compelling voice in secondary education than the five-paragraph you-know-what, unless it is no writing at all. I will take time here to talk about this popular, formulaic structure and the myths about writing it has spawned.

James Moffett explains that Montaigne "coined the term *essai* from *essayer*, to attempt" (1983, 171). The essay has been marked by colorful language, free-ranging expression, and exploratory surprises. Moffett had this to say of the essay, which should give pause to anyone teaching essay writing as a strict formula:

> [T]hrough the essays of Swift, Lamb, Hazlitt, and DeQuincey to those of Orwell, Virginia Woolf, Joan Didion, and Norman Mailer, English literature has maintained a marvelous tradition, fusing personal experience, private vision, and downright eccentricity, with intellectual rigor and verbal objectification. In color, depth, and stylistic originality it rivals some of our best poetry. (1983, 171)

Students think none of these things when they think *essay*. They think of completing the assignment, as Meg notes in the epigraph. When students think *expository*, they think dry, dusty, boring. They think of a kind of writing I don't want to spend my one wild and precious life reading. No publications I know feature five-paragraph you-know-whats. They are not the preferred mode of expression that literate people seek out to read. The five-paragraph you-know-what has no currency beyond the classroom. In fact, with many of my colleagues across the nation in English and education departments, it has no currency in the classroom either. It is not uncommon for teachers of first-year composition to talk about the bad habits that students must unlearn, bad habits derived from the superstructured pseudo-essays they wrote in high school.

I'm not against students learning to take and state a clear position and explain why they believe it. It doesn't follow, though, that students need to memorize a form for the purpose, a bogus, simplistic form that puts the lie to the "color, depth, and stylistic originality" that Moffett wrote about.

Five-paragraph you-know-what advocates argue that the form teaches students to organize their ideas and present them in a structured way. Bruce Pirie, author of *Reshaping High School English* (1997), thinks that idea is an illusion:

> The five-paragraph essay doesn't "teach structure" any more than a paint-by-numbers kit teaches design. We teach structure by sitting down with students who have something they care about saying, helping them sort out how they might try to say it, and looking at examples of how other writers have structured their work. . . . It takes time, and the first results of students' own shaping definitely don't look as neat as formulaic essays, but perhaps our eyes, like art teachers' eyes, must learn to appreciate the inevitable messiness of the learner. (78)

One English educator pointed out to me the usefulness of the five-paragraph you-know-what by likening it to a ticket. "It gains students admittance," she said. "With the five-paragraph essay, they can pass proficiency tests and written exams. Once they have that ticket, then they can learn the many wonderful other ways to write."

I have doubts about the rosy future predicted for properly ticketed writers. Like Meg, many of my students claim that the only writing they did in four years of high school was five-paragraph you-know-whats. I haven't run into students yet who learned to write five-paragraph you-know-whats their freshman year of high school and wrote them only sporadically after that. On the contrary, the form sticks. Students come to view the five-paragraph you-know-what as *the* way to write academically. Pirie believes that

> [the] assumption that students can easily discard their earlier learning underestimates the importance of what goes on in classrooms. Early experiences are foundational, and we have to ask exactly what foundation we think we are building. (76)

Better than learning a form and using it in every instance of academic writing, I would rather students learn about the flexibility of written language, its playfulness, its possibility, its room for (Dare I use the *c* word?) creativity.

I had a student address the issue of foundational experience—with some amount of ruefulness—another way:

> From where I stand now, waiting until after high school to unleash your creativity is too late. By then, at least from a teacher's point of view, you could have lost a student's interest in higher education.
>
> *Katherine Converse Goodwin, College Junior*

We want students to become versatile with words on paper. We want them to become flexible, logical, inventive, and resourceful. Pirie thinks that inculcation in the form of the five-paragraph you-know-what might actually harm or delay students' ability to write:

> Writing, at its core, is a matter of *finding and making the shapes of ideas*, not a matter of cramming ideas into a universal pattern. Well-intentioned teachers believe they are giving students a helpful boost by handing over a prefabricated structure, but they may in fact be denying students the opportunity to do the very thing that writing is all about—making order, building a structure for the specific ideas at hand. In an important way, those students are not doing real writing. They are creating clever, almost lifelike facsimiles of writing, but a key element is missing: they have never asked themselves, "What shape is demanded by what I am trying to say?" (1997, 77)

The five-paragraph you-know-what has spawned many mythical features of good writing for academic audiences:

- An essay must be thesis-driven.
- An essay cannot use *I* or embody the personality and voice of the writer.
- An essay cannot be personal, but rather must be objective.
- An essay can contain no humor, no dialog, no narrative.
- An essay must end with a final paragraph that restates the thesis and summarizes what has already been said.

An essay must be thesis-driven.

I have been in the company of students, teachers, and others whose minds worked in thesis-driven, deductive ways: They experienced a piece of literature or a set of circumstances and quickly formulated a stance. They made a succinct statement, then argued its truth point by point. At a workshop in Holland, Michigan, years ago, I read Raymond Carver's short story "The Bath" to a large group of teachers. Then we wrote about the meaning we made of the story. Volunteers began reading aloud what they'd written. One fellow read a classic literary essay in which he eloquently stated a theme he saw in the literature, explicated it convincingly, and ended with a rhetorical flourish that left us breathless—all this in one ten-minute quick-draft! Ruth Nathan (1988), no slouch herself at analytical thinking, exclaimed, "How did you do that?"

He was practiced in it, that's how. And I've a hunch his mind was adroit in working that way. Not everyone's is. Many of us are incredibly messy, tentative, and groping in our initial writing. Anyone who writes—even on-the-spot analytic superstars—knows that the act of writing leads to thinking, leads to thinking that would not have been thought unless the act of writing had been under way. Many advocates of the thesis-driven essay believe you develop a thesis *before* you begin your essay. You do this from your consideration of the data at hand, from your weighing of evidence. Then you write your essay proving the thesis—a classical Greek notion of writing in which the writer knows what she wants to say and simply finds language to dress up her thoughts (Knoblauch and Brannon 1984).

Years ago I visited a former student who worked in a steel mill by day and took a college literature course at night. On the coffee table was an essay Mark had written about three short stories. His definitive thesis statement fairly bristled with "I dare anyone to challenge this." In the following paragraphs Mark expanded his position, ferreting out nuances of plot and character, illuminating thematic similarities and differences among the stories. Mark was the owner of a first-rate linguistic intelligence. In high school he had been a poor speller, a haphazard student, and an excellent writer. His virtuosity with language and ideas was exciting to behold and fulfilling to read. Mark's literary essay reached a thrilling climax—language, imagery, argument, and echoes from each story coming together in a final, triumphant paragraph *that was in direct opposition to his thesis*—the thesis he had put together, of course, before engaging in the deep thinking that the actual writing led to.

Easily fixed, you are thinking. Mark merely needed to go back and revise the essay—particularly that thesis—to match what he finally came to think and so eloquently explicated. He could surely do that, if, indeed, the thesis-driven essay were the only way for writers to express their thinking. Sometimes writers do well to take a stand early—write a thesis statement and defend or explain it. But top-down, urgently argued, thesis-driven essays are not the only way to share perceptions and communicate ideas. Sometimes writers are better off unfolding a story and revealing surprises to the reader. Sometimes they are better off posing a dilemma, then exploring and discussing it.

Five-paragraph you-know-whats are the ticket students need for success in their classes? Not in mine. And I am an academic.

An essay cannot use *I* or embody the personality and voice of the writer.

I ran into this dictum when I student taught. It was a coup for me in 1970 to student teach in a high school with a teacher who had created and taught a one-semester composition course. I learned from Phyllis Neumann, a woman who valued literature *and* fine writing by teenagers. Students wrote argumentative, thesis-driven essays modeled after the method of writing them in Lucile Vaughan Payne's *The Lively Art of Writing* (1970). The book was big on dictums. Elimination of *I* was one of them. Lucile's reasons involved wordiness and power.

> I believe the USA's unilateral foreign policy is arrogant and damaging to its image as a democracy.

The statement would carry more force and authority if "I believe" were cut. In addition, the deletion would eliminate words without affecting meaning, always a good idea. "I believe" is also redundant: if the sentence occurs in your essay, the reader knows that it is you who believes it.

Seems like harmless advice. I, too, strive to make my writing clean and forceful, sans redundancy and wordiness. The personal pronoun myth is related to another one, which is the one that really causes damage to students' voices and integrity: the objectivity myth.

An essay cannot be personal, but rather must be objective.

This is sham. Essays cannot attain objectivity; I don't care who writes them. Our personal tastes, our proclivities, our biases always assert themselves in one way or another. But couch the writing without first person, without personal stories to support a position, without acknowledging any humanity or fallibility on the part of the writer, and the essay *seems* objective. I must ask: Didn't we learn anything from Shakespeare? *Seeming* is not *being*.

I reject the notion of the objective essay. In fact, I welcome informed, reasoned, and voiceful subjectivity. I love seeing one mind at work in the business of writing, one mind probing, reflecting, recounting, explaining, thinking.

In a compelling essay in *College English*, "I Stand Here Writing," Nancy Sommers (1993) explains eloquently how the personal must exist in academic writing.

> At the outset, many of my students think that personal writing is writing about the death of their grandmother. Academic writing is reporting what Elizabeth Kubler-Ross has written about death and dying. Being personal, I want to show my students, does not mean being autobiographical. Being academic does not mean being remote, distant, imponderable. Being personal means bringing their judgments and interpretation to bear on what they read and write, learning that they never leave themselves behind even when they write academic essays. (425)

It's hard to learn to do this. It takes experience, confidence, and courage. It takes judgment to know when using the first-person *I* will not clutter the writing and when it will effectively get the reader on your side. It takes judgment to know when a personal story of your own will enhance your argument, illustrate your point, help your reader see what you see, come to meaning where you come to meaning.

An essay can contain no humor, no dialog, no narrative.

I reject these out of hand. I'll admit my bias: lightness and humor are important to my mental well-being. Voices are important to my thinking. Story helps me understand my experience, which includes the experiences of reading and writing.

The omission of humor must be a holdover from the attitude that essay writing—especially academic essay writing—is serious business where there is no room for frivolity, foolery, or joking. Dialog? Some people want purity in their genres. Dialog, they maintain, is meant for plays and fiction. No room in essays for people talking.

In some of the best writing I read, however, I see genres blurring. I see techniques in one genre used to great effect in another. Think of how the new journalists of the 1960s commandeered fictional techniques to great effect in their nonfiction. And no narrative in essays? Look at the work of great essayists: Michel de Montaigne, Annie Dillard, James Thurber, Henry David Thoreau, Barbara Kingsolver—those writers used narrative effectively in making their points.

Consider this personal essay by Leslie Robinett, a college junior when she wrote it. She was charged to write about an experience with literature that turned her head around:

> **Understanding Dad**
>
> When I was young, I loved to bundle up on the couch and watch the snow fall. I even had a favorite blanket, a camouflaged poncho liner. It was so smooth and light and warm.
>
> There was one problem with my wonderful blanket. I have three younger brothers who also liked it. They said they liked it because it was camouflage,

but I know they just wanted it so I couldn't have it. My brothers and I would fight over it, often trying to pull the blanket in four different directions. The poncho didn't survive the fights intact. It got a tear here and a smudge there, until it got pretty rough looking.

My dad went ballistic every time he saw one of us with it. "Keep your damn hands off my blanket!" he said. "It's not yours, so don't touch it!" There were lots of hurt feelings. I always asked my dad why he got crazy over a stupid blanket. He just ignored me.

Just recently, I was assigned to read Tim O'Brien's *Going After Cacciato*, a novel about the Vietnam War. I don't read about Vietnam. I don't usually watch movies about Vietnam. I don't like the images of horror, pain, and death the war conjures. The war also symbolized everything I do not know or understand about my dad.

I do know he was a sniper in the war and saw a lot of his friends die. He killed people, and he doesn't like to talk about it.

When I read about the war, I think I am seeing it through my father's eyes. I think about my dad and everything I do not know. Then I think about all that he must have gone through, and I cry.

I read *Going After Cacciato* only because it was assigned. I never would have read it otherwise. Throughout the book, I managed not to feel much. But there was one part, one line really, that brought some old feelings into the open. A soldier is sitting guard on a cold, wet night. Then "he found his poncho liner, wrapped himself in it, then lit another cigarette." This one line would mean almost nothing to most people. But to me it meant the world.

All those years ago, when my brothers and I fought over that poncho liner, I had no idea what it meant to my dad. I didn't know until I read that line. I might never have known.

The poncho represents that one cold, lonely soldier who had nothing else to keep him alive. It represents comrades whose bodies were once covered with a poncho liner awaiting the trip home. Dad's poncho liner was his link to all those who died and all those who live with the memory of death, more than any medal or picture ever could.

That poncho came home from a hateful war intact, to cover me and keep me warm. I never knew then why my dad got so upset. I didn't understand his rampages or all that was behind them.

Now I know.

"He found his poncho liner, wrapped himself in it, then lit another cigarette."

Leslie Robinett, College Junior

If you were as moved by this essay as I was, take a deep breath right now and savor it before reading on.

Would Leslie's essay have been better if she had written a general first paragraph that ended with this sentence: "My dad's experience as a soldier in Vietnam became clear to me once I realized that the poncho liner he brought home from the war symbolized the horror and pain he had experienced"?

Who knows for sure?

But I'm glad she didn't write it that way. I can't imagine Leslie achieving the same emotional impact by cramming this material into the form of a thesis-driven essay. Leslie uses narrative to pull me into her memory and create atmosphere. I find humor here, too, in the image of the children's four-way tugging. Leslie uses dialog to characterize her dad. Her essay is told without self-consciousness. She is personal and reflective, the use of personal pronouns *I* and *my* not intrusive or redundant. All this leads to that wonderful reflective paragraph near the end when Leslie analyzes what the poncho symbolizes and finally understands a part of her dad that has been a mystery to her. She helps readers understand with her. She uses a three-word paragraph to emphasize the profound nature of her discovery. For the final sentence of the essay, she quotes that subdued lonely line from O'Brien. The ending, it seems to me, is damn near perfect. I am moved and grateful for the reading experience. How many student-written essays do you say that about?

An essay must end with a final paragraph that restates the thesis and summarizes what has already been said.

Sometimes yes, sometimes no. Hard to restate a thesis in those pieces of writing that don't start with a thesis, like Leslie's. And would you have really wanted Leslie to engage in a summary in the final paragraph? But that is what she might have done had she believed that this realization of hers would have to fit into the structure of a five-paragraph you-know-what.

One of my Miami students wrote this about his evolution as a writer:

> For years I struggled with my own writing, staring at page after page on the computer screen, wondering why it felt so dry and lacking. This, of course, was back in high school where the five-paragraph essay held dominion over all other forms of writing. I never understood how something so lacking in personality and flavor could be praised, no matter how technically accurate it was.

> Then one day during my junior year of high school I asked my friend Johnathan what the plan was for Mr. Burton's class. He looked at me, begrudgingly rolling his eyes. "It's an essay day. More robotic writing," he groaned.
>
> *Jason Robinson, College Junior*

Yes, no robotic writing. Please. It's hard enough to break through to authentic voice.

15

Of Buts and Burrs and Bad Advice

I stand before a group of fourth graders ready to lead them in a writing workshop. My goal is to get the children writing about topics they care about, confer with as many of them as I can during writing time, and gather them together near period's end to share some of their writing. I also want to teach the children to "hit dem senses." On chart paper I write *see, feel, hear, smell,* and *taste*, and talk about how writers often use language of sensory detail to help readers experience their words. On the overhead I place a poem I have written, read it aloud, and ask the children to identify words and phrases that hit the senses.

Morning Coffee

An hour before the sun lightens the black sky
I pad downstairs in soft slippers to the kitchen.
I pour coffee beans into a grinder
and burrrrr them into grounds.

Coffee suddenly colors the air,
speaks yellow butter melting
into steaming biscuits topped with peach jam.
But the air goes gray as I get used to the smell.

A minute later boiling water wakens the grounds,
the air now red with scent.
Soon I press my lips against the porcelain rim of a cup,
sip hot coffee, spread flavor over my tongue.
The taste is good, black and bitter,
But not the best I know is coffee.

Tomorrow morning, after I grind coffee beans,
I'll pour the grounds into an empty jar,
tighten the lid and take it to my office
to set at the edge of the desk.

Every now and then
I'll unscrew the lid, sniff
like a careful animal in the woods
and really wake up.

—Tom Romano

The children are bursting to talk of the senses.

"I see that butter melting."

"When you write 'boiling water,' I hear the coffee maker."

"You say the flavor spreads over your tongue. How can you like that? Coffee's yucky."

"I smell the coffee when you sniff."

"You got feeling in there when you write about that whatever-it-is of the cup on your lips."

Then one girl says, "That last sentence of the second paragraph—you start it with *but*. You can't do that."

"I can't?"

"No, you can't start sentences with *and* or *but*."

"You know what?" I say, and I draw a quick box around *But*. "I did."

"But you can't do that."

"What? Will the but police come after me?"

She raises her eyebrows, grins, and says with a lilt in her voice, "They might."

"What about *burr*?" I ask. "I spelled *burr* with five *r*s. Can I do that?"

She says nothing, just keeps those eyebrows aloft. The children look my way for the answer. Nothing like playing loose with rules to rivet attention. "Why do you suppose I added those *r*s?"

One girl wraps her arms around herself and says, "That's how you spell *burr* when you're cold."

16

Grammatically High-Strung

I like the way you teach writing in the book with the ideas and what a student is trying to say having most importance, that you can fix it up later. That's so much better than what I went through, day after day diagramming those sentences. I didn't get nothing.

MAE ROMANO CARNAHAN

That's my mother speaking in a letter to me a month after my first book was published. Mom didn't finish ninth grade. She dropped out of school in May of 1930, about seven months into the Great Depression. I'm guessing that the sentence diagramming she did was more about correctness and the knowledge of subjects, predicates, and parts of speech than it was about teaching writing and the wonderful flexibility of American English.

I feel persistent, low-level tension between my role as an English educator responsible for helping students become secondary school English teachers and my passion as a writing teacher who moves students to cut loose with language, trust the gush, write voicefully, focusing on meaning, language flow, and straight, honest perceptions, to hell with correctness, decorum, and propriety.

In a memoir titled *The Blood Runs Like a River Through My Dreams*, author Nasdijj writes,

> I know nothing about the technical stuff of writing or where to put a comma. What I know about writing goes beyond where to put your commas. What I know about writing has to do with where you put your heart. (2000, 112)

This is where I land every time in matters of correctness versus voice, form versus meaning, commas versus heart. I want students to experience the energy of their voices. I want them to feel power rising in them to use those voices to describe and explain, to analyze and narrate. I want them to understand the voice they are and to imagine voices they might become. I want them to realize how their natural voice can be engaging, colorful, and effective. I also want them to realize that if their writing is a mechanical disaster, their natural voice might be dismissed by others, regardless of how authentic, colorful, and pointed it is. I want them to keep gaining and learning, getting more education, and becoming savvier in the ways of written English so they have access to many voices.

A young, intelligent friend of ours cannot abide the voices in her workplace, her coworkers whose work skills are competent, in some cases excellent, but whose speech features liberal use of *ain't*, subject-verb disagreements, and double negatives. Our friend has that not uncommon prejudice against regional, non-standard dialects. I fear that if she had the power, she would silence the songs of her coworkers until they got their grammar and usage straight.

On the page our voices get translated into symbols and punctuation. There are standards and traditions for how those symbols ought to look and sound. Many years ago when I was a young teacher, I brought a short story written by one of my high school students to a nonteacher friend. In my four years of teaching, I'd never read a short story written by a teenager that was so sophisticated, literary, and disarmingly honest. A paragraph into reading, my nonteacher friend began carping about the atrocious punctuation and manifold spelling errors. Indeed, those were all present. Although a capable writer and reader himself, my friend said nothing about the story's surprising observations, deepening plot tension, vivid characterizations, evocative detail, and distinctive voice.

I'm glad that *I* am my students' writing teacher and that some of my educated, intelligent friends are not. With strong-voiced, technically unskilled writers, I must slip in my work at getting them correctionally proficient, while not causing them to retreat, hold back, play it safe in their writing—like the third grader I worked with once who wouldn't use any word she wasn't certain of spelling at that moment, because a previous teacher had made her correctly spell out ten times any misspelled, first-draft guess she made. In other words, when Melissa behaved like a real writer, she got nailed. She scuttled her substantial oral vocabulary and derailed the flow of her thinking in the name of correctness. Every writing teacher understands the dilemma and reasoning of Melissa's teacher. That doesn't mitigate, however, the damage the teacher's practice had on Melissa's writing process.

I don't want to become the kind of writing teacher one of my Miami students described when she wrote about arbitrary rules of writing:

> I always just knew it was okay to begin a sentence with "and" or "but" if it helped your point. Whenever a random grammatically high-strung teacher circled that usage and called it a mistake, I dutifully corrected it but knew in my heart that wasn't how I really wanted to say it.
>
> *Jenn Ellison, College Sophomore*

Not all students have the self-confidence that Jenn had to keep her own council about how she wrote.

I know that writing involves more than putting the heart on the page. I know that audiences react irrationally to errors in the amenities of writing. As part of their development in becoming strong, voiceful writers, I want students to steadily improve their skills in language and in producing written texts that reflect the norms of standard edited English (and to break those norms when they can do so meaningfully). I also want my English education students to learn the higgledy-piggledy ins and outs of language use, like the difference between *exert* and *excerpt* or why "between she and I" is hypercorrective or why "we ain't gonna go" won't raise an eyebrow in some contexts but will have people's eyes widening in others.

There is no magic bullet to ensure that all students write with textual correctness and standard grammar and usage. If all students came from a family and neighborhood in which conservative, standard, edited English were spoken and written, then there wouldn't be much of a problem (though I imagine adolescent speech communities would surely put that asunder).

My bottom line value in teaching writing is voice. I want nothing to stand in the way of my students' evolving their voices. Experience tells me that for many students a primary emphasis in writing on grammar, usage, and punctuation—a close kin to strict form in writing—is a voice blocker, a voice skewer, a voice silencer.

Here is the dilemma for me summed up in one student: I taught Angie one semester of her sophomore year of high school. She was feisty, alert, and intelligent with not much motivation for formal education. Just like her personality, her writing was direct, colloquial, and pulled no punches. After one of her pieces of writing, I wrote her a note, complimenting her on her honesty and naturalness of voice, pinpointing strong sentences, and calling attention to her myriad punctuation errors. Angie wrote me back:

> I agree with what you say. I would have had more of them two best sentences but I realy didnt see where else they fit in good. I probably do have alot of punctuation errors but thats me and I want my writing to say Angie and not Perfect. I don't quite understand what you are saying about the "honesty" and "naturalness of voice."

"Voice," I wrote back to her, "is the part of your writing that says Angie most loudly and clearly. A little more attention to punctuation will help your reader experience the *you* in *your* writing."

I talked to Angie recently over the telephone, first time in seventeen years. I was so happy to hear her voice that "my heart soared like a hawk," as Old Lodge

Skins would have said. Angie had graduated a year early from high school, had owned her own temp business for a while, and now was a valued employee in an optometrist's office. She was mother to an eight-year-old daughter, and the family was just closing on a new house. Angie hadn't attended college. Any dialect features and nonstandard usages she retained hadn't worked against her. Her voice was strong and clear and forthright—and maybe could still get feisty when it needed to. And I hoped that when she had occasion to write anything, Angie's words continued to say *Angie*.

I usually have more success with students in getting them both to write with voice and to learn some of the rules. I think that's because I show such keen interest in their meanings, perceptions, and thinking, however incomplete, clichéd, or unsophisticated they might be. I'm there to get students to examine their thinking and write the best they can. But I still feel strong responsibility in alerting my students to the amenities of writing. Most of them are English education majors and will have students of their own one day. I want them to nurture their students' voices *and* to know the amenities of writing so they can teach their students.

What pays off in teaching students standard usage and punctuation is our slow, steady, attentive work, one or two skills at a time on each piece of writing that students take through a writing process. Students have to write a lot, and they have to read a lot so they constantly experience printed possibilities. Teachers have to decide when to give students minilessons and then systematic practice in a mechanical writing skill. It doesn't make sense, for example, to teach students the use of the semicolon when they are still developing sentence sense and learning to halt them with periods.

On some matters of correctness, especially with debatable rules like variant word spellings and minor comma splices, and on arcane rules of little use to writers like when to use the subjunctive mood, I say step back. Go easy. Watch and learn. Ask questions. Less is more. (I cringe when I think of all the error accounting I did on Angie's paper.) Don't adversely affect someone's drive to write, someone's eagerness to proclaim herself on the page, because of your own grammatically high-strung obsessing. Don't be a Romano to an Angie. In matters of correctness in punctuation, usage, and grammar, focus your work for maximum effectiveness. When students write something that features characters talking, that's the time to teach the use of quotation marks.

Here is an admission and a resolution: I still get bothered when students place periods and commas outside quotation marks instead of inside them. That's much ado about little, it seems to me now. I intend to change. I'll teach the skill in a minilesson but won't mark it on papers anymore. Why should a teacher—especially one with plenty of papers to read for meaning and voice—be concerned about that copyediting idiosyncrasy? Yet there I have been, writing in the transpositional mark whenever I encountered commas and periods outside the quotation mark. If I am going to live or die about some aspect of writing, it sure should not be periods and commas inside quotation marks. I want students to remember me being concerned about more important matters. I want them to feel power in their voices and in the meanings they work hard to make.

I want them to remember me as a teacher who created a classroom in which they were empowered to speak defiantly on the page, lovingly, lasciviously, reverently, boldly, tenderly—the whole range of emotions that humans feel and might appropriately write from. I want students to remember me as a teacher who helped them refine their meaning, indeed, get to meaning in their writing that they hadn't intended on. I want them to remember me as a teacher committed to getting at what was important in his own writing, who was as meticulous as he could be about the amenities himself, was even more meticulous about the meaning he was making and the sound of his words.

If any of my students become reluctant to trust the gush for fear of making grammatical, usage, or punctuation errors, I've become one of those grammatically high-strung teachers. They won't achieve what I want. They won't remember me as I want them to. And I won't have helped them to voice.

As my mother might have put it, they won't get nothing.

17

Whatever It Takes: Breaking the Rules in Style

Reading exploratory, imaginative writing gives me ideas for my next paper. The alternate style is the spark of creation for pieces yet to be born. I think, "Hmm, maybe I'll try that," or "Oh! That would be fun." Grammar B is like getting in the car and being the only one on a deserted country road, with a guarantee that you won't be caught for speeding. There are no grammar cops in sight, so you step on the gas. A little harder. A little harder still. Before you know it you're flying down the road with the wind in your hair, never looking back. How fast am I going? you wonder. But it doesn't matter; you're free. You're creative. You're breaking the rules in style.

MEG MCKINNON, College Junior

In Brian De Palma's film *The Untouchables* (1986), Eliot Ness—played by Kevin Costner—tries to enlist the aid of a tough Irish street cop named Malone—played by Sean Connery. Ness wants Malone to join his fledgling group of crime fighters to battle the Chicago mob led by Al Capone—played by Robert De Niro. Malone is reluctant to join, even a little hostile. He has seen his share of prima donna crusaders. He needs to see how serious Ness is.

"What are you prepared to do?" Malone asks.

"Everything within the law," says Ness.

"And then what are you prepared to do?"

I could ask you the same question: What are you prepared to do to move students to write with strong voices?

Think about that a moment.

How far will you go? To what lengths? What sacrifice will you make?

Donald Murray reminds us of a key point in our approach to language:

> It is the responsibility of schools to teach the rules educated people follow most of the time when they speak, write, and read, successfully communicating with each other. But it should also be the responsibility of schools to teach the other times when the rules can be broken to achieve clarity. Language should not be taught as an absolute, a matter of clear right and wrong. The history of language is the history of change; the rules evolve. (1998, 161)

It is the last three sentences of that passage that interest me most, that part about showing students the flexibility of language, the possibility it offers for productive rule breaking. Since the mid-1980s, I've been interested in pushing students to break rules of standard written English as a way of communicating with élan and voice.

In the effort to ignite students' voices, I'm down for just about anything. Rule breaking is the most drastic pedagogical tack I've taken. This idea quickened in me when I read Winston Weathers' wonderful book (though ignominiously out of print for some time now) *An Alternate Style: Options in Composition* (1980).

In a scholarly treatise, Weathers looks to professional writers, both classic and contemporary, to discover the many ways in which they have broken the rules of standard written English and written exceedingly well. He cites rule breaking from the writing of Robert Frost, e. e. cummings, Virginia Woolfe, Tom Wolfe, Tillie Olsen, Anne Sexton, John Dos Passos, E. M. Forster, and many more.

I formally introduce students to ways in which they can break the rules in style. They read two chapters I've written about what Weathers has called Grammar B, the alternative to Grammar A, which is the standard, traditional, conservative form of written English enshrined by most publications, standardized tests, and just about every English teacher who has ever written *frag*, *awk*, and *RO*, including me (Romano 1995). I demonstrate how professional writers and past students have effectively used sentence fragments, lists, double voice, labyrinthine sentences, and orthographic variation (respelling of words). These unconventional language moves leave the norm of Grammar A. They break the rules. It isn't anything students haven't seen before.

> In high school I began to notice that we were reading books that didn't adhere to the rules we were meant to. I found it hypocritical that I was being berated for doing the same things my teachers were praising as great literature.
>
> *Julia Porter, College Freshman*

Look at the first six paragraphs of sportswriter John Erardi's Cincinnati *Enquirer* piece about a high school basketball rivalry, "Woodward vs. Withrow":

> Maurice Williams, 13, sat on his bed in his room in his mother's apartment on Reading Road in Avondale, dribbling a basketball. Left hand, right hand, left-right-left-right, leftrightleftright, so quickly that it was a blur to even him.
>
> *Woodward, Withrow, Woodward, Withrow,* he whispered.
>
> He dribbled the basketball around his legs, between his legs, out the other side. Leftrightleftrightleftright.
>
> *Woodward, Withrow, Woodward, Withrow.*
>
> "I grew up watching Woodward-Withrow games," said Williams. "I wasn't sure where I'd wind up going to school. I was hoping it would be one school or the other. I wanted to play in that game someday."
>
> That someday is tonight. (1996, A1)

In the second sentence, Erardi uses a sentence fragment to contain a hyphenated word he's invented, then he removes the hyphens, jams the words together to further show the speed of the dribbling. The boy's spoken words—cast in italics instead of quotation marks—become a psychological mantra three lines later. The boy is passionate, single-minded, trancelike. Erardi's rule breaking to make written language match the physical action of dribbling a basketball and the boy's obsession with the two schools makes the writer's voice playful, dramatic, and respectful.

In an *Esquire* piece, Ron Rosenbaum writes about "dangerous women." At one point in his article he uses double voice to throw two points of view into sharp contrast:

> Lauren . . . argue[s] that men are really talking through their hats when they say they want Dangerous Women, because when they find one, they just can't handle it, particularly when it comes to sex.
>
> Lauren has been dangerous in her time: A deceptively seductive yet innocent-looking blond, smart and knowing, she has strong feelings about men who say they like dangerousness.
>
> "I prefer to call it intensity," she says. "Men always say they want real intensity, particularly in bed, but if you *really* show it to them, it scares them. They run."
>
> She talked about the way the male vocabulary for dangerousness in women so often misses the reality she sees. And so, as an educational public service to men, here is what one Dangerous Woman thinks is really going on:

When A Guy Says . . .	**What He Really Means Is . . .**
"She's too neurotic."	"She's smarter than me."
"She's too intense."	"She's more interesting than me."
"She's too difficult."	"She's more independent than me."

"She's too out of control." "She's not under *my* control."
"She's too dangerous." "She's braver than me."

(1996, 108)

Writing that bends and breaks rules is out there, and not just in the world of email, instant messaging, and journal writing, but in mainstream publications, too. Most of my students take readily to breaking the rules in style. For some it's like unleashing a long-pent-up need:

> Dr. Romano, why have you been holding out on us like this? I have been waiting for Grammar B to be professionally noted and praised my whole life. Breaking the rules of traditional standard English is the reason I go on writing. Well, I don't write to specifically break the rules, but being able to break the rules is that little something extra that keeps me going. It makes it fun and exciting. It makes it original. Sure, all writing is original, but breaking the rules inside of already original writing is where kings are born.
>
> *Sir Nathan Stevens, College Junior*

The Sentence Fragment

One useful tool for rule breaking is the sentence fragment, that sometimes verbless, sometimes subjectless, sometimes bothless group of words that appears in students' writing, usually unwittingly. Most of their writing lives, students have been nailed for using sentence fragments, regardless of whether they intended the fragment or not. Professional writers, however, don't hesitate to use fragments when their use makes meaningful points. Michael Pollan's first chapter in *The Botany of Desire* (2001) is about the apple, which originated in central Europe. We learn all kinds of facts about the history and mythology of the apple and its chief proponent, John Chapman, aka Johnny Appleseed. In the section that precedes the following excerpt, Pollan writes about how the apple figures into Protestantism and the view of America as a new Eden. His sentence fragment could have easily been unfragmented by hooking it to the previous sentence with a comma. Instead, Pollan uses a sentence fragment to emphasize his point. He even gives it a prominent position. What should properly be the final words in a paragraph become the opening words of the next paragraph:

> [R]ecreating a promised land anywhere in the New World without an apple tree would have been unthinkable.
>
> Especially to a Protestant. There was an old tradition in northern Europe linking the grape, which flourished all through Latin Christendom, with the

> corruption of the Catholic Church, while casting the apple as the wholesome fruit of Protestantism. Wine figured in the Eucharist; also, the Old Testament warned against the temptations of the grape. But the Bible didn't have a bad word to say about the apple or even the strong drink that could be made from it. Even the most God-fearing Puritan could persuade himself that cider had been given a theological free pass. (20–21)

One of my students wrote a multigenre research paper about punk rock. As befits her antiestablishment subject, she purposely broke a lot of rules in her writing. "I didn't know a thing about punk rock," writes Jamie in the preface to her paper. "Really. Nothing, not the name of one band, the origins of the movement, the significance of it. Just this past weekend, there was a small punk rock concert outside Havighurst Hall. I quote the drummer: 'I wrote this song when I was pissed off.' This seems to be the overriding fuel behind punk rock's fire today."

In one part of her paper, Jamie embodies some of that anger by creating a character. Note Jamie's use of sentence fragments and the key three-word repetition that she alters slightly in the last three sentences when she presents readers with an unexpected insight:

> "I AM PUNK," she screams. Eyes wrenched shut, mouth stretched wide, teeth crooked in defiance. As if she wanted that one word to swallow her whole identity. Punk like the posters that sheathe her walls, the edges curling down. Loud labels and semi-famous rockers curling with them. "I am punk." She's become angry now, as if you wished to strip her of the title she's earned by wearing a dog collar and cutting her hair short. "I am punk." She stamps her feet, a maniacal dance tribute to her idols. Rebelling against everything, until there is nothing left to rebel against. An unexplainable need to cry "Fuck you" at the world, at those controlling her, at the countless grabbing hands, coming at her from every direction. Shouting, shaking fists at the air she believes is choking her. She is punk, to hide that, deep inside, she is soft, a girl who likes to be pretty. She is punk along with thousands of others so that she'll never have to feel alone with herself and her anger. Kept safe here, she is punk.
>
> *Jamie Fuhrman, College Freshman*

The List

The list is another strategy that assumes prominence in the alternate style. The words or phrases often appear just like a grocery list diagonally down the page. They can, however, appear as part of a perfectly grammatical sentence, though it isn't often that you see long lists such as the following one by Joy Fowler. Joy is a writing teacher at the Cincinnati School for Creative and Performing Arts. She earned a doctorate in creative writing and children's literature through the Union Institute. For part of the requirements of her dissertation, Joy wrote a young adult historical novel, *Redheaded Angel* (2001), set during the American Civil War, or the War of Northern Aggression, as she sometimes calls it. The narrative is told from the southern point of view through the eyes of an eleven-year-old girl named Cully. In an epilogue to the novel, Joy has her expository say about the ghastliness of this particular nineteenth-century war. In this excerpt, she uses a long list to communicate some of that horror and misery:

> I cannot imagine living on a daily basis for years with the likelihood of being shot, shooting someone, having a limb sawed off on the edge of a corpse-strewn field with no anesthesia, sleeping on frozen ground, fording rivers in the winter, having all my clothes freeze stiff to my skin, being blinded by gun powder burns, never seeing my family again, having my house burnt, being raped by the enemy, being dismembered, riding twenty-five miles without sleep or food on horseback, often, then staying awake to scout, fight, or do sentry duty, seeing my friends explode, having my eardrums burst from cannon fire, watching my leg rot yellow from gangrene, dying of measles, dysentery, pneumonia by the thousands, deserting, getting caught, court-marshaled, captured, imprisoned, tortured, hanged, having my horse shot out from under me, reading untrue newspaper accounts of my actions when I was trying my hardest, hearing of a sick, maybe dying, family member and not being able to go home, being responsible for so many other trusting souls, having to keep my spirits up for appearances, keeping on in the face of insurmountable odds, believing the odds are not insurmountable.
>
> *Joy Fowler, Teacher*

Students can often use the list to cover a lot of territory and build momentum, even reaching insight, as Joy did in her final item. Students' voices are revealed in the details, meaning, and urgency of their lists.

Double Voice

Another alternate style device popular with students is double voice. I'm not talking about dialog here but rather two voices, perhaps within the same author: an objective voice and a subjective voice, a rational voice and an emotional voice, a factual voice and an imaginative voice. Roisin O'Brien writes from competing feelings she had after she learned she had been accepted into the graduate program in English education at Teachers College, Columbia University. Look how Roisin uses an internal debate to reveal her exhilaration and anxiety. One internal voice is conservative and safe, the other liberal and risky.

> *We got in!*
>
> Yeah, I know. Now what?
>
> *What do you mean?*
>
> How do we explain to people why we turned down a chance to live in New York?
>
> *We're not turning down a chance to live in New York. We're going. "New York, New York it's a wonderful town. The Bronx is up and the Battery's down. The people ride in a hole in the ground. New York, New York."*
>
> You can't be serious. We've lived in Boston our whole lives. We can't just uproot ourselves now and move to a city where we know almost no one. How sadistic! How depressing! Not to mention what we're in for. I mean you read the packet the English Ed. Department sent. We have to do two semesters of student teaching as part of our graduate program.
>
> *Yeah.*
>
> In two separate schools.
>
> *Yeah.*
>
> In two separate New York City public schools.
>
> *Yeah!*
>
> How can that sound appealing to you?
>
> *It's life, man. How is that not appealing? I mean, come on, whatever happened to that stuff we learned in college? Didn't anything sink in? Whatever happened to sucking the marrow out of life and choosing the road less traveled? You know—poetry from experience that speaks to people like us in a time of decision. What about Shakespeare? To thine own self be true. Remember? We're only hurting ourselves if we let this opportunity pass us by.*
>
> Yeah. (sigh). I forgot about Shakespeare. That one gets me every time. So, we're moving to New York.
>
> *Roisin O'Brien, Teacher*

In the same multigenre paper, Roisin wrote a piece about how students dealt with her name and also how she dealt with the sexual tension and intimidation that young female high school teachers often contend with in the classroom. She communicates this through alternate style techniques—multiple voices, word fusions, graphic textual variety, the dispensing of conventional paragraphing, and labyrinthine phrasing within a sentence fragment to more closely reflect her interior turmoil and professional resolve. Note that the first and last sentences are in perfect Grammar A form, but, oh, the inbetween is royalty:

> **Rasheen Dawg**
> At West Manhattan Outreach Center, the students wrote to me. Hey Rashene Hey Risheen Hey Rashid my paper is late cuz my kid was sick last night and I had to care for her. Once I got a Rasheen Dawg after I wrote to a student that his last poem was totally inappropriate so go back and rethink it. He respected that so the Dawg was a gift of acceptance. Unlike Lenny who used to call me RaSHEEN with a smirk like he knew something about me that was secret an' lowdown dirty like it was an intense turn-on to call me because we were closer in age which made me a possibility in his eyes. One night he sickened me as I read his poetry portfolio at 3 a.m. full of raped words forcingthrustingslapping on every page until I stopped and said NO. I'M NOT GRADING THIS LENNY. But miss, I did it. Ha' com? Smirkwink. It's offensive, Lenny. What? Where? C'you sit with me an' work out where? Smirkwink. Why don't you go back and put on the mindset of a woman. Then take out anything that offends you. Got it? I received it back the next day in gradable form.
>
> *Roisin O'Brien, Teacher*

My students know we're in dangerous territory with our use of alternate style techniques. But as Meg notes in the epigraph to the chapter, the rule breaking is exhilarating. And many of my students are given pause. Most of them are going to be English teachers one day. They will be responsible for preparing students to take standardized writing tests and to write academic essays in high school and college. Their students will be required to produce "correct" writing for writing worlds in which imagination, creativity, and meaningful language play are not expected and often not recognized as revealing intelligence, intentionality, and meaning.

My students and I have vigorous discussions about "proper" grammar, audience awareness, variant word spellings, topic and voice restrictions, language change over time, grammatically high-strung fastidiousness, and the place of Grammar B in academia. One evening even a colleague of mine—a reading teacher, fine writer himself, and dedicated teacher of writing—heard our talk from the hallway and stepped into the classroom to join our discussion.

I've heard many arguments against Grammar B:

- Students need to know the rules before they break them.
- Students will produce maverick essays on formal tests of writing skills.

- Students will become irresponsible writers, sacrificing depth for glitz.
- Students will develop a great sense of freedom but no discipline.
- If students are allowed to break rules, they will not develop respect for them.

These arguments don't sway me. I teach Grammar B and also emphasize Grammar A. They are not mutually exclusive. We learn of the black space between the stars at the same time that we admire the stars. Without the dark night sky, we wouldn't even see the stars. Learning how to effectively break rules helps us learn awareness of rules. As students learn to forge and manipulate language, their respect for the craft increases. Crucial in any writing circumstance is audience awareness; alternate style techniques are not always appropriate. Smart writers scope out the needs and biases of their audience. My initial response to a student's writing always addresses meaning. When style and voice do not contribute to meaning—when they are just for show—that's bad writing. For writers the flip side of freedom is discipline. Responsible teachers emphasize both. Good writers cherish both.

> Your students, like mine, might benefit from purposeful rule breaking. Prepare a handout with examples of effective sentence fragments, double voice, orthographic variation, labyrinthine sentences, and lists. Over a series of class periods, require students to break the rules in style. I encourage you to experiment with each alternate style device, too. The sharing of writing and talk about rules will lead students to deeper understanding of "correct" language use and the possibility for effective writing that breaks the rules.

Some years back I brought a piece of writing I was working on into a classroom of high school seniors. I put the poem on the overhead and began reading. Before I got far, one student interrupted me: "Hey, wait a minute. You can't break rules like that."

I could. And what's more, I did. You can too. So can your students. Purposeful rule breaking might help their voices break into the open.

Again, what are you prepared to do?

The Day School Gives Out
this poems gonna make you mad
maybe madder then you every been before
you seen this coming din't you
its june and your sick is rising
to many papers to many nights with them

so alls you can do now is
get your finger and thumb up under your glasses
and rub the sides of your nose

this making you mad yet
how could it miss when I aint
doing what you want and I don't
care cause its your headache not mine
in ten minutes I'll be summer
and wont touch pencils til september

so see it dont matter if this
poem fufills its purpose like you always bleive they should
you can make it say what you want
you can shove in terpretations where you damn well please
just like you done with emily dickersons poems
she been dead so long it dont matter to her anyway
an five minutes from now—just five minutes
when I'm driving my pickup

the windows down so wind blows in
rock cranked and jumping
Julie beside me with her hair mussed
an her hand against the back of my neck
my fingers slipped through the rip in her jeans
her naked knee and all that means mine
it sure as hell wont matter to me

—*Tom Romano* (1990)

18

Mischief, Rebellion, Attitude

While I don't want to place overmuch importance on gender,
I know that reading the work of men who approach art, life,
and kids in this spirit of mischief and disregard for authority . . .
has enlarged my horizons.

JUDITH MICHAELS, Poet, Teacher

I am drawn to bold voices, ones laced with humor, irony, and irreverence, voices that make me remember the thrill I felt when one of my grade school peers broke a rule right under the teacher's nose, skating fast over ice so thin that catastrophic consequences were just a glance away. *Mischief* and *rebellion*, Judith Michaels maintains in *Dancing with Words* (2001, 89), are qualities to be searched out and valued in students. And how I appreciate *deviltry*, another of Michaels' dancing words.

Second week of school during my new job at Miami University, I assigned my students to read several chapters in my second book, *Writing with Passion* (1995), chapters that deal with multiple genres and purposeful rule breaking. I didn't know the students well yet, could put names with only a few faces, but I was about to know one young woman indelibly. In the first paragraph of her one-pager, Jenny describes beginning to read the assignment:

> Brain swollen. Body bloated. Senses paranoid. **P**recious **M**ommy's **S**weetheart, **P**re **M**enstrual **S**yndrome, **P**issed-Off **M**aniac **S**truggling. I call home, Mom says, "Stay away from chocolate and salt. Drink lots of water." Yeah, right. I think I'll have a fudgepop and some pretzels. I am a prisoner of my body. I pop a Premensyn and strap myself down with a highlighter and a bad attitude. I am ready for orders. ATTENN—TION! I've been under contract for almost thirteen years from textbooks, teachers, and political curriculums. Page sixty-nine. I laugh bitterly and then honestly. My dramatic

> analysis of *A Doll's House* for theatre 101 was "well-researched, thorough, and inquisitive" according to Professor Dean. I know the truth. My paper was not provocative and it was not original. It was adequate.

In the second paragraph Jenny really revs up the ideas she is writing about:

> I read Chapter Five and I find tools—repetition, repetition, repetition, sentence fragments, a labyrinthine sentence, double voice, the list, and the sharpest, strongest tool of all—ORTHOGRAPHIC VARIATION. Say it again—it feels so powerful—ORTHOGRAPHIC VARIATION. No standard five sentence paragraph for me anymore. With these newly identified allies I press against the red-brick, ivy covered walls that surround me. Are my estrogen levels rising? Am I on the upswing of my PMS cycle, or am I finally breaking out of the academic bonds that tie me down? I read on and in Chapter Six the ugly brown caterpillar I've been breaks out of my cocoon, stretching my cramped, dusty exotic wings that have been locked up by the chains of single-minded writing.

Two paragraphs later, when I finished Jenny's one-pager, I was metaphorically breathless. I wrote at the top of her paper:

> "Who is this woman?!" Absolutely wonderful to read this, Jenny. You've captured the spirit of *Writing with Passion*.

At the end of the semester in her portfolio, Jenny includes her PMS one-pager and explains to me in the cover letter why it is important to her learning:

> First impressions . . . first impressions . . . first impressions. . . . In my mind, brain cells were fighting for breathing room. Not one part of my body was under my control, and even things that are extensions of my body (my laptop and printer) were out of control. I knew my problem was severe PMS—the kind women in my family are famous for, but trying to figure out what was wrong with the rest of the world was driving me out of my mind! All I could think of was that I had a "one-pager" due at the end of the weekend, and I wanted to make a first impression. I wasn't sure if I wanted to make a good impression or a bad impression, but I knew that if I wrote some blasé, neutral, "oh, isn't that nice" kind of piece I would be really, really ticked off. I just wanted to shoot a bullet and leave an impression. I knew that *Writing with Passion* had ignited a long-dead fire in me, and I wanted to show you that I was ready to give it my all, and to resurrect the life in my writing.
>
> When you called and left a message on my machine to call you back, I was hesitant. I didn't run to the phone. I had a bowl of cereal, read some mail,

> and collected my thoughts. You see, by the time I turned the paper in, I was pretty much over the PMS and back to normal. You asked if you could read a part of my paper in class, and in a calm voice I said yes, but the voice inside my mind did a few backflips and screamed at the top of its lungs. I had met my goal—you had noticed my paper.

Jenny's bite and brass made me pay attention. She dived into her writing with a spirit of mischief and disregard for authority. I was the fortunate bull's-eye for the bullet she fired. She had written with attitude: "Back off," she seemed to say. "Give me room to write. I'm learning here, and I'm going to stretch and test some boundaries."

In *The Right to Write* (1998), Julia Cameron has this to say about academic writing and vigorous style:

> It is a rare teacher who takes the time and care to praise the kind of writing that doesn't fit into an academic paradigm. It's as though scholastically we're on a pretty strict diet: "Not so much pepper here."
>
> Not so much pepper. Not so much spunk. Not so much humanity, please. Academically we are inclined to a rather pedestrian prose denuded of personality and passion, perhaps even a bit elevated in tone as if writing is something to be done only from the loftiest of motives, a kind of distillate of rationalism trickled on the page. (2)

Jenny hadn't used much pepper, either. She'd gone beyond pepper. She had used jalapeño seeds. It's nine years since I read Jenny's one-pager. I remember her look, where she sat in class, and most of all, that first piece of writing. The mischief and disregard for authority that Jenny displayed bespeak another attitude that's useful to a writer: the readiness to risk.

Anne Lamott puts it this way:

> Write straight into the emotional center of things. Write toward vulnerability. Don't worry about appearing sentimental. Worry about being unavailable; worry about being absent or fraudulent. Risk being unliked. Tell the truth as you understand it. If you're a writer, you have a moral obligation to do this. And it is a revolutionary act—truth is always subversive. (1994, 226)

Sometimes students develop an edge to their writing because they reach a breaking point. Desperation mixes with frustration and they are determined to be themselves, consequences be damned. Here is one such circumstance:

> In the cumbersome final weeks of second semester of my freshman year, I staged a revolt. I had three essays to write and couldn't stand to type another

boring and lifeless word. For my final paper in Eng. 112, I wrote a spirited analysis of *Othello*. I didn't care anymore. I was going to write something that for once didn't feel like a waste of paper. I wrote in a fashion that was in keeping with my personality and actual voice. Humor, irony, and wordplay reared their heads for the first time in years. My authentic voice only improved with each revision of my paper.

Jeff Slutz, College Junior

Ask your students to take fifteen or twenty minutes to write rapidly, laying down words with candor and spice, writing with an edge, driving directly to the emotional center of something they care about with no holding back. I predict that many of your students will surprise themselves with the power of their voices. Write such a piece yourself before you ask students to do so. Show them you are one of those rare teachers who appreciates such writing.

Assuming a risk-taking stance can be just the attitude adjustment that developing writers need to step forth and seize control of their writing. Here is Robin explaining a significant part of her semester's learning, Robin, who is respectful, thoughtful, intelligent, and now determined to add feistiness to those qualities.

One of the biggest things for me this semester is that I feel as though I am starting to take risks. In the past, if I had been asked to write a one-pager, I would have written it straight, no commentary, no spice. This one-pager, though, is one I can be proud of—it has candor, spice, and a little bit of spunk. And . . . it's not boring.

Robin Perlmuter, College Junior

Spunk, spice, deviltry, rebellion,
and dead seriousness about the integrity of your mind at work.
No way to avoid voice.

19

Many Voices

For all my words about a writer's authentic voice, we have, in fact, a number of voices and voice variations available to us. We aren't monologists; at least, we don't have to be. Many voices exist outside us. Other voices are part of our identity. Within me, for example, I have a sincere, sympathetic voice I use to communicate to friends and relatives undergoing hard times. I have an earnest, precise, slightly indignant voice I use to communicate with businesses that have wronged me. I have a sardonic, irreverent voice I use to communicate with readers I think will join the fun this voice has with hyperbole, irony, and attitude. Multiple voices have I. And sometimes, I must admit, a voice I choose to use misses the mark. Sometimes that sardonic voice, for example, is read as flip, opportunistic, callous, and disrespectful. That's the risk I take when I use such a voice.

I have other voices in me, as well. Some scholars suggest, though, that I have but one voice within me, one that I vary the register of, depending on the rhetorical situation. In music the term *register* refers to the range of an instrument or voice. Bill Strong suggests that I "modulate" my one authentic voice, "its level of formality, its appropriateness for certain situations, its consideration of context" (personal email, 29 November 2002). Donald Murray believes that we have one voice that we "tune" to different occasions (1998, 162).

Regardless of the register, I aim for directness, clarity, and vivid language. It matters not if I'm writing a report to the state office of education or an email message to a friend. I try to demand of myself clear, strong language and a pointed manner.

I also recognize humor as part of my authentic voice. Even in situations that wouldn't seem to allow it, I sometimes inject lightness into the writing if I think it will help make my point. I work in academia, which can, on occasion, exhibit a full measure of pomposity. This is often reflected in the register of the writing that is done within it. One of my missions in my little space of academia in Miami's Department of Teacher Education is to make anything I am associated with writing clear, vivid, and pointed. And sometimes I can inject a little humor into the prose and perspective of a document to break up the dead seriousness and to call attention to an item of importance.

I recently served on an ad hoc committee whose purpose was to articulate guidelines for probationary faculty to follow in their quest to gain tenure and promotion. Under the category of Research, Scholarship, and/or Creative Achievement, we listed the "best" decisions that assistant professors could make. Here is an excerpt:

Best Decisions

- Carve out blocks of uninterrupted time to do your research and writing.
- Seek out readers for your manuscripts in progress.
- Write and publish that writing in respected, refereed journals and books.
- Establish a research area and gnaw that bone. Your publication record should show focus and be continuous.

"Gnaw that bone" gave members of the department pause. After all, tenure and promotion are serious business to junior faculty members. We're talking livelihoods here. Tenure and promotion are also serious business for departments that have invested time and money in hiring new faculty and wish to mentor them into leadership roles.

Our committee was aware of all that. We thought the humor of "gnaw that bone" made the concept of "research focus" stand out. We also liked the metaphorical language (another rarity in in-house academic prose). The metaphor suggested working at a research interest until every shred of usefulness is extracted. If you have watched a dog gnaw a bone, you've observed its single-minded purpose. Get down on your belly, we were saying to untenured faculty, get involved in your work. Keep at it. Examine it. Gnaw that bone.

Voices from Without

Teachers have the responsibility to teach students to write successfully in academic settings. Part of what this means is that students must learn to weave other voices into their own texts: the voices of other writers and researchers from previously published sources, the voices of others from interviews, conversations, and observations.

In *Coaching Writing* Bill Strong writes that

> the idea that a single voice has greater power than multiple voices seems a dubious claim at best. In most areas of our experience—but especially in writing—multiple resources are an asset, not a liability. (2001, 109)

Quoting others gives writers the opportunity to include multiple voices in their writing and to build upon words of others to illustrate a concept, strengthen a point, introduce a counterclaim. A pertinent quotation can add variety and energy to the texture of writing. Sometimes the words of another cannot be improved upon. Admitting the voices of others into our writing doesn't have to steal our voices, silence us in deference to another, and make for a numbing kind of academic writing that no one I respect wants to read.

Teachers complain when students jam quotations into their writing, piling one quote atop another. Learning to weave quotations seamlessly and substantively into writing is a skill we have to teach students. We can't assume they will know how to do this.

Middle school English teacher Julie Westerberg took a class called Literature for Teachers that I taught one quarter at Utah State University. I required students to write literature relationship papers (Romano 1998). Such a paper narrates and reflects upon a significant experience that the writer has had with a piece of literature. In the following excerpt from her portfolio cover letter, Julie writes about that literature relationship paper, the meaning it holds for her, and what she has learned from observing classmates and reading theory about teaching literature.

> Writing the paper and listening to other students' papers helped me realize how our own experiences color our connections with literature. For instance, Biffy Johnson had an entirely different experience with *Of Mice and Men* than I did because of events in her life. In his article, "Five Kinds of Literary Knowing," Robert Probst states, "The literary transaction is, first of all, a way of knowing something about the self" (Probst 1991, 63). He continues with this paragraph:
>
> > It seems reasonable that learning about oneself might be a legitimate purpose for the study of literature. The significance of introspection and reflection on one's own values and beliefs, one's own place in the culture, should be recognized, and our teaching should invite and encourage such exploration. (Probst 1991, 64)
>
> I agree.
>
> *Julie Westerberg, Teacher*

I like Julie's combination of personal experience and the citation of important passages from Probst. The two enable her to contextualize, articulate, and consolidate her learning. Julie deftly handles the quotations, naming the article and author and providing a taste of Probst that appears on one page of the article, then laying out a longer quote by Probst from the following page of the text. She ends the passage with her own two-word sentence. As a reader I feel completeness in Julie's weaving of the personal and the academic.

Author Barbara Kingsolver shows another way to use the words of someone else to communicate pertinent information and then to surprise the reader by using some of the author's language in a sentence following the quote. This excerpt comes from Kingsolver's essay "A Fist in the Eye of God." Kingsolver makes a case for maintaining biodiversity in growing food for the world. Cultivation of only one strain of a crop is not nature's way. Nature wants diversity. Nature wants a hedge against catastrophe that might befall one strain.

> Recently I heard Joan Dye Gussow, who studies and writes about the energetics, economics, and irrationalities of global food production, discussing some of these problems in a radio interview. She mentioned the alarming fact that pollen from genetically engineered corn is so rapidly contaminating all other corn that we may soon have no naturally bred corn left in the United States. "This is a fist in the eye of God," she said, adding with a sad little laugh, "and I'm not even all that religious." Whatever you believe in—whether God for you is the watchmaker who put together the intricate workings of this world in seven days or seven hundred billion days—you'd be wise to believe the part about the fist. (2002, 107)

Kingsolver foregrounds the quote with information about the speaker she is citing, then folds into her text Gussow's metaphorical quotation. In a final sentence of her own then, Kingsolver writes of the common ground shared by believers and nonbelievers. A fist in the eye is not a good thing. A fist in the eye is damaging. A fist in the eye hurts. It is disrespectful, maybe enraging. A fist in the eye sets the stage for retribution. And a fist in the eye of God? That's foolhardy. That's reckless. This elimination of natural corn strains, we understand, is urgent. Kingsolver uses Gussow's quote to build her own argument against genetically engineered food. She reiterates in a slightly different way Gussow's metaphor and ends the paragraph with the strong word *fist*. That's skill. That's style. That's an experienced writer with a distinctive voice using another remarkable voice to strengthen her purpose.

> Each day for one week, have students bring in a quotation they like—from the newspaper, television, film, literature, conversation, or famous people. Either in class or as homework, assign students to weave the quotation into a paragraph of their own. With practice, incorporating useful quotations in their writing can become natural.

Dialog

When my daughter was four years old, she came to me where I sat reading aloud a chapter from *Adventures of Huckleberry Finn*. The scene I orally interpreted featured Huck and Jim engaged in dialog. I was practicing so that I could read the dialect smoothly and expressively the next day to my high school sophomores. Mariana, a talker herself only three years then, was drawn to the sound and sense of Jim's speech.

"You read me that book, Papa?" she asked, peering over my shoulder at an E. W. Kemble illustration.

I paused. Twain's masterpiece was much longer than anything we had read at bedtime. I didn't want to ruin Huck for her. I foresaw all Twain's satire and side trips becoming tedious to a four-year-old. I imagined her struggling to listen but reluctant to tell me to quit since she was the one who asked me to read the book. I shuddered. She might develop a Huck Finn phobia!

"I'll read the book to you," I said, "but you have to promise that if you get bored and want me to stop, you'll say so. OK?"

It was a deal, and for the next forty-three evenings we sat on her bed, our backs leaning against the wall, me reading aloud a chapter each night of *Adventures of Huckleberry Finn*. It's a memory we've cherished almost thirty years. The scenes in the book Mariana liked best were ones in which Jim spoke. Twain's rendering of Jim's dialect—and my faithful oral interpretation—captivated her. And it sustained her through that long novel when she was but four years old.

The sound of people talking can be powerful. I want my students to know that dialog isn't just for fiction writers. By using dialog we can admit other voices into our nonfiction, other intelligences, other points of view, other ways of speaking and knowing. We can add depth and drama to our own expository voices by including the revealing things that people say.

One of my students explains why she likes to both read and write dialog:

> [D]ialog is fun for the reader. When I read dialog, I like to adjust my inside voice to suit my image of the character. This gives the writing some variety. Instead of reading my thoughts or descriptions, the reader hears another voice.
>
> *Amanda Peller, College Junior*

Amanda illustrates her fondness for dialog in the following excerpt. She had completed a two-week field experience in the classroom of a junior high school English teacher in an urban school. In one part of her multigenre paper, Amanda sets up this dialog exchange that reveals her own tentative first steps as a teacher and her mentor's values, enthusiasm, and way with words:

Room 117, 7:30 A.M.

> AMANDA: Mrs. Miller, would it be all right if I did a lesson tomorrow?
> MRS. MILLER: Oh, girrrl, you do whachu want. Ain't gonna bother me none.
> AMANDA: I thought I could bring in some magazines and my craftbox and have the kids create a collage abo—
> MRS. MILLER: Ooo, that sounds like fun. They'll like that. May get rowdy but you be okay.
> AMANDA: Yeah, I thought the collage could be about easy and hard life. Be—
> MRS. MILLER: MMhm. That's good. Real good. Cause these kids know about life, you know? They got to deal with stuff most people can't imagine.
> AMANDA: I figure we could read "Mother To Son" together and discuss the use of analogy in the poem. Then we could make the collages and try to write a poem about life. It will relate to their lives and the Struggling For Survival Unit you're teaching.
> Mrs. Miller: You go for it, girl. These kids will have plenty to say. You know all they really need is some luvin. Too many ain't had no love in their life. You know, I just believe that our main goal should be to love these children. So many people tell you not to get attached, but you can't help it. Workin with these kids every day, Lord help me but I done got attached. You know?

Amanda Peller, College Junior

In a last example to illustrate how our own voices can take on strength and energy through other voices, look at this excerpt from a reflective narrative by Lisa Ayers. Lisa also writes about her field experience, this one at a high school. She deftly renders many voices. There is an academic voice that describes, explains, reflects, and analyzes. There is an italicized inner voice that Lisa uses to show her anxiety and lack of confidence. There are voices of dialog in three registers: the mentor teacher's, Lisa's, and the students'. Just like Twain, Lisa alters the spelling and syntax of some characters' speech to capture its flavor and sound:

> As I walked to my classroom on that second day of my field experience, my heart pounded its fists against my chest. A million thoughts swarmed through my head like bees around a honey hive.
>
> *Why are you so nervous, Lisa? This isn't your first field experience. You've taught lessons before. You'll be fine. But, that was to a very obedient class of middle-school students who wanted to learn. It was pretty easy to get them motivated. This is different. These kids hate school. Some of these students probably won't even last the school year. How am I supposed to get these kids to love poetry, let alone learning? They're going to eat me alive.*

I showed my lesson plan to my cooperating teacher before school began the next day. I hoped to have a discussion about the role of the speaker in "Incident in a Rose Garden."

"You're going to have a discussion?"

"Is that okay?"

"Oh it's fine, it's fine. The questions you wrote down here are good. I don't know how much talking you're going to get out of them. These kids aren't eager to take risks in front of the class."

"Should I change it?"

"Oh no, it's fine. It'll certainly challenge them, though."

"I'm sorry."

"For what? For challenging them? It's good for them. I'm just warning you not to expect too much from them."

I didn't want to believe him. I wanted to believe that if my lesson was engaging enough, the students would naturally flock to it. But as much as I didn't want to believe him, I knew what he said was probably true: I shouldn't expect too much. When the clock hit 7:37, I stood at the front of the classroom armed with a complete forty-minute lesson plan in the hopes that if I had enough planned, they wouldn't be able to get off-task too easily. "We're going to talk about poetry today." I could almost hear their eardrums shutting off. "But I think you'll find this activity fun." They didn't buy that. These kids were going to need a hard sell on poetry if they were going to learn anything from me.

"Do I have a volunteer to read the first poem, 'Incident in a Rose Garden'?" Nothing. Complete silence. Not a single hand budged. "No one wants to volunteer to read?" Finally, a reluctant hand reached towards the ceiling. *Phew!* "Thank you, Sharee."

The remainder of the class period mirrored those first few minutes. I asked questions continuously, and practically reached down their throats for answers. Although it was a struggle, gradually, they began to respond. And their answers were good. Real good. By the end of the period, I was drained. The whole class period had been a battle, but I had succeeded in engaging them in discussion. With three minutes left in the period, I wanted to keep them engaged. So I asked if anyone had comments on the lesson. Amazingly, Tyrone raised his hand. "Muss Ayers, where d'ya'll git dis poem? It's pretty tight."

"You mean you liked the poem?"

"Yeah, dis slammin'."

"Pretty sweet," another voice piped in. "Dits cool how that one guy thinks Death is comin' fer him but he's really getting that other guy." All of a sudden I was bombarded with comments and nods from all directions. I couldn't believe my eyes and ears. They didn't hate me for challenging them!

Every day that week I taught first period, and every day I struggled to hook them with the language of poetry. Every day they gave me a hard time, but every day they also gave me a little bit more than the day before. Although I was thrilled that I had engaged these seemingly apathetic students in analyzing poetry, I couldn't help feeling surprised and a little disappointed at my constant struggle. I thought they would follow me like the pied piper, dancing to whatever beat I played. Instead, every day was the first day again and another struggle against their anti-school barrier. Their resistance, however, did not discourage me; it inspired me. Every day they kept me on my toes because I had to find new ways to reach them.

Lisa Ayers, College Junior

One of the hardest things I do as a teacher is listen to students, listen to their voices in the classroom, listen to their voices on paper. I have my agenda. I have a note card in my shirt pocket with a list of things I must do. I have classes to prepare, meetings to attend, messages to read and write. It takes great concentration on my part to pull myself away from all the to-dos and to attend to my students' voices.

Lisa is learning to do that. So is Amanda, who pays her mentor teacher the great respect of reporting her words and capturing the rhythm of her voice. By their attention to the voices of others, by their respect for them, their inclusion of them in their writing, Lisa and Amanda increase the power, presence, and democratic stance of their own voices.

20

Imitation

When I began to write with some seriousness, something beyond classroom assignments or the occasional need to transfer my most intense emotions to paper, I naturally imitated other writers. Establishing my own voice took many years of experience and creative growth.

KEN BREWER, Poet and Essayist

Should I go around trying on author's voices until I find one that works for me? Should I begin writing using words like "pish" and "o'er" as Shakespeare does? "O, pish. I've thought 't o'er and I'd dare say not."

KARA WARREN, College Junior

Cheryl was a high school junior, a reading and writing dynamo who taught me literacy possibilities on many occasions. One morning she handed me, unbidden, this "book report." Here is an excerpt from it:

> **Do You Really Want to Hear About It?**
> If you really want to hear about it, J. D. Salinger's *The Catcher in the Rye* is a damn good book. Now, you take most books, the characters are either phony as hell or too real to be true. My kid sister reads the too good to be true brand, which is maybe better than the phony books that my mom is always pushing at her. Nothing against my mom or anything—she's nice and all—but she has a thing for books about this girl detective that she used to read when she was a kid. The author must be a goddam century old but she still turns out a book a year on these madman mysteries. The detective has been 18 years old for about 50 years, never once behaving like a normal kid, and, of course, never

failing to solve an unbelievable mystery that never would have happened in the first place. It's enough to make you puke. . . .

When I read a book, I like to get to know the characters. And if you start thinking about it, the only way to get to know somebody is to have them talk at you about the way they feel about something the moment it hits their brain. What I'm saying is you have to get inside their brain and hear them think while at the same time seeing what they do on the outside. I read a half-assed idea somewhere that no one ever really knows anyone. I don't know about that. I do know that I can go around and think I have someone all figured out and then they'll do one thing and ruin my analization. I guess it just goes to show you, you shouldn't analyze people's personalities unless you have a goddam Ph.D. in psychology.

You've probably read *The Catcher in the Rye* but maybe not. It's about this guy who obviously comes from a family that has a fair amount of bucks. I mean, Holden goes to one of those fancy as hell prep schools and all. The thing is I don't know about Holden. If I had the bucks and the brains and the connections to be accepted at one of them classy Eastern schools, I'd somehow manage to keep my goddam grades high enough so I could stay there. But Holden, at the beginning of the book, leaves the fourth school that he has flunked out of. It's not that Holden isn't smart; in fact, it's my guess that he has a real high I.Q. He has mental problems though and his teachers continually report that he isn't applying himself. I really don't know what to tell you about the book besides the character of Holden. Holden is the book. If you really want to know the truth, not a goddam lot of stuff happens in the book. Don't get me wrong or anything; it's a great book. Holden is the one that makes it great. Maybe the book wouldn't appeal to me if it was told with a third person narrator. All I would see is a crazy teenager walking around New York wondering where the ducks in Central park go in the winter. You have to hear first hand what Holden is thinking before you can appreciate him.

I could tell you about Holden's hangup with phoniness and his views of people in life, but I really don't feel like it right now. And you have to feel like doing something before you can do it.

Cheryl Musselman, High School Junior

I saw soaring and swooping and barrel rolling that morning, a high school junior confident in her voice, steeped in literacy, fueled for a test flight. Writing teachers live for surprises like that. *The Catcher in the Rye* had captured Cheryl's moral imagination. She was synchronized with Holden's voice so well she could imitate it as second nature. Cheryl had no problem cutting loose a voice. She produced almost nine hundred words, critiquing Nancy Drew mysteries, launching into opinionated and illuminating tangents (as Holden was wont to do), and creating a mini "analization" of Holden's character. Cheryl uses Holden's cynicism, slang, and sensitivity to fly forth with the language rhythms in her from the reading, appropriately ending the piece with a typical Holden-style cop-out in the final paragraph.

Even Henry James

Imitation of an author's ways with words can create a gush of language. Imitation can cut loose a voice and let writers experience the power that comes with a little recklessness, a little letting go of the self and learning the language rhythms and voice habits of another.

One of the memorable writing experiences I had in college came my sophomore year when a frustrated writing professor, tired of our safe, academic voices, charged us to write brief pieces the following week in the voices of three big-time American writers: Hemingway, Faulkner, and James. (No big-time women writers mentioned by the prof in 1968, though most of the class was female. Seems we all could have profitably learned by imitating Gertrude Stein, Virginia Woolf, or Eudora Welty.)

Hemingway and Faulkner I had read, so I knew something of their voices. Henry James I hadn't heard of. I went to the library and read enough of his voice to learn how he handled vocabulary, dialog, sentence rhythms, and narrative. The assignment marked the only A I got in that class. Although the professor judged my Hemingway and Faulkner imitations mediocre, my Henry James satire earned an A, and the professor read it to the class.

I was glowing from the success I'd finally achieved and chagrined that my James imitation had earned plaudits (it was my Hemingway I was proudest of). I remember the Henry James piece to this day. That voice was not so distant from my experience as a writer in high school, where great value had been placed upon sounding scholarly: lofty vocabulary, long, wending sentences, and, instead of vivid showing, elegant telling (at least I shot for *elegant*).

The imitations helped me grow as a writer. They let me flex my syntactical muscles and experience three distinct voices from the inside. They let me range over choices in diction, trying to be hard-boiled and direct in one writing, flowery and long-winded in another (my Faulkner imitation is long out of my mind).

Imitation of other writers is profitable for students to try. In one of the foundational books of the teaching profession, *Language and Learning* (1970), James Britton writes, "Trying other people's voices may for the adolescent be a natural and necessary part of the process of finding one's own" (262). His conjecture is also a call, I think, to make sure that contemporary authors are a significant part of our students' reading diets. After reading Sandra Cisneros, Barbara Kingsolver, Jane Smiley, Kent Haruff, Stephen King, or Sherman Alexie, students ought to try writing like the author.

After students have read several authors either as an entire class or independently, ask them to write a piece in which they imitate the voice of an author. It might help students before they write to meet in groups and discuss aspects of the particular writer's voice they intend to imitate. Ask students to deal with specific information in their discussion: "I like how Robert Cormier uses metaphors, like on page 64 in the third paragraph."

Then turn students loose to imitate the author to see what they can learn.

Copy-Change

Students can experiment with voice and meaning by imitating the form and structure of other writing. Stephen Dunning and William Stafford write about the technique of the *copy-change* as a way for beginning writers of poetry to develop " 'a poetic way' of looking at the world" (1992, 90). Students can try copy-changes with prose or poetry. I've seen this done most prominently, perhaps, with William Carlos Williams' "This Is Just to Say" and "The Red Wheelbarrow" ([1938] 1951). When creating a copy-change of a poem, Dunning and Stafford suggest that the writer give credit to the poet with something like "In the style of William Carlos Williams" or "After Williams's 'Red Wheelbarrow'" (1992, 90). On a recent self-assessment at semester's end, one of my students wrote this poem to indicate what she had learned about becoming a teacher:

Introduction to Teaching (EDT 428-style)
You asked us to take our souls
and search them for caring
like a mother hen
or stretch a long arm out and lend a hand.
You say drop diversity onto a classroom
and watch it explode like wildfire,
or walk beside our students
and guide the way to the light.
You want us to dig deeper
into the realm of writing
and help our students learn as we learn.

But all we want to do
is sit back and continue being students
while you torture us with preparations.
You make us rewrite, relearn, reread with a vengeance
and we start to understand what teaching really means.

This poem is a "rewrite" of "Introduction to Poetry," by Billy Collins. It was inspired by the lesson that Nate and Dave did for their thematic unit. I didn't follow the structure or meaning of the poem to a tee. (The poem ends on a cynical note) but I think this works better for my purposes.

Julie Gunzenhaeuser, College Junior

Have students try their hands at copy-change. Have them each choose a favorite poem or excerpt of prose, then write their own pieces, using the literature's structure to guide them. In this case, the structure of the self-chosen piece can give voice, not block it. The copy-change will teach students about forms and rhythms of language.

I Am What I Am

Megan Fulwiler was a graduate student at the University of New Hampshire enrolled in my multigenre writing class one summer. Students were required to teach a lesson that led their peers into writing. Megan introduced us to an imitative writing prompt that I have used with students ever since. The imitation hasn't failed yet to launch students' voices and get them to dig into subject matter they care about.

Here is the piece of literature that Megan gave us to imitate:

I Am What I Am
I am what I am and I am U.S. American   I haven't wanted to
say it because if I did you'd take away the Puerto Rican but now
I say go to hell   I am what I am and you can't take it away
with all the words and sneers at your command   I am what I
am   I am Puerto Rican   I am U.S. American   I am New
York Manhattan and the Bronx   I am what I am   I'm not
hiding under no stoop   behind no curtain   I am what I am   I
am Boricua as Boricuas come from the isle of Manhattan and I
croon sentimental tangos in my sleep and Afro-Cuban beats in
my blood and Xavier Cugat's lukewarm latin is so familiar and

dear sneer dear but he's familiar and dear but not Carmen Miranda who's a joke because I never was a joke I was a bit of a sensation See! here's a real true honest-to-god Puerto Rican girl and she's in college Hey! Mary come here and look she's from right here a South Bronx girl and she's honest-to-god in college now Ain't that something who wouda believed it Ain't science wonderful or some such thing a wonder a wonder.

And someone who did languages for a living stopped me in the subway because how I spoke was a linguist's treat I mean there it was yiddish and spanish and fine refined college educated english and irish which I mainly keep in my prayers It's dusty now I haven't said my prayers in decades but try my Hail Marrrry full of grrrace with the nun's burr with the nun's disdain it's all true and it's all me do you know I got an English accent from the BBC For years in the mountains of Puerto Rico when I was twenty-two and twenty-four and twenty-six all those young years

I listened to the BBC and Radio Moscow's English english announcers announce and denounce and then I read Dickens all the way through three or four times at least and then later I read Dickens aloud in voices and when I came back to the U.S. I spoke mockDickens and mockBritish especially when I want to be crisp efficient I know what I'm doing and you can't scare me tough that kind

I am what I am and I'm a bit of a snob too Shit! why am I calling myself names I really really dig the funny way the British speak and it's real it's true and I love too the singing of yiddish sentences that go with shrugs and hands and arms doing melancholy or lively dances I love the sound and look of yiddish in the air in the body in the streets in the English language nooo so what's new so go by the grocer and buy some fruit oye vey gevalt gefilte fish raiseleh oh and those words hundreds of them dotting the english language like raisins in the bread shnook and shlemiel zoftik tush shmata all those soft sweet sounds saying sharp sharp things I am what I am and I'm naturalized Jewish-American wasp is foreign and new but Jewish-American is old shoe familiar shmata familiar and it's me dears it's me bagels blintzes and all I am what I am Take it or leave me alone. (Morales and Morales 1986, 138–39)

I—or a student who can speak Spanish—will read the authors' declaration aloud with all the heart and attitude we can muster. Then we talk about the various identities that are depicted, the metaphorical language, the vocabulary, the unconventional spacing, the implicit punctuation. I read pieces by former students to show what they have done with the imitation. I use two or three pieces to immerse students in the structure. Then I turn them loose to create their own version of Morales' "I Am What I Am."

> I am what I am. I am a mistake that was thought impossible, and I am loved, because sometimes the biggest mistakes are the ones you hold closest to your heart. I am what I am. I am a defining moment to a young girl almost a woman; a horror, a disbelief. I am a memory that holds no color, no substance. I am what I am. I am a life change, a 180. I am a dangerous projection. I am unannounced and undecorated. I am what I am. I am a casualty of heart's warfare, a by-product of immaturity, a waste product. I am unwanted, a regret. I am what I am.
>
> I am love, baby soft and peachy sweet. I am joy and I am surprise, I am a dream that plays over and over. I am what I am. I am a thousand castles, a thousand cracks. I am what I am. I am fragile and I am persistent. I am a life project and a tax write-off. I am what I am. I am a daughter, a sister, a dependent, a burden, a bargain package, a done deal. I am what I am.
>
> I am the collaborative effort of many hearts, love's masterpiece, the knowledge that some of life's greatest gifts are the ones we aren't expecting. I am what I am.
>
> —*Andrea Bailey, College Junior*

This prompt often impels my students to travel to the heart of their identity. Andrea's "I Am What I Am" also demonstrates how the imitation often takes a turn to reveal a second side or complexity. Andrea may have been a 180 in her mother's life, but she is also love's masterpiece.

My daughter took a new teaching job in a new state. She gave her high school students the "I Am What I Am" assignment so she could engage them in language, begin getting to know each of them, and taste their voices. Mariana wrote the assignment herself so the students could see how it might be done and also begin to know their new teacher's values, personality, and background:

> I am what I am. I am Mariana Annette Romano. I am a natural blonde so don't ask. I am the granddaughter of an Italian immigrant and no he wasn't from the north and despite your stereotypes I do look Italian. I am what I am. I am a daughter, a

dreamer, and an only child (and I hated it). It doesn't mean that I am rotten and selfish, either. I am older than twenty-two but younger than thirty-five. I am what I am. I am an Ohio transplant to Evanston, Illinois, at the brink of a new life. I am Ohio River Valley, fields of Indiana corn, and college towns. I am a Hoosier grad. I am a former resident of New York City and Rome, Italy. I am a lover of stories and talking and late nights with my friends. I am an enthusiast of history, reading, and writing. I am an NPR junkie. I am a procrastinator who knows how to get her work done so don't give me excuses but I can empathize with your plight. I am what I am. Listen to me and maybe I can help.

I am what I am. I am a rebel and a conformist. I am a supporter of radical ideas and a promoter of behavioral temperance. I am what I am. I am skeptical of exclusivity, but I want to belong. I am a woman who believes in equality and fairness. I am respectful of all people, but I expect respect and if you disdain common decency I will let you know even if I have never met you before. I am what I am. I am imperfect. I make mistakes, but I don't like to be exploited for my frailties. I like only to have them pointed out so I may learn from my stumbles. I will treat you with the same courtesy.

I am what I am. I am a voyager of the world and of words. I am the spirit of Whitman, Dickinson, Fitzgerald, and Lee. I am the mouthpiece of Kingsolver, Smiley, Morrison, and Gibbons. I am a teacher who pushes her students to speak the rude truth, write, and think. I am the instructor, the facilitator, the learner. I am a believer of deadlines and keeping them and honesty when the work doesn't come in. I am what I am. I am a disciplinarian if I need to be. A parent-caller and a referral writer, but only if my previous interventions leave me no choice. I am not one to harbor resentment, but I remember disappointment. I am what I am. I am a student's loudest cheerleader or the person who will relentlessly nag you for fear you are giving up or copping out or unable to see the value in yourself and your efforts. I am a believer of integrity and expect you to have some. I am what I am. I am your English teacher. Accept it, or it will be a long year.

—*Mariana Romano, Teacher*

Immerse students in examples of the "I Am What I Am" prompt. Talk about what the author is doing in each example, then let your students try it. I find this assigned writing works well as a ten- or fifteen-minute in-class writing after we have read examples aloud so that students have heard the language rhythms. Point out to students how the repetition of "I am what I am" not only creates rhythm but also gives writers time to think during writing.

21

"It's Alive! It's Alive! It's Alive!"*

Nate Stevens was hard to resist. He was a junior in college when I met him. He was smart, irreverent, and respectful. In class he spoke up for what he believed. He could be feisty. He reminded me of Calvin in the comic strip "Calvin and Hobbes." There was nothing bland or mediocre about Nate. He had an unruly shock of hair like Calvin's too. In his presentations, class participation, and writing, Nate had distinctive presence. His voice was irrepressible, his sense of humor ever ready.

Nate never signed his papers the same way twice, and he never signed his papers simply "Nathan Stevens." One paper he might sign "The Honorable Nathan Stevens." Another, "Sir Nathan Stevens." Another "Constable Stevens." Or in a recent postcard from Germany: "Doktor Stevens." He never ran out of titles for himself.

Nate decided to student teach on the Navajo Indian Reservation in Many Farms, Arizona. Before student teaching started, I got a postcard from him (see Figure 21–1).

Nate had put on the mask of a mad scientist to send his former teacher a postcard declaring his passion for writing workshop, personal choice, and student voice. He was confident, idealistic, committed, youthful, and inexperienced. I knew that student teaching on the Navajo Indian Reservation was going to challenge him. I couldn't wait to talk with Mr. Stevens when he returned to Miami.

*Colin Clive as Dr. Henry Frankenstein, *Frankenstein*, 1931

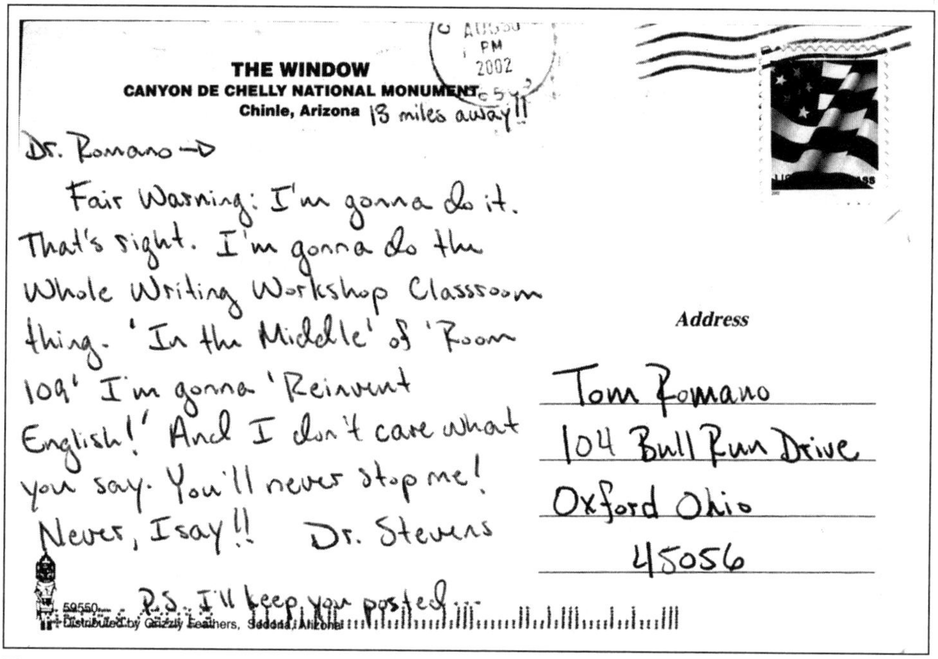

THE WINDOW
CANYON DE CHELLY NATIONAL MONUMENT
Chinle, Arizona 13 miles away!!

AUG 30 PM 2002

Dr. Romano —>

Fair Warning: I'm gonna do it. That's right. I'm gonna do the Whole Writing Workshop Classroom thing. 'In the Middle' of 'Room 109' I'm gonna 'Reinvent English!' And I don't care what you say. You'll never stop me! Never, I say!! Dr. Stevens

P.S. I'll keep you posted...

Address

Tom Romano
104 Bull Run Drive
Oxford Ohio
45056

59550 Distributed by Grizzly Leathers, Sedona, Arizona

Figure 21–1. Postcard

22

Wear a Mask, Unleash a Voice

Writing is this enormous costume closet. There is so much to try on, try out, so much to parade around in.

College Student

When I was a child in the 1950s, I watched a lot of television. I liked old movies best. My favorite actor was Edward G. Robinson. He had an Old Country look, like my Italian uncles. In my estimation, Robinson's tough guys surpassed James Cagney's and Humphrey Bogart's.

One evening my parents sat in the living room, my dad taking some uncharacteristic time to relax from his work downstairs in his beerjoint. On a chair was Dad's coat and fedora. Below them were his shoes. On the telephone stand was an "It's a Boy!" cigar that a proud customer had given him. I went into the bathroom, retrieved a towel, and wrapped it around my neck the way Edward G. Robinson had done in *Key Largo*. I put on my robe, dropped his fedora on my head, slipped into his shoes, grabbed one of my toy cap guns, and shoved the cigar in the side of my mouth.

I clopped into the front room, hat over my ears. The towel was ruffled around my neck. The toy gun I pointed showed I meant business. "Yeah," I snarled. "I know you two mugs. I seen ya before. Now, get a move on before I lose my temper, yeah."

Years later my mother told me that she never saw my father laugh as hard and as long as he did that night.

I'd watched so many Edward G. Robinson movies that putting on his gangster mask was a cinch, yeah. I knew that character. I wasn't eight-year-old Tommy when I walked into that living room. I was Johnny Rocco, ruthless mobster, terrorizing Bogey, Bacall, and Lionel Barrymore, waiting out a hurricane in an old hotel on Key Largo so I could escape to Cuba with my loot as soon as the weather cleared.

I was imitating, but I was wearing a particular mask, too, much like Cheryl in Chapter 20 was imitating but also wearing the mask of Holden Caulfield, much like Dr. Stevens wore the mask of a mad scientist in the previous chapter.

Students can often write with voice and find truth by wearing a mask. Sometimes the mask isn't as distant as we think. Of playing characters, Edward G. Robinson wrote in his autobiography, "Every one of us bears within him the possibility of all passions, all destinies of life in all its manifold forms. Nothing human is foreign to us" (1973, 310).

Megan Fulwiler, the graduate student who introduced me to the "I Am What I Am" prompt, wrote a multigenre paper about Captain Ahab's wife that summer at UNH. You might be wondering how on earth she wrote such a paper, since Ahab's wife is fictional and mentioned only twice that I can see in *Moby Dick*: ". . . whole oceans away, from that girl-wife I wedded past fifty, and sailed for Cape Horn the next day, leaving but one dent in my marriage pillow—wife? wife?—rather a widow with her husband alive! Aye, I widowed that poor girl when I married her . . . " (Melville [1851] 1964, 533).

Two mentions in 566 pages. That's it. Ahab had a wife? Who knew?

In an American literature seminar the previous semester, Megan had written a straight research paper about Melville and *Moby Dick*. She was steeped in information about this womanless masterpiece of American literature. Her feminist instincts were roused. To get at Ms. Ahab Megan researched whaling wives of nineteenth century New England. And then she put on a mask and imagined:

> **I Am Not Melville's Muse**
> I am what I am trapped between sentences a pause a phrase a fragment I am what I am the white space between ink letters a brief mention an offhand remark a passing reference a literary device a distant memory an afterthought I am the classic case of an undeveloped character I am never analyzed imagined or remembered I am not part of any narrative arc I am not even on the goddam boat
>
> I am what I am a model of Christian faith an emblem of redemption in a wool dress the patient pious wife of a whaler I am a waiting room a safe harbor a home port an empty vessel I am every woman who ever waited too long to remember why
>
> I am what I am I am meridian and magnet I am shoreline and lighthouse a distant port true north shelter in the storm a known quantity a sure thing a safe bet I am a comfortable arrangement a convenient situation a no brainer all nighter last minute reminder I am every sailor's dream
>
> I am all these things and none of these things I am more

I am strong black tea on a Sunday morning and the curl of my child's palm   I am cool melon and soft skin   I am rest   I am a typhoon   I am snipping thread   cutting twine   baking bread writing letters to a man I don't know and praying to a god I can't see   I am the soft rustle of silk around the corner   I am the long hot night and the cool early morning   I am stronger than you'll ever know   I am a slammed door and an open invitation   I am tangled cotton on a tall bed   I am a slow smile and a long loving   I am bone and muscle   I am liquid   I am salt and the hollow of a throat   I am bare feet when no one's looking   I am lavender and muslin and milk   I am a missed opportunity

and my name is not wife

—*Megan Fulwiler, Graduate Student*

Give students opportunities to try on masks and write rapidly from those points of view. Watch them find voice by being who they aren't, except for that core of truth they share with other human beings. They can become literary characters or characters from films. They can become a character of another gender, another ethnicity, another age. They can wear a mask and tell the truth.

23

The Generative Power of Parallel Structure

The most important aspect of voice is rhythm. How can you play any instrument without rhythm? It's like making orange juice without oranges, like playing football without the pigskin, like driving a car without gasoline. Rhythm is everything in the voice of the author. It makes the clock tick. It makes the wind blow.

DAVID MCCREA, College Junior

Walking. Running. Swimming. Skating. Shoveling snow before dawn. Rhythm is all. Pitching baseballs, passing footballs, returning tennis balls, massaging someone's back with aromatic oils. My wife works in an emergency room. Patients arrive with chest pain. They are given oxygen and hooked up to a cardiac monitor. If the heartbeat is irregular, that could mean trouble. Nurses and doctor go to work. Rhythms begin, sustain, and perpetuate life.

My mother at eighty years old had read forty pages of Sue Grafton's *L Is for Lawless*. I asked her how she liked the latest Kinsey Millhone mystery. Mom looked me dead in the eye and said, "It's witty and sharp and good." Three adjectives rolling on a rhythm, moving in a cadence, the *it's* and the *ands* taking the offbeat so the accent lands on the adjectives.

I heard a woman talk about her company's annual Christmas party: "I'm not going," she said. "I'm not going. If she's going, I'm not going." That last qualifying phrase before *I'm not going* provides variation that makes the repetition interesting and satisfying. She's not going and we know why.

In the backyard of John and Cathy Gaughan's house one summer afternoon, I chased their daughter Amy, six then, and two of her friends. I played the role of crazed wildman, huffing and puffing and growling. When I got hold of one of the girls, I threw her into the air and caught her on the way down, my growl reaching a high point when I heaved her. Amy's sister, two-year-old Kelly, watched from safety, behind her mother's legs. She was fearful. She was envious. She shouted, "Tom is chasing the big girls and throwing them in the sky and I want to be holded!"

Listen for rhythmic speech. It's all around you. People naturally gain a rhythm to their language, a cadence to their spoken words, a rock and roll and movement to their speech.

These cadences, these patterns of language and phrases and sentences appeal to our ears and our sense of meaning making. When rhythmical language appears on the page, our eye gets involved, too.

In *Writing to Be Read*, Ken Macrorie wrote clearly about the effect of rhythm and repetition in writing:

> [S]trong repetition is the heart of all good writing, in fact, the heart of all good music making, hurdle racing, hammering, walking, or courting. Repetition sets up patterns. Only with pattern can you achieve emphasis and variety. Da-da-da, da-da-da, da-da-dum. That *dum* is smart because it comes after all those *da's*. It picks up its power as you wait through all those da's for something to happen. Repeat and vary. That is the secret to achieving significant form in all art and communication. (1984, 35)

I require my students to experiment with language rhythms, to consciously let themselves slip into repetitions. No maybes about it. I give students a two-page handout of examples of effective parallel language structures I've collected, some from speech, some from previous students' writing, some from the work of professional authors. I've recently read Scott Russell Sanders' *The Country of Language* (1999). Sanders is a master of rhythm and repetition. Next handout I'll put passages from him to spur my students to write with rhythmical language patterns.

Here Sanders writes about learning to read. He sets up patterns in listing the names of animals. He strings along verb phrases that begin with the word *couldn't*. Then he turns that around and uses a series of three independent clauses that begin with *we could*, varying the length and the beat of the last one:

> All the while our dog Rusty took almost as many hours of reading and writing lessons as I did. He lay beside us listening or nuzzled our laps as Sandra and I studied, his tongue dripping on the page. Yet he never learned even the first letter. I tried briefer experiments with the cow, the billy goat, a pet raccoon, and a rabbit, with the same results. This did not fool me into supposing that animals are dumb, for I had seen all of them do amazing things; it merely convinced me that reading and writing must be our own best tricks. We couldn't run as fast or jump as high, couldn't hole up all winter

> underground, couldn't make honey from flowers or dams out of sticks, couldn't fly like birds or swim like fish, couldn't do a thousand fabulous things the other animals could do; but we could read, we could write, we could name everything under the sun. (17)

I also like how *fish* repeats the short *i* sound in *swim* and *sticks* before it. The entire passage begins descriptively and sedately with sister and brother and Rusty studying on the floor, names some triumphs of the animal world, then builds to an exuberant climax affirming what we can do with language.

In this second passage Sanders sets up small parallel structures of single words and larger parallel structures of independent clauses connected with semicolons. I altered the way this passage appears on the page to point up the rhythms and repetition:

> What little I knew about teaching had come from watching my own instructors over the years. While preparing for the semester, I recalled
> the best of them,
> the ones who had opened my eyes
> and ears
> and
> heart.
> Although distinct as individuals, each one impressive in his or her own way, these forceful teachers did have a few qualities in common:
> they enjoyed using their minds;
> they paid attention to what was going on outside
> the classroom;
> they were demanding
> and generous
> and patient;
> they cared passionately about learning;
> they lived in light of what they knew.
> They left their mark on me not merely because they
> passed on knowledge, although that was crucial, but
> because they demonstrated ways of being
> fully
> and richly
> human. (74)

I can't read Sanders' prose without getting swept up in the rhythms of *how* he says as well as *what* he says. The parallel language structures he uses seem to make me a faster reader.

After we have shared plenty of examples of parallel language structures, noting what the authors are doing with words on paper, reading the language aloud (crucial), so we physically feel those sound waves of rhythm, I ask students to focus freewrite, letting themselves slip into language patterns in both in-class quick-writes and homework assignments. Using parallel language structures turns on the passions.

Kara has read an article about breaking some of the so-called standard rules of writing in an effort to free the voice and write powerfully. She is hopped up, passionate, ready to risk:

> I am looking forward to pushing my writing style to a point of rebellion. I'm nervous, frightened, afraid of failure, but I have faith. Not a blind faith but a faith rooted in the fact that I have the skill, the talent, the experience, as we all do, to "render experience," to convey our thoughts as powerfully and as honestly as we feel them.
>
> *Kara Haubert Hass, College Junior*

I ask students to analyze their own writing to ferret out what they think are markers of their authentic voices, then explain what they find in a paper that uses that authentic voice. Jamie has fun varying the end of prepositional phrase patterns:

> I could recognize my style of writing in a stack of fifty similar papers because of certain phrases I love to use, sentence fragments I delight in, images I thrill in creating. My writing speaks of my life and the way in which I long to live it . . . with a bit of romance, a bit of the unknown and unsuspected, and a bit of the refined all wrapped tightly together with my name branded on them all.
>
> *Jamie Furhman, College Freshman*

Laura has read John Gaughan's *Reinventing English* (2001). She writes a one-page analysis of the book that contains this passage that strings together verb phrases in the second sentence to get at the substance of Gaughan's teaching:

> Gaughan believes that teaching literature and writing should happen in meaningful contexts. Teachers can use literature and writing to encourage students to reflect on their beliefs, consider different perspectives, develop into responsible citizens, question the status quo, understand another point of view, and defend their own point of view. Literature and writing are effective tools for allowing students to empathize, explore, interpret, and grow.
>
> *Laura Strandberg, College Junior*

And lastly, Julie has read Jane Yolen's *The Devil's Arithmetic* (1988), a novel about a contemporary adolescent girl's firsthand look at the Jewish Holocaust of World War II. Julie writes this sentence in which she reflects upon her own family and the subject matter, using a series of phrases beginning with *why*, the last one quiet and sobering and reverberating:

> I finally understood why my grandfather wouldn't talk about the past, why my great grandmother always tried to hide her wrist from the world, and why my dad's family was so small.
>
> *Julie Gunzenhaeuser, College Junior*

Professional writers use repetitive language structures abundantly and in many ways. I want my students to be alert to it. I want my students to employ parallel language structures in their own writing, want them to make effective rhythm and repetition a habitual part of their voices.

When you encounter parallel structure in a stylebook, the emphasis is upon keeping the parallel language structures grammatically consistent, on not producing a sentence like this:

> I sat on the carpet with the second graders, leading them into talking about their writing, wanting them to say smart things and help each other out, prodding them to listen closely, and glowed when they performed well.

The Generative Power of Parallel Structure

Emphasizing correctness in the matter of using parallel language structures misses the mark. It is wasted time and needless warning. If students are invited to write with parallel language structures after seeing and reading examples of them, they get it right most of the time. Then, if the writing is going somewhere and not merely an exercise, they can work with removing redundancies in the parallel structures. If the parallel structures begin to carry too heavy a meaning load, students can break the structures down into more sentences.

What is rarely mentioned in the grammar and stylebooks is *the generative power of parallel language structures*. Rhythm and repetition can begin, sustain, and perpetuate thought. Setting up language patterns and following them can lead writers to say more and discover meaning. Example: I wrote an email message to a young teacher who had contacted me about an impending confrontation with her superintendent. She had inspired her students to write letters of protest to whomever they wished. Make your voices heard, she exhorted them. Speak of the wrongs that you see. Students wrote to the president of the United States.

They wrote to congressmen, celebrities, and local businesses. And as high school students who spent nearly half their waking hours five days a week in school, they wrote letters of protest to the school principal and district superintendent. Part of the assignment was to actually send the letters, so students would see that they were not ineffectual, that their voices counted, that their concerns would be addressed if they made themselves known.

The teacher was stressed about her upcoming meeting with the superintendent. After reading the students' letters, she had been exhilarated by their voices, impressed by their tact and tone and the specificity of their protests. Now she despaired. She worried about being chastised, reprimanded, maybe even fired. I wrote to her:

> You keep your cool. Take deep breaths. If the superintendent launches a withering barrage, let it fall around you. Keep your steady center. You did right by the kids, right by the profession, right by the idea of responsible citizenship, and right by your school district.

That last sentence of my email message is a prime example of a parallel language structure leading to new thinking. When I wrote, "You did right by the kids," I set up a language pattern that I followed. The very pattern itself made me think: you've done right by the profession of teaching, too, a profession that believes in spurring students to reflect and write. You've done right by the idea of being a citizen in a democracy that depends on the active participation of the people. There was more: You've done right by your school district and the people who hired you—the thinking and writing and, in some cases, social activism that the students engaged in is, I thought, exactly what a school district ought to want for its students. Because I followed the language structure I'd set up, I extended my thinking beyond the kids. And in this paragraph, because I followed the pattern of those independent clauses starting with *you've*, I did further specific thinking even here.

So lead students into writing with rhythm and repetition, setting up parallel language structures and following them. Their writing will be pleasurable reading. The repetition of language structures will also make them think.

Parallel Structure and Writing About Literature

My students read Francisco Jimenez's *The Circuit: Stories from the Life of a Migrant Child* (1997), a collection of closely knit short stories about an illegal immigrant family's experience as farm workers in California. My students at Miami are mainly white and middle class. And they are going to be secondary English teachers. Like

Laura's earlier writing about John Gaughan's *Reinventing English*, I wanted my students to look at the world from another perspective, to understand another point of view, to question the status quo, and to reflect on their beliefs. After we had explored our responses to Jimenez's book about family, illegal Mexican immigration, and migrant farm working, I asked students to freewrite about their thinking. One stipulation I made about the writing, however, was that students were to let themselves fall into parallel language structures. I knew the patterns they invented would assist them in generating meaning.

Keri uses the pattern to name what *The Circuit* is about. She discovers a key word and extends her thinking about it:

> *The Circuit* tells a story about sacrifice, about hard work, and about loss. Loss of dreams, loss of pride, and loss of innocence.
>
> *Keri Allen, College Junior*

In the following freewrite Paige starts in what might seem an unpromising way by mentioning tedious matters of time and the naming of repetitive actions of the family. But she has faith and keeps writing in her parallel language patterns, eventually leading herself to say something specific about the struggle that marked every aspect of the family's life, something specific about both the difficulty and the success Panchito experienced in school, and about the persistent upbeat feeling the reader has that the boy will one day transform himself:

> Minute after minute, hour after hour, day after day, month after month they all drag on. They all hang overhead. They all glome together. Picking cotton, picking strawberries, back to picking cotton. Changing soiled diapers day after day. Day after day, struggling to find friends, struggling to speak English, struggling to understand English, struggling to wake up day after day.
>
> Waking up early, working late to again wake up early and work late.
>
> Working and picking and gathering and weighing to wake up and do it all again. After being read to in English not understanding what was read, waiting to draw, drawing animals and butterflies, coloring animals and butterflies.
>
> Watching the caterpillars grow, seeing the caterpillar spin its cocoon, observing the caterpillar emerge, watching the caterpillar escape to the sky.
>
> *Paige Patton, College Junior*

The one African American student in class sets up a pattern of questions that she follows, leading her to the basic question of freedom and her own identity:

> While reading *The Circuit*, I found myself wondering. Wondering what will become of the family? Wondering why they continued to have babies?

Wondering what happened to Miguelito? Wondering why *la migra* had to catch up with them? Why Panchito? Why his family who had worked so hard? Why his little brothers and sister who were born in America? Who were supposed to be free—a boy and his family. Who were in search of a promised land, who were more willing to work for America than most Americans. Most Americans see them as a virus—most Americans see them as nameless faces—most Americans see them as thieves, robbing us of our resources. But I see them as humans. I see them as brother and sister. I see them as me.

Courtney Foy, College Junior

Acquaint students with parallel language structures by sharing rich examples of them with your students. Let students try their hands at creating such language structures in their own fast-draft writing. They will discover the power of parallel structures. Ask students eventually to write about the literature they are reading together. Give them a few minutes to edit what they have written, then do a read-around so that parallel language structures fill the air and the meaning of the literature expands.

24

"Who Said That?"

David Schuster, College Junior

In writing, just as in everyday life, there are many voices in my head. Not all the voices are uniquely mine. I hear the world influencing me to think what is important. I hear my family pressuring me what to do and think. I hear my friends thinking about me.

And then there are my voices. I have a selfish voice and an unselfish voice. I have a worried voice and a peaceful voice. I have a fearful voice and a hopeful voice.

I trust my voices, but not all of the time. I am starting more and more to not trust the voice of the world. What the world thinks is important, I do not. I listen to my family, but am starting to hear my voice as separate from theirs.

So I guess this begs the question of "Whose voice do I write with?" It's a good question. I have heard several voices come through my writing since I have been here at Miami.

My first year, I definitely had my "write what the teachers want to hear" voice. This is similar to the world's voice. The world was telling me that grades are the most important part of college. The world went on to say my first year, "Don't worry about coming up with your own voice, but just write what the teachers want to hear. They have the power to give you the grades, they have the power to give you a job, they have the power to give you success in life."

I don't listen to this voice anymore.

My second-year of college I started to hear another voice loud and clear. I heard my friends, and I listened. They told how to be cool, and they told me that they would really like me if I did certain things. These things made me cool, and I was unhappy.

My third year of college was a battle of the voices. I didn't hear the world's voice very loud, and my friends' voices were getting softer, but there were two very loud voices in my head. One was selfish. The other was unselfish. This battle of the voices was a boxing match. Each round was won by a different voice. I didn't know who was to win.

The knockout came like this. The unselfish voice showed love. The selfish voice brought destruction. The unselfish voice showed compassion, yet overcame evil. The selfish voice was ruthless, but did not know which way to go. The unselfish voice brought peace. The selfish voice brought turmoil. This was a war, but in the end the selfish voice could not stand. The prideful, selfish voice would not get up from the mat. The humility of the unselfish voice prevailed and still prevails today.

This year, my fourth and final year of college, I listen to the unselfish voice more and more. It is not quite my own voice yet, but it takes control of my life a little more everyday.

This voice tells me it is better to give than to receive.

This voice tells me the first will be last, and the last will be first.

This voice tells me this life is not about me.

This voice tells me love never fails.

Part IV

Crafting Authentic Voice

Antipasto
Squirming, Fretting, and Fraud

"The voice is so authentic," said Vicki.

The voice she was talking about was the voice in my second book, *Writing with Passion* (1995). We were using it as a text in a summer class I cotaught with Susan Stires at the University of New Hampshire.

"What's authentic voice?" I asked.

"When the voice in the writing matches the personality of the writer."

"Yes," said another student, "in class you're genuine. And so is your book. We read your words and hear you talking to us."

My personality in my writing. The real me. Authentic voice. I smiled and nodded. Inside, I squirmed and fretted.

I should have been beaming, but I knew the truth. I knew how un-me my writing voice is. In speech, I am sometimes stumbling and inarticulate. I don't say what I mean or I say it poorly, inadequately, unremarkably, and my words are misinterpreted or dismissed. Sometimes when I'm speaking I run out of words altogether, leaving my point unexpressed, unexampled, unpunctuated. In writing, these things happen less frequently, since I have time to revise and refine first words and initial thinking. Without the chance to craft language, I doubt I would write.

I believe in plowing ahead when something needs to be written. Grab words and begin to write, I say. Write with faith and fearlessness, faith that more words reside in you and fearlessness in moving down the page with them.

The most important part of my writing voice, what enables me to stamp my identity and values and perceptions on my writing is *craft*—how language can be generated, considered, shaped, and strategically used. I write words and listen to how they take life, rhythm, and meaning on the page. Or don't. I listen closely over a series of many drafts. I take time to reread my words, over and over, saying them aloud, tinkering, manipulating, saying more, taking words out, saying more yet, "fooling with words," as Bill Moyers put it (1999).

Authentic Voice?

Eventually.

25

Enter Craft

I like saying, but I love shaping that saying. Trust the gush, then control the flow. Writers pinpoint and refine meaning through the craft of revision. In this process they tinker with language and make their voices distinct and precise.

In 1855 Walt Whitman wrote, "I sound my barbaric yawp over the roofs of the world." I found that line bold and empowering when I read it at nineteen. I still do. I take it to heart. I, too, have a barbaric yawp, and I, too, can sound it. When I began to teach, I saw that my high school students also had barbaric yawps. Helping students sound those yawps was the best part of teaching English for me. More than teaching literature, language, or film.

I delight in the spontaneity of expression. I value writing when passion to say is upon us. Such writing sustains our writing workshops and injects a creative current into our classrooms. But I also know that when I craft my yawp, when I bring to bear on my first utterance what I know about language and how words work on the page, I can make my writing tighter, stronger, and smarter, more interesting, vivid, and accessible. I am first blurt for sure, but I am more than first blurt, too. I am first blurt considered and crafted.

One of my students recently took stock of her writing and had this to say:

> This year I have taken more care than ever before with crafting my work. In years past, I wrote a paper, gave it a once-over, and turned it in. I caught my spelling errors and most of my usage issues, but I didn't care much for revision. I turned my words in to my teachers the way they came out—for better or for worse. I stuck with the way I knew how to write—the way my mind created it. Then, I enrolled in one of Don Daiker's classes and he explained that revision is not the devil. Through kind prodding, he showed me that I could look at a piece of writing and change more than a word here and a word there. He showed me that revision would only help my writing.
>
> After nearly a semester with some of the "craftiest" (that is, in terms of how often they speak of *craft*) teachers I have ever known, I feel as though

writing is no longer a simple event. Now, I must examine what I have written—more than a once-over in search of errors. I ask myself questions: "Is this really what I'm trying to say?" "Can I show this more?" I simplify. I complicate. I make sure that whatever I have written makes sense.

Robin Perlmuter, College Junior

Robin is a writer and she is gaining sophistication as she learns the pleasure of working with language. She is discovering the enormous possibility for invention, precision, and voice that exists between her words already on the page and the nimbleness and creativity of her own mind. Most writers are passionate about fooling with words. Don Murray writes,

> I enjoy cutting, reordering, developing, shaping, polishing my drafts. Never have I failed to make a text better by my revising and editing. . . . There are few things more satisfying than this form of participatory reading, where the acts of reading and writing incite new reading, new writing, line by line. (1990, 171)

Once their first-blurt voices are launched, I teach students to craft their writing, to shape their voices. I'm one of those crafty teachers Robin refers to.

Look how the words work on the page.

Look what happens to your sentences when you use verbs of muscle, when you eliminate unnecessary adverbs and adjectives, when you change the rhythm of the words in a sentence.

Look what happens when you create pictures in your writing, when you use sensory detail, when you invent striking metaphors, find living leaping words.

Look at the effect on readers when you fashion words, sentences, paragraphs that draw them irresistibly in and when you discover endings that are intellectually meaningful and emotionally satisfying.

Look what happens when you take care how your writing appears on the page.

That's craft.

And craft is what this section is about.

26

Making It Rougher

One year at 7:30 each morning, I taught a class of twenty-two sophomores: one girl and twenty-one Skoal-dippin', Hank Williams Jr.–lovin', I'll-write-but-I-won't-like-it-and-I-won't-write-much boys. Not all of them, of course. There were Tim and Les and Dwayne, who seemed to take quiet pleasure in saying on paper. Most days, though, it seemed that all twenty-one boys were agin me. The challenge revved me up every morning. If I failed, it would not be because of a lack of determination and enthusiasm in me.

After the semester was under way, I began talking about revision, about looking at writing with fresh eyes and crafting the language. "Put your writing under a good light," writes William Stafford. "Turn your brights on and look at it" (1998, 140).

I used the overhead projector to show students various drafts of my own writing. You could see my thinking sprint, stumble, wander, take flight, lose momentum, get lost in verbiage, and find its way to meaning. With all my deleting, adding, combining, dividing, and rewording, I was doing the same things E. L. Doctorow did and Marge Piercy, Mary Oliver, Robert Cormier, and Shakespeare. "I work with language," said Bernard Malamud. "I love the flowers of afterthought" (quoted in Murray 1990, 184). I surely did.

Writer David Huddle describes the demands of revision this way:

> I am always telling my stories that I can finish them in three or four drafts, and they are always telling me that I can't finish them in fewer than seven or eight drafts. . . . Right this minute I have several unsuccessful stories of my own on my desk at home, and these mock me each time I look at them. "You did not give us enough," they say. "When will you come to us and give us everything?" (1991, 17)

I didn't want *everything* from my Skoal dippers, just some reflection and rethinking. I wanted them to interact with their own initial voices and find their way to new thinking, crisper language, accurate assertions, a little "wild exactitude," as Adam Gopnik wrote to describe that first generation of writers for the *New Yorker* (2000, 46).

One student named Jeff battled me at every turn. He sighed his resignation and pulled out fresh paper. He placed it beside the rough draft I had just handed back to him and began to recopy it.

"Oh, no," I said, moving to Jeff's side. "You saw my revisions. I want to see you mark up that rough draft, revise your thinking and language before making a new copy."

Jeff didn't look up, just kept copying. "I like to rewrite instead of marking it up, 'cause I have bigger ideas instead of those piddly little changes you make."

The students laughed, as did I. Jeff looked up, pleased, surprised, and maybe a little embarrassed at the laughter he'd evoked.

I stooped to desk level. "There's a big difference between rewriting and revising."

"You don't say," Jeff said, his eyes somewhere between bored and baleful.

"Recopying is usually mechanical, not much thinking to it," I said. "But revision is seeing again. Revision is creation. Revision is you bringing your mind to bear on what you have written. When you have revising in mind, I'd hate to see you get in a groove of recopying and miss opportunities to clarify and develop your first words. So, Jeff, I'd like to see you mark up that rough draft."

"And make it rougher," Jeff said.

I left him and began circulating among the other students, helping, questioning, cajoling, kidding. When I came by Jeff's desk again, I found he had taken my advice. He had worked at rethinking right on his paper, and it did indeed look rougher—blissfully, gloriously rougher. Jeff had crossed out sentences and passages, added words, phrases, and sentences between lines and in the margin. He'd even added a half page to the end.

"Jeff," I said, "you mind if I show the class the movement you've made?"

"Whatever," Jeff said and leaned back in his desk. I held Jeff's paper aloft and said to the other students, "Look what Jeff has done."

Across the room Scott glanced up, squinted. His face registered horror. "Look!" he said, "Jeff ruined it!"

27

Mind Pictures

I create voice through images.

LISA AYERS, College Junior

Yeah, Yeah. We know. Show don't tell. Explode the moment. Create word photos. Make movies in the reader's mind.

All good advice. Writing teachers have told their students such things for years. But I'm here to tell you, such advice misses the mark.

Here's a secret: Writing with specific detail, showing not telling, creating vivid imagery, exploding a moment . . .

It ain't for the reader.

It's for the writer.

Oh, it's for the reader eventually. But first—and most importantly—showing with vivid imagery is for writers to use in their mental writing workshop. Specific language works magic in the mind. When writers create images with words, they see what they are saying. Pictures take shape. Visual stimulation evokes more language, and the additional language evokes more images, and the new images spark more. . . . You get the picture?

Detail teaches. And it is the writer who is taught first, not the reader. Here is a story from my childhood I have known about most of my life, but never fully got until I used language in my journal to describe and visualize and name what I knew.

We Three Kings

For twenty-four years my dad operated a beerjoint and two bowling alleys right on the square in Malvern, Ohio, population in the mid-1950s about fourteen hundred people. The name of the place was Red's Nite Club, but it wasn't really a nightclub. It was a beerjoint. A working man's bar, my mom called it. No music.

No dancing. On Fridays after work, though, regular customers got their paychecks cashed. Saturday afternoons guys sat in the high-backed booths against the wall and played hearts or euchre or five hundred. After high school athletic events, the place filled with sports fans wanting sandwiches, beer, soft drinks, and talk. Dad did a brisk lunch business, too, thanks to the small Diebold plant outside of town and his famous Coney Islands (a hot dog on a steamed bun topped with chopped onions, mustard, and a spicy, tomato-based sauce with ground beef). The recipe for Coney sauce came from my mother, who learned it during her waitressing days at a diner in Canton, Ohio, during the early 1930s.

Outside the beerjoint above the sidewalk hung a huge neon sign with an arrow pointing toward the building, flashing "Red's Nite Club, Red's Nite Club, Red's Nite Club" from the time the place opened at 8 A.M. until closing at 2:30 the next morning.

We lived in a spacious four-bedroom apartment above the bar. Our living room overlooked the street and town square through a wide bank of six tall windows. Mom had begun oil painting in the early 1950s. She was passionate about it, traveling during summer to surrounding environs to paint landscapes or historical buildings, and when the weather turned colder painting still lifes in an art teacher's studio.

After Thanksgiving one year, maybe 1955, Mom began a huge project—to paint her tribute to the upcoming holiday season so everyone passing through town would see it. From inside she painted on the bank of windows facing the street. On the far right window she painted a star hanging in the night sky, a beacon radiating light over the countryside. In the other windows, moving surely toward the star, she painted three men wearing crowns and dressed in colorful robes, each riding a camel, their eyes fixed on the distant star. Every bit of each window was covered with paint: the blue night sky, the brown rolling earth, the camels and colorfully robed riders, and that distant, constant star.

As I wrote about this scene in my journal with all the detail I could remember and imagine, I found myself seeing Mom's mural from the street as people in cars would have when they waited at the lone traffic light in town. I was suddenly startled and delighted! Not until that moment of writing with detail and imagery did I realize that flashing intermittently over my mother's pastoral, reverent scene was the lurid red light of the neon sign. Yes, we three kings, that star was your goal and your guide, but lighting the way was Red's Nite Club, Red's Nite Club, Red's Nite Club.

It was the language of imagery that propelled me beyond just remembering what my mother painted in 1955 on those windows overlooking the street. The specific language, thought and written, led me to visualize the painting in more detail than ever before. Finding words to describe what I imagined made me see the effect of the neon sign. What a sweet irony: Bethlehem Above Beerjoint.

The writing teaches. The showing illuminates. First for the writer, then for the reader. Both benefit.

A Lie, from Which We Get the Truth

Not long ago with a group of teachers I wrote about a memory from my adolescence. It was one of those indelible moments that has stuck with me for years. Betrayal, heartache, and humiliation realized in one instant of recognition:

> Saturday night. One in the morning. Under the street light on the square. Me. Sixteen. Dateless. My girl visiting her grandparents for the weekend. Snow sifting through the street light, landing dry on the pavement, the curb, the sidewalk, the Ford Galaxy pulled to a stop thirty yards in front of me, idling at the traffic light. That blonde head seated next to the driver, swiveling, that blonde head, black-framed glasses glinting, hair shiny and bright from the street light, that blonde head—the whole body really—rotating, seeming to rise up, looking away, wanting to crawl into the back seat, that blonde head so often on my shoulder, now pinned under the street light, snow falling lightly through the crisp February air, falling on the road, on the car, on me.

I often place this piece of writing on an overhead to share with students and teachers.

What was the weather doing? I ask them.

Cold, they say, snowing that dry snow you can brush off the pavement with a broom.

The truth?

I can't remember. But soon after I started to write, I saw snow falling this way: You look against the black sky and can't tell whether it is snowing or not. You turn to a streetlight, however, and you see snow falling through the air. I wrote down the detail of snow sifting through light.

What kind of car was being driven?

A Ford Galaxy, they say.

The truth?

I can't remember. But the year was 1965, so a middle-class family car could very well have been a Ford Galaxy.

I remember it was late. I remember my girl was with another guy. I remember her blonde head trapped under the streetlight, she turning this way and that to escape my gaze.

I am happy with my final line that names what the snow is falling on, each prepositional phrase getting shorter, isolating at last the "me." Cold, humiliated, heartbroken me.

I never would have come to that ending if I hadn't been specific in that first labyrinthine sentence fragment after all the shorter fragments. Snow sifting through the streetlight sharpens the mental picture I am experiencing as I write. Snow becomes part of my consciousness as I imagine and write it. Snow remains in my subconscious as I move on to other detail. I don't realize it when I write down that image, but the snow sets the stage for the wonderful magic of language, writing, and imagination: in the final lines of what turns out to be a prose poem, I find myself writing about the snow.

I couldn't have planned that. Not me. Couldn't have outlined or webbed or listed details that would have led me to that ending before I was engaged in writing it.

Don't write in generalities. Don't write in abstractions. Be specific. Write visual images. They enable writers to see more clearly. The better writers see, the better the writing will be, the better the chance for surprise, the better the chance for voice.

For Readers, Too

The words are eventually for readers other than the writer. As writers we want our voices full of images that appeal to readers. I ask students to read literature with an eye toward noticing vividly rendered passages, this to alert them to writing that creates pictures. Students copy these passages and explain why the words moved them so much. One student chose this passage from Ken Kesey's *One Flew Over the Cuckoo's Nest:*

> His arms commence to swell, and the veins squeeze up to the surface. He clinches his eyes, and his lips draw away from his teeth. His head leans back, and tendons stand out like coiled ropes running from his heaving neck down both arms to his hands. His whole body shakes with the strain as he tries to lift something he knows he can't lift, something everybody knows he can't lift. (1962, 120–21)

Missy explained why she chose this passage:

> Kesey paints a picture-perfect description of McMurphy's maximum effort to move something he knows he can't move. His word choice shows detail and action. I see his "veins squeeze" and his "lips draw" and the "tendons

standing out like coiled ropes." I am happy that the author did not just tell me that McMurphy tried very hard to lift the panel. He let me witness the blood-pumping, sweat-beading strain.

Missy Lee, High School Senior

Charge students with finding and then typing or writing out vividly rendered scenes from their reading. Ask them to describe in writing why the passage appeals to them, just as Missy did. Then share the gold.

The Craft of Showing in Revision

This chapter about using visual detail to enhance our voices could have been included in the section of this book titled "Trust the Gush." Visual detail propels our voices. It generates further detail and understanding. I place the chapter here, though, because shaping a scene or description is a matter of craft, too. We can revisit our drafts with an eye toward revising what we've written so that the visual image is stronger for us as writers. When writers see and understand a scene better, so do readers.

Here is some seeing and masterful reseeing by a student who writes about an encounter with a friend he hadn't seen in years:

> When we found each other again, it was at a rave—the true club/gay night-life dance party. He was in the bathroom. Shooting. That is, he was shooting junk. Heroine to be exact. I saw him but he didn't see me. He looked thin and wasted, in every sense of the word. I ran from the bathroom through waves of overwhelming guilt. I did that to him. And, I'll never forgive myself.

Casey Browning, College Junior

Casey revises the passage so that both he and his readers get a full look at what he saw:

> He looked thin and wasted in every sense of the word. His hair, normally longish and a gleaming, rich black, was cropped tightly to his head and dyed an impossible white-blonde. Many of the other club kids had similar haircuts, but against his now anemically yellow skin it just made him seem sickly. The worst were his arms. The way he sat on the edge of the yellowed urinal I saw them too clearly. They hung in front of him like a scarecrow's. Tortured blue veins barely under porcelain skin. Red, irritated pocks peppered up and

> down. He looked up at me, through me, grinning. Not seeing me. I looked at the ghost a moment longer. I ran from the bathroom through waves of overwhelming guilt.

Show what you are writing. Show so that it etches itself in the mind. In your mind. In your readers' minds. Bring a camera to bear on your drafting so what you're writing builds in you and makes your writing experience deeper. Give yourself the benefit of revisiting what you've shown, as Casey did, to see it again and show it better, to glimpse some flower of afterthought. Your voice will grow strong.

> Ask students to describe a strong but brief memory. Collect the pieces and hold them for three or four days. Redistribute the writing and ask students to read them and note what images they see beyond what the words suggest. They might do this with a partner so they will be sure to articulate their thoughts. Have students add language to deepen the picture they are creating. Use Casey's description of his friend to demonstrate how this might be done. Lead a discussion on the relationship between language and mental pictures.

28

Hit Dem Senses

I convey a sense of feeling in my writing that is both a sense and a feeling. I appeal to the senses in my writing. "Smell the freshman fear," "pat-pat of hands gently clapping," "smiles spreading," and "feet like lead" all elicit the senses. We smell the freshman fear, hear the pat-pat of hands, see the smiles spread, and feel the lead feet.

AMANDA PELLER, College Junior

When Amanda analyzed her writing to identify traits of her authentic voice, she found that she "appeal[ed] to the senses." I remember teachers using that expression. I pictured someone on his knees, wearing a desperate expression, hands outstretched, appealing to a higher authority. "Oh, please, don't let my writing be unappealing. Anything but that!" I do have sensory memories, though, of appeal in other ways. I remember seeing someone dig a thumbnail into an orange peel, citrus mist spritzing into the air. I remember the peel of Rocky Longo's 1965 GTO, blue smoke roiling into the air from beneath the tires and a prolonged, wailing scream reverberating off buildings on both sides of the street, a sound I still find chilling and dangerous.

I don't use the word *appeal* when exhorting students to write with sensory detail. "Hit dem senses," I tell them. I heighten students' attention to language that carries a sensory load by creating a handout of excerpts from Diane Ackerman's *A Natural History of the Senses* (1990). Ackerman writes vividly about each of our senses, providing feeling and fact, folklore and science, loading her own writing with sensory detail and illustrative metaphors. She is a master at producing colorful, playful, sensory-laden language. The book is must reading for every writer and writing teacher. "It is both our panic and our privilege to be mortal and senseful," Ackerman writes. "We live on the leash of our senses" (xiii).

Ray Bradbury knew this. He was especially attentive to the sensory experience of his characters so readers would accept his science fiction settings:

> [I]n order to convince your reader that he is *there*, you must assault each of his senses, in turn, with color, sound, taste, and texture. If your reader feels the sun on his flesh, the wind fluttering his shirt sleeves, half your fight is won. The most improbable tales can be made believable, if your reader, through his senses, feels certain that he stands at the middle of events. He cannot refuse, then, to participate. The logic of events always gives way to the logic of the senses. (1966, 43)

My Ackerman handout immerses students in interesting information and colorful writing about how we come to know the world. Ackerman is both humanist and scientist as she writes a luscious, redolent prose that is pure pleasure to read aloud, which we do, and then talk about.

> **Smell**
> Smells detonate softly in our memory like poignant land mines, hidden under the weedy mass of many years and experience. Hit a tripwire of smell, and memories explode all at once. (1990, 5)
>
> **Taste**
> Adults have about 10,000 [taste buds], grouped by theme (salt, sour, sweet, bitter), at various sites in the mouth. Inside each one, about fifty taste cells busily relay information to a neuron, which will alert the brain. Not much tasting happens in the center of the tongue, but there are also incidental taste buds on the palate, pharynx, and tonsils, which cling like bats to the damp, slimy limestone wall of a cave. (1990, 138)
>
> **Touch**
> [T]he skin is . . . alive, breathing and excreting, shielding us from harmful rays and microbial attack, metabolizing vitamin D, insulating us from heat and cold, repairing itself when necessary, regulating blood flow, acting as a frame for our sense of touch, aiding us in sexual attraction, defining our individuality, holding all the thick red jams and jellies inside us where they belong. (1990, 67)
>
> **Vision**
> Seventy percent of the body's sense receptors cluster in the eyes. . . . Lovers close their eyes when they kiss because, if they didn't, there would be too many visual distractions to notice and analyze. . . . Lovers want to do serious

touching, and not be disturbed. So they close their eyes as if asking two cherished relatives to leave the room. (1990, 230)

Hearing

In the robust festivity of a dinner party, a waiter pours a luscious Liebfraumilch, whose apricot blush we behold, whose bouquet we inhale, whose savory fruitiness we taste. Then, wishing one another well, we clink our glasses together because sound is the only sense missing from our full enjoyment of the wine. (1990, 177)

Being alert to sensory detail affects the way we look at writing. Take note of writers—like Ackerman—who write in sensory ways. Choose passages to share with students. Have students catalog and share strong sensory impressions they have experienced. Form the habit of using sensory details when describing or explaining, narrating or arguing.

I include *explaining* and *arguing* right along with *describing* and *narrating*. Exposition and argument are not modes of writing we often associate with sensory detail. But emotional impact is not mutually exclusive of clear, logical thinking. In our examples, anecdotes, and details that support our positions and illustrate our points, sensory detail helps readers experience our writing, not merely understand it. In her quest to make us realize the extraordinary work our senses do, Ackerman writes in the fullness of sensory detail herself: memories hiding in a thicket of years, bats clinging to the slimy limestone walls of caves, red jams and jellies inside us. Keep in mind Whitman's assertion:

Logic and sermons never convince,
The damp of the night drives deeper into my soul. ([1855] 1981, 52)

Logic and sermons have convinced me many times, but I know the spirit of what Whitman is saying. I believe in "the logic of the senses." I try to dwell there in my own writing. Connect logic and points of argument to sensory experience—*to the damp of the night*—and your chances of convincing readers improve.

I'll end this chapter with an example of student writing that hits dem senses. Jenie had read Sandra Cisneros' *The House on Mango Street* (1991) and was moved to write about a particular place (Box Canyon) and time (her childhood). Jenie hits dem senses in a way that casts you amid the experience:

Big Mouth Spring bubbled up, and you'd put your face down there and suck. It was like a liquid crystal ball, cold on your lips, on your face, on your fingers. The water was different, fresher than anything, fresher than the forest ground after rain. Almost like magic, like it came from the middle of the earth. I thought it might make you magic, give you something nobody else ever had, making you different. It flowed out, and I felt under my toes that it turned the moss into something special, like it was the carpet of a magic castle. . . .

The bushes in Box Canyon were full of berries, red and purple. Huckleberries you could eat. Huckleberries you could never get enough of. We were like the bears, we loved to pick and eat, pick and eat, all day turning our fingers purple and filling us purple. Most of the time we had buckets, old Shwann Man ice-cream buckets to fill and bring back home. Mom made jam, or huckleberry pancakes. Dad made homemade ice-cream: soft, white, purple huckleberry ice-cream, sweet and cold.

Jenie Skoy, College Junior

Get students reveling in sensory experience. Taste a drop of honey on the tip of the tongue. Crush basil leaves between fingers and hold under the nose. Listen to fingertips tapping letters on a keyboard or a pen scratching across a page, an *i* being dotted, a dash being slashed. Sensations mean you are alive, just as your writing will be when you hit dem senses.

Have students choose an important time and place, as Jenie did. Ask them to list all the sensations they remember associated with it. Have them talk these sensations over with a partner, putting language to memory and seeing what further sense data can be caught. Have them write a descriptive piece that brings the time and place to sensory fullness.

29

What the Ear Knows

Deafness is a much worse misfortune [than blindness]. For it means the loss of the most vital stimulus—the sound of the voice that brings language, sets thoughts astir and keeps us in the intellectual company of man.

HELEN KELLER

That quotation surprised me. I read it in Diane Ackerman's *A Natural History of the Senses* (1990, 190). The most well-known blind person in America lamented her deafness more than her blindness? I spend so much time reading that the idea of blindness makes me shiver. Still, Helen Keller knew what she was talking about. She knew both silence and darkness. Her words made me remember how I, too, value hearing as part of my process of creating a voice distinctive, fluent, and musical.

Oral Interpretation

I make a big deal in my classes about the sound of writing. *Oral interpretation* is how we name the skill of using voice and expression to breathe life into words on paper. Readers animate words. They use voice modulation, pitch, and pace to bring language alive for listeners. Those oral interp classes I took as an undergraduate so many years ago were offered, appropriately enough, by the theatre department. Effective oral interpretation requires a tad of acting.

I model oral interpretation by reading aloud my own writing to students in a clear, expressive, appropriately paced voice. Sometimes I read from my journal or a quick-write I've done on the spot. Sometimes I place my writing on the overhead projector and read it aloud. Sometimes I simply read aloud my words from a text

I have in hand. Always, though, I give my words the respect of a clear, expressive, appropriately paced reading.

A Poem a Day

I begin every class period by reading aloud a poem. Some teachers take attendance at the beginning of a class. Some tell a joke. Some chitchat. I read a poem. It's the Romano ritual. The only poems I read are ones I like. Doesn't matter if the poems have been revered by anthologists or critics. If I don't like the poem, I won't read it. Ninety percent of the poems I read are contemporary and free verse. The voices of contemporary poets are some of the most varied and literate in the land. Students don't hear enough of those voices. If a traditional literature curriculum is in place in their high schools, students might go through four years without hearing contemporary voices. If students are going to write, they need to regularly experience the best modern voices in the land, the voices of their time. When I read aloud, I don't hide emotions the poem makes me feel. You won't hear me reading in a detached monotone. I strive for expressive, clear, appropriately paced oral interpretations. I want to interact with the language of the poem to see what kind of voice it enables me to create.

When I taught high school, a poem each class period meant that my students heard ninety intelligent, inventive, compelling voices each semester. We didn't take time to analyze a poem, take it apart, or deconstruct it. We just listened and tried to resonate to the careful use of language.

Making Music

> When we read aloud, often and well, we fill our classrooms with the sound of words, well placed and well written, and that sound wraps its arms around the work of young writers who are hard at work learning their craft. (Ray 1999, 68)

That goes for writers of any age.

I expect students to read aloud their own writing to peers in clear, expressive, appropriately paced voices. I want students to gain a sense of audience beyond the teacher. I want the writing to become more than mere academic exercise. For inexperienced writers, reading aloud causes them to reenter the geography of their drafts, moving through them from beginning to end, reexperiencing and reassessing the whole of their work even though it may have been created in fits and starts.

I want my students to realize they are creating music when they write. I want them to hear that music and check to see if it is hitting the right notes. I want a voice to arise from the text. I want writers to become sharply aware of the connection between their spoken voice and the symbols they place on the page. Students are responsible for those words, just as much as they are responsible for what comes out of their mouths when they speak. I want students to use their ear to write well.

Richard Marius writes,

> I still read everything aloud. I have a fundamental conviction that if a sentence cannot be read aloud with sincerity, conviction, and communicable emphasis, it is not a good sentence. Good writing requires good rhythms and good words. You cannot know whether the rhythms and the words are good unless you read them aloud. Reading aloud is also the easiest way to see that prose tracks, that it runs on smoothly from sentence to sentence, idea to idea, section to section within the larger whole. Reading aloud also makes the mind consider connotations of words and perhaps above all their relations to each other. (Quoted in Murray 1990, 134)

I've published four books, written two others that have gone unpublished. At some point in their creation, I've read aloud every word in them several times. I've taken my writing seriously over forty years. I've developed a good sense of how my words sound when I read them silently. Even so, I read aloud all my high-stakes writing.

The way I test my words for their contribution to the music I'm seeking is to read them aloud in a clear, expressive, appropriately paced voice. I use first gear, holding back my reading speed, making sure I give each word shape and breath and respect. It is a practice that might be out of step with today's frenetic world of faster cars, faster computers, remote controls that fly up and down the television channels, fast food, fast service, instant credit.

But deliberate reading pays off.

If you picture me, sitting in front of my computer monitor, elbows on my chair, hands folded on my lap, saying every word slowly, listening for hitches in rhythm and music, adjusting language as I need to, sometimes diving into deeper revision in which I'm not just tinkering with words and phrasing, but also altering meaning, then you are picturing me accurately.

This act of reading aloud isn't drudgery. It is bliss. I'm doing the important work of crafting a linguistic musical score. I enjoy this act of listening to my language as much as any part of the process of writing. There is a chunk of ego involved, I admit. I know I am gazing at my reflection, but it is necessary gazing, and I am not passive as I watch and listen. I'm as close to art as I can get. I want to make the reflection I see and hear pleasurable to myself. That's how I know it will be pleasurable to readers.

Tonal Writers

I think I am a *tonal* writer. *Tonal* is a new word I learned from an essay by Adam Gopnik about James Thurber and Harold Ross of the *New Yorker*: "[Thurber] was also probably the best tonal writer we've ever had. No one worked harder or went farther to slim down the space between the way we talk and the way we write" (2000, 44). The tonal writer, Gopnik says, tries to make readers forget they are reading and just think they are hearing (44).

How does tonality work in my writing?

In working with Chapter 1, I read aloud this sentence:

> I've read voices fraught with nonstandard usage, little punctuation, and spelling aberrations, yet the meaning of the words was unmistakable, the presence of the writer undeniable.

Two sentences above that passage I had already used the word *fraught*, so that little-used word bonged when I said it a second time. I liked *fraught* better the first time I used it. The ill-sounding bong also made me stop to consider a meaning problem: How could writing be fraught with little punctuation? *Fraught* means "full of" or "in abundance." I was talking about writing of scant punctuation, not abundant punctuation. Sound and meaning drove me to recast the sentence:

> I've read voices riddled with spelling aberrations, nonstandard usage, and incorrect punctuation, yet the meaning of the words was unmistakable, the presence of the writer undeniable.

I like *riddled*. The spelling, usage, and punctuation I'm describing were hopelessly askew. The word *incorrect* covers punctuation that is both inaccurate and absent. I changed the order of my list of three items, too. When I read aloud and listened, I liked the sound and rhythm of two-syllable *spelling* coming first, followed by the three syllables of *nonstandard* and *incorrect*.

In a novel about high school football, sex, and grief, I wrote a scene in which a high school football coach speaks to students at a pep assembly. He singles out one of his players for praise. The fictional passage reads:

> Coach Raymond looked into the stands. "Angel," he said, "please stand."

I'll bet you have a finger in your ear right now, itching out the bad repetition. For *stands* I substituted *audience*, and the tone was to my liking.

Recently, Kathy and I decided to make osso bucco, that wonderful Italian dish of veal shanks in a rich sauce, the meat almost falling off the bone. We got out a reliable cookbook: Jeff Smith's *The Frugal Gourmet Cooks Italian* (1993). In the preface to the recipe Smith writes about the wonderful osso bucco he's eaten at restaurants both in New York City and in Italy, then I read this sentence:

> I think you can do better on your own, providing you can find a butcher who can provide quality meat. (326)

I hear a clang and wince. The writer in me has pushed aside the cook. *Providing* and *provide* so close together? How about *supply* for *provide*? How about "a butcher who *sells* quality meat"? Or maybe drop *providing* and write instead, "*if* you can find a butcher who can provide quality meat"? There is usually more than one way to amend sound and make music.

The osso bucco, by the way, was delicious and not as hard to prepare as I thought it would be. When reading cookbooks, my stomach wins out in the end. I'll take a wonderful recipe with a clang in the language over one with musical prose and unpalatable results. But I am what I am—anywhere writing is involved, I'm listening.

A Wild and Stormy Poem

In January 1979 southwestern Ohio was hit by a fearsome blizzard that shut schools down for days. When the snow abated and roads were cleared, we went back to school, but not for long. High winds drifted the snow from the fields over the roads. The snow turned to ice. Schools closed again.

My daughter was eight then. She and I were housebound while Kathy was transported to the hospital to work by a volunteer driving a Jeep. During one of our homebound afternoons, Mariana wrote a poem she aimed to send to *Cricket* magazine (see Figure 29–1).

I asked Mariana to make lines out of her words in places where she heard natural pauses. She inserted slashes where lines might break. Then I asked her to read her words aloud and listen.

Melt
The gray clouds
are drifting away.
The ice is thawing

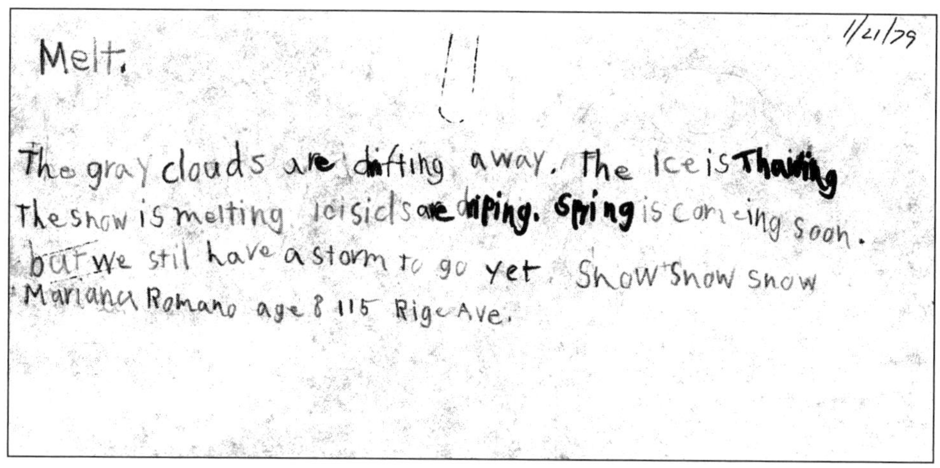
1/21/79

Melt.

The gray clouds are difting away. The Ice is Thawing
The snow is melting icisicls are driping. Spring is comeing soon.
but we stil have a storm to go yet. Snow Snow snow
Mariana Romano age 8 115 Rige Ave.

Figure 29–1: Mariana's poem about snow and spring.

> The snow is melting
> icisicls are driping.
> Spring is comeing soon
> but we still have
> a storm to go yet.
> Snow snow snow.
>
> —*Mariana Romano, Second Grade*

"That doesn't sound right," she said.

"What doesn't?"

"*Yet.*"

"Drop it and see how it sounds."

Mariana erased *yet* and added a period after *go*. She read aloud: "'but we still have / a storm to go. / Snow snow snow.' Now that sounds better!"

In his essay "Three Mysteries at the Heart of Writing," Peter Elbow argues that some writing is easier to read because the writer is able to somehow make readers "*hear* the meaning coming to us from the silent words on the page" (2003, 16). Elbow thinks it would be a good thing if more student writers learned how to do this:

> I'm not asking students to reproduce speech on paper, I'm asking them to write sentences that are inviting and pleasing to read aloud—that feel good in the mouth and sound good in the ear. (2003, 20)

Demonstrate the craft of listening for music in words on paper. Place a draft of your own on the overhead. Read your words aloud with clarity, expression, and respect. Slow down and enunciate. Don't mumble. Don't hurry. Trust your ear. Listen for music. Listen for clangs and bongs and missing beats, too. Let your pen move to amend the page to make the music you want to hear.

Set students to reading their own writing aloud, quietly, trusting their ears to know when words need altering.

30

Linguistic Inebriation

In the last year I taught high school students, writer and teacher Donald Murray spent a one-week residency at nearby Miami University. In addition to teaching a writing workshop for faculty, giving a public writing demonstration, and talking with students, Murray offered to meet one evening with area K–12 teachers. The Ohio Writing Project based at Miami kicked into gear to spread the word, and one evening twenty-five teachers sat in a circle with Murray at the Edgewood High School media center in Trenton, Ohio. For an hour we talked the shop of writing and teaching.

After the session, we drank punch and ate cookies, everyone lingering and chatting, extending this stimulating evening. One of our graduates—then a political science major at Miami—had arranged to interview Murray for a Cincinnati radio station where he worked. Chad had been a go-getter in high school. He had acted in school plays (Mr. Applegate in *Damn Yankees!*), written a column for the school newspaper, and played goalie for the soccer team. Chad had been a delight to have in class. His mind was nimble, his sense of humor quick and ironic. He didn't hesitate to participate in discussion. He loved to write and then to use his resonant voice to give additional volume, emphasis, and texture to what he had written. His senior year Chad delivered the morning announcements, broadcast athletic events, and emceed school assemblies. Anything that needed a voice, Chad got involved in.

At one point during the Murray reception, Chad took the author aside for the interview. My former stellar writing student and my friend and mentor from New Hampshire—I couldn't help but stand within earshot. I cringed as Chad tossed around big words like horseshoes. A few were ringers but most clanged and bounced, not even close.

"When you talk about your writing, you talk about psychological, maybe psychosomatic stimulations. . . . How should elementary teachers go about coercing their students at that young age to write. . . . Tell me, Mr. Murray, has your ineluctable commitment to writing affected your theoretical stance as a pedagogue?"

I moved over to the punch bowl, aghast. What had happened to Chad's straight-shooting style? His directness? His disdain of all things pretentious? Chad had been among the finest high school writers I'd taught in seventeen years. When had he started to talk like that? When the interview ended, I went to Murray and asked how it had gone.

"Bright young man," said Murray. "Enthusiastic, professional, and drunk with language."

31

Living Leaping Words

The language is always offering us bonuses.

William Stafford

Words were living and leaping in Chad's mind when he interviewed Donald Murray that fall evening at Edgewood High School. I got over my cringing. I am, in fact, embarrassed by it. My chagrin that evening caused me to abandon two key concepts of my philosophy of teaching and learning: growth and development. Chad wasn't quite nineteen in 1988. He was developing as a sophisticated language user. He was trying out new, fascinating words. He was probably a little nervous and intimidated at the prospect of interviewing a major figure in the development of composition in the second half of the twentieth century. Chad was smart and bold and no doubt feeling his intellectual oats that evening. He may have been trying to sound impressive by putting on the "war paint" of "big words" (Hoffman 1986, 61).

For students who are intelligent, verbal, and willing to take risks, drunkenness with language is a natural stage of development. I went through it, and I wasn't near the writer Chad was when I was nineteen. When students get a little drunk with language, it might be time for smiling. It might be a time for discussion about audience, word meanings, and malapropisms. But it is *not* a time for cringing or embarrassment or frustration on the teacher's part.

> Appropriating a style and making it your own is difficult, and you'll miss the mark a thousand times along the way. The botched performances, though, are part of it all, and developing writers will grow through them if they are able to write for people who care about language, people who are willing to sit with them and help them as they struggle to write about difficult things. (Rose 1989, 54)

Chad didn't stop growing as a writer and speaker at nineteen. He kept working with words. He kept reading and talking and discussing. He kept growing and developing. He toned down his Walter Winchell delivery. He crafted a crisp, direct style of speaking and writing. Chad earned an undergraduate degree in political science and a graduate degree in communication. He announced the news, conducted interviews, and wrote copy for Miami University's local National Public Radio affiliate. After graduation, Chad traveled to Washington, D.C., secured a job at C-SPAN, and later moved to National Public Radio, where he produced news segments for different programs and wrote and delivered the news. He was no longer drunk with language. He'd grown out of that. Now he controlled language and used it to explore and communicate.

Chad loved words. Still does. He loves putting language together that explains complexities, interprets events, and argues positions. He lives near Washington, D.C., today. He writes a column every three or four days on a current event. I'm among many he emails them to. The columns teach, provoke, and enlighten. I'm grateful for what I learned from Chad about language growth and development. Writers don't stay the same. They take in more. They lose naiveté. They sharpen their ability to perceive, expand their vocabulary. They learn how to put things together faster and more accurately.

It is words that writers work with, and it is words that create their voices. The title of this chapter comes with a debt of gratitude to Judith Rowe Michaels' clear voice in *Dancing with Words* (2001, 45). She is a teacher and writer who knows about growth, development, and living leaping words.

The Words Themselves

Vanish. Bedazzled. Beneath. Catastrophic. Fibrous. Wrath. Passion. These are words I am fond of that come to mind right now. I like the way they look. I like the way they sound. I like considering their meaning and using them in speech and writing. One verb, one verb-adjective, one preposition, two adjectives, two nouns. This list could be much longer. I can fall in love with many words, given the right context.

I even love wrong words. In an essay about *Julius Caesar* a high school sophomore wrote, "They acted real jealous about Caesar getting crowned to be king, which I think was very shellfish of them." A junior in high school once wrote that "[t]he Dinah Shores were extinct." Bonuses for me, the language lover with a sense of humor.

Those word misfires are delightful instances when experience, word knowledge, sound, and sense making collide instead of harmonize. They were handwritten, before the days of computers. Today those misfires could have been spellcheck errors. Not errors of the *there–their–they're* variety, but the kind of spellcheck error that occurs when writers are too quick in making choices, the kind of errors akin to seafood and celebrities. Here are some splendid spellcheck errors from my college students.

- A Jewish friend invited me to Satyr Dinner.
- My main purpose in the internship was to teach kids the impotence of reading, writing, and critical thinking.
- The poem was by e.e. cummings, an author who deified the rules of grammar.
- Her problem is low self-esteem and hidden hatred of our mother, who is somewhat to blame for her anorexia. My sister finally agreed to canceling.
- During prep hour, the English teachers gather together in the writing center, talk about their classes, gossip, exchange lesson plans, eat bagels, and drink Diet Cock.
- I'll work as a graduate assailant next fall.

I am not immune from rash choosing either. I wrote a memo once and almost sent it addressed to the Ohio Department of Elucidation. One of my colleagues claimed that anyone who has ever dealt with a state department of education knows I was being satiric.

I love to write, but once I made this spellcheck error: "I spent the morning at my desk writhing."

That one's been all too true occasionally.

Turning Language on Itself

William Stafford tells writers to ask themselves, "Does the reader find early and sustained rewards?" (1998, 140).

Writing can offer many rewards and pleasures: The reward and pleasure of information, meaning, logical thought, narrative, plot, revelation, characterization, personal identification, musical rhythms. And there are little rewards and pleasures like those that come from authors alert to the language they are using and playing off that language to extend meaning.

In *The Botany of Desire* (2001), Michael Pollan devotes a chapter to the potato. In one section he writes about a genetically engineered potato he experimented with: a New Leaf potato. The New Leafs were disease resistant, fleshy, long lasting, and large. But Pollan had qualms. How would long-term mass production of New Leaf potatoes affect the environment? How would mass production affect the diversity of the potato seed bank? How would New Leaf potatoes affect human beings who ate them? Pollan harvested some of his New Leaf potatoes, then delayed doing anything with them until an invitation arrived:

> But I was still left with my bag of New Leafs sitting there on the porch. And there they sat until Labor Day, when I got an invitation to a potluck supper at the town beach. Perfect! I signed up to make a potato salad. The day of the supper, I brought the bag of spuds into the kitchen and set a pot of water on the stove. But before the water even had a chance to boil, I was stricken by this obvious thought: Wouldn't I have to tell people at the picnic what they were eating? I had no reason to think the potatoes weren't perfectly safe, but if the idea of eating genetically modified food without knowing it gave me pause, I couldn't very well ask my neighbors to do so. (That would be rather more potluck than they were counting on.) (237)

I am rewarded by *potluck* in the two contexts (as I imagine Pollan was rewarded in the writing). He was paying attention to language. He wasn't just laying down words and moving on. He was aware of what he was saying, what he had said, and how he was saying it.

In a summer course for teachers recently, we read Esmé Codell's *Educating Esmé: Diary of a Teacher's First Year* (1999). We read half the book and wrote one-page, single-spaced responses to it, chasing our thoughts on paper, sometimes explaining, sometimes interpreting, sometimes critiquing. We could say our say, whatever it was. High school English teacher Kate McDonell loved the book. She admired the author's feistiness, honesty, and great compassion for children. Kate wrote, "Esmé's journal is where she let it all hang out—bravado, arrogance, judgment, and she does. In spades. And in hearts."

Kate turns the language on itself and takes advantage of multiple meaning, injecting life into the well-worn expression of saying something "in spades"—the suit that trumps all others. Kate extends the metaphor with "And in hearts" and points the way toward the most moving part of Esmé Codell's stance toward education—her great love of children, books, and learning.

Repeating a Key Word

Sometimes a word is so surprising, distinctive, and perfect that writers use it only once. Esmé Codell writes this of her indolent, unsupportive, exploitative principal: "My pose upon his departure was that of pure maliciousness, as Snow White's stepmother looks into her mirror with squinting, plotting, viperous eyeballs" (1999, 133). The adjectival form of *viper* isn't a word we run into often. *Viperous* is one of those living leaping words that Judith Michaels writes about. Best choose a powerful place for it (in Esmé's sentence, the last in a series of three effective adjectives), and use it once.

In other contexts, however, meaning can be enhanced by repeating a word. Ken Macrorie points out that writers with voice "repeat words with power, not weakness. If they want to hit a word hard, they repeat it" (1984, 77), and sometimes they "shift the form of the repeated word, or play with it in some way" (78). Look at this paragraph by Lottie Hawkins, a thirty-five-year-old mother of two and former member of the United States Air Force:

> When I assert my feelings, I occasionally use repetition or key words throughout to solidify my point. For example, I believe that a person of the male gender can father a child. However, I do not believe that fathering a child makes a male a daddy or a man. Being a father involves donating a small amount of sperm to fertilize an egg. Being a daddy involves loving the child and supporting the child financially, spiritually, and emotionally. A male is not a man when a court system has to make him provide financial support for the child he fathered.
>
> *Lottie Hawkins, College Junior*

The Counterpunching Perfect Word

Sometimes a writer rewards readers by using a word that reverses the tone of a piece. Heather Johnson has fun writing about her devotion to chocolate. She establishes an elitist's notion of fine chocolate, then swiftly refutes it with a final, hyphenated word:

> I have taste-tested chocolate from some of the finest regions of Europe. The Swiss pride themselves on their creamy mountain-milk chocolate. In Salzburg, Austria, they package their chocolate in extravagant wrappers and boxes in the shape of Mozart's profile. The Germans sell inch-thick blocks of dark, rich chocolate by the pounds. I have seen the wrappers, tasted the mountain cream, and eaten pounds of chocolate; there was pleasure in every bite. But even in the Alps of Switzerland or the streets of Germany I would have been satisfied with a Kit-Kat.
>
> *Heather Johnson, College Junior*

The Invented Word/The Unconventional Word

Making up a word that fits perfectly and communicates swiftly takes cleverness, creativity, and intelligence. Word invention is a sophisticated move by a writer. I am surprised when I read a third grader's narrative and encounter this sentence: "I ate blugurt in the morning." Justin explains to me that *blugurt* is his invented word to describe his favorite breakfast—blueberry yogurt (Romano 1995, 91). I'm envious. I don't know that I have ever made up a perfect word in my own writing (which says something about my cleverness, creativity, and intelligence).

Writers also surprise us when they employ an unconventional or little-known word and put it in just the right place. In an essay stating her gratitude to independent booksellers and lamenting the passing of their stores, Barbara Kingsolver imagines a miracle in which one bookseller is saved at the eleventh hour:

> People would show up there in droves with cash in hand . . . to prove that their hearts had not been sold after all for the three-dollar markdown. The prodigal readers would return, and those who had never left would also come back to scour the aisles, looking for the enlightenment and passions and how-to manuals that filled our lives before TV stultified and bumfuzzled us. (2002, 221)

I thought Kingsolver had invented a word. But *bumfuzzle*, I found, is in a dictionary. It is an informal word used in the southern United States meaning "to confuse somebody." *Stultified* is a terrific word to describe the effect of too much television. But *bumfuzzled* is a capper, a surprise, a pleasure, a reward. Notice that Kingsolver places *stultified* first and saves *bumfuzzled* for the final payoff spot.

Our language is rich, and humans are endlessly inventive with it. If you invent or unintentionally stumble into a made-up word, try using it in your writing. Likewise, be alert for spots where you can use an unconventional, informal word that's perfect for tone and meaning and surprise.

> Talking about language is worth the class time it takes. Have students bring five interesting or favorite words to class. Spend time sharing them and talking about the delights of language. I organize small-group sharing first so everyone has a chance to speak. Such activity sends the message that individual words are what we work with. Language choices are crucial to shaping authentic voice.

Authentic Voice and Academic Audience

When my college undergraduates analyze their writing for authentic voice, they often tell how academic writing has adversely influenced their voices. I don't doubt it. Listen:

> In high school my writing was full of words meant to impress, simple ideas dressed in elaborate sentence structure. And what is even more disturbing is that my teachers ate it up! I was praised endlessly for my writing, and it was effortless. I was master at the game of teacher-pleasing.
>
> *Melinda Humbarger, College Junior*

> My formal writing has only the whisperings of my true authentic voice. I think the quote, "It is human to want the world to see us as we want to be seen," pretty well sums it up. In formal writing, I attempt to make everything sound ingenious and inventive. I rely heavily on my thesaurus, but I only use words that I should have been able to think of myself. For example, I was trying to find a word to replace "energy." I came up with vitality, dynamism, pep, pizzazz, demonic energy, power, and intensity. Even though dynamism is a great word and fit the use perfectly, I used vitality and pizzazz. In normal dialect I would never use the word dynamism and therefore it has no place in my formal writing. I want to come off as intelligent, not like I tried too hard.
>
> *Jodie Kelly, College Freshman*

> I have the ability to write what the professor wants to hear and I can meld my words around to make it candy for the professor. An example: for one of my education classes I have used the term "paradigm shift," not because I have a great vocabulary or anything intellectual like that, but instead I have heard the professor say it several times in class. I included it on one of my papers and it got circled with an exclamation mark indicating that my term was effectively used. What a joke that exclamation mark was—worth nothing to me but a better grade on the paper. I sell my crafting-authentic-voice soul by simply writing how the professor talks in class.
>
> *David Kunkle, College Junior*

> I also "craft an identity" in my writing. I use the vocabulary and discourse required in writing papers and assignments according to the subject. Words

such as "on-task," "learning activities," and "pedagogy" (which, by the way, wins the "Ugliest Word in my College Career" contest) are difficult to work into conversations, but they succeed in writing by making me appear to know what I'm talking about. Those words also stretch and deepen my thinking. I may shape myself into a living, breathing teacher.

Rhonda Clinger, College Junior

I don't weep for those academically defiled voices. These students are smart. Though they are consciously altering how they say on paper in order to get the grade they want, they are also, like Chad at nineteen, trying on language new to them, entering different discourse arenas and trying their hands at writing in them. If they keep making meaning with words on paper, keep learning about language, keep noticing how writers they admire and respect write, they will come out all right. They will write in ways that retain their individual voice: Melinda's exclamatory indignancy, Jodie's knack for specific examples, David's penchant for metaphor, Rhonda's mix of humor, hope, and sincerity.

Developing our voices, finding comfortable ways to say and communicate takes time and practice and patience. The voice that fits us at thirteen has changed when we are seventeen, has altered further when we are twenty-one, has grown confident when we are thirty, thirty-five, forty—provided we keep writing. We learn more about language and expression. Our vocabulary expands. We enter new writing milieus. We learn more language moves. We mature. We gain confidence. And one day audiences no longer intimidate us. We're eager to speak to them. One day we say our say without the need to impress, without the need to phony our voice.

Here I am. This is what I think. This is why I think it. These are my words. This is me.

32

Who's Got the Action?

Active verbs rarely fail to live and leap. Wilma sprinted. Olga soared. Monica aced. Pete slid. Joe stole. Tony homered. And Megan shoo-eed.

Megan what? She shoo-eed, that's what. She shoo-ees every day. We all do. The origin of that verb comes from the expression "Shoo-ee!" When Megan's mother, my friend Laney Bender Slack, changed her daughter's diaper, she sometimes found herself fanning the air, exclaiming "Shoo-ee!" The expression caught on in the household, even became a verb. "Mama, I shoo-eed" or "Do you have to shoo-ee before we get in the car?"

This invented verb is regular and perfectly serviceable. Today she shoo-ees. Yesterday she shoo-eed. Tomorrow she will shoo-ee.

"Look for verbs of muscle," advises Mary Oliver (1995, 89). *Shoo-ee* has muscle aplenty.

I'm always after my students to check their verbs when they revise their writing. Are they muscular or anemic?

Jason, a high school sophomore, had written this sentence: "His eyes had hatred." I liked the detail, told him so. I knew what he was talking about. I've seen people simmering and burning behind a gaze. But I pressed Jason to find a stronger verb than *had*.

I stooped by his desk and fixed my eyes in a blaze of malice.

"What are my eyes doing?" I said.

Jason looked alarmed. I moved closer, increased the intensity of the blaze.

"What are my eyes doing?"

Jason drew back. I moved closer still, almost going cross-eyed, I was bearing down so hard.

"What are my eyes doing?"

"Gettin' to me!" cried Jason.

I don't remember if my histrionics incited Jason to muscle up his verbs, but one thing he knew and all his classmates knew: their teacher would go to great lengths to get them to pump up their verbs.

Revise for Strong Verbs

One of my college students asked some honest questions in a one-pager she wrote about voice:

> Does everyone's authentic voice consist of verbs that muscle over mealy-mouthed adjectives? That really works for people who ARE strong, who ARE full of conviction. Suppose you have wishy-washy students? Would you expect their authentic voice to be the same as the most assertive students in your room?
>
> *Jennifer Armstrong, College Junior*

No, I don't expect the voices of different students to be the same. But I do want all my students to express themselves with as many interesting, active verbs as their writing will bear. Verbs move forward writing. Verbs carry action. Verbs eliminate wasted energy and verbiage. Active verbs, my linguist friend Max Morenberg says, move readers across the white space.

I said that I want my students to use as many interesting, active verbs as the writing will bear. I say "will bear" because sometimes a verb can be too active and interesting. Consider this sentence: "Desperate and alone, she walked down the empty street." Although quite pedestrian, *walked* might be just the right active verb, instead of livening up the sentence with a unique verb: "Desperate and alone, she *perambulated* down the empty street."

She what?

Perambulated?

There goes mood, there goes tone, there goes meaning.

> Ask students to take the verbal temperature of a piece of their writing. Is their language warm and vivid with active verbs? Or is it cold and lifeless with passive verbs, adjectives, and adverbs? Instruct students to tinker with the text to find strong verbs. Illustrate this with an excerpt of your own writing, or take a piece of professional writing, replace the strong verbs with weak ones, then show students both versions.

Take a look at the following paragraph, whose audience is new university faculty members beginning the road toward tenure and promotion:

> It would behoove you to submit proposals and joint proposals to present sessions, panel discussions, and workshops at professional meetings at national, regional, and state levels. It is important that your presence begin to be felt

> at the national level. Several national presentations are especially important by year six. Presentations at conferences alone do not gain a faculty member tenure, but presenting at conferences is important in gaining notoriety for your work and in meeting professionals who might someday serve as external reviewers. If you write and publish and if you present at national conventions, other important things will begin to be set in motion. You will begin to be contacted for consulting opportunities. You will begin to be contacted for professional service opportunities. You will find that your scholarly activities will have an influential effect on your teaching.

Here is the same content, tinkered with to highlight and strengthen the verbs. See how the prose is less wordy and the verbs are upbeat and capable:

> *Submit* proposals and joint proposals to present sessions, panel discussions, and workshops at professional meetings at all levels. *Begin establishing* yourself as a national presence. Several national presentations by year six *strengthen* your tenure application. Presentations at conferences alone *do not gain* a faculty member tenure, but such presentations *help* you *achieve* notoriety for your work and *meet* professionals who might someday serve as external reviewers. If you write and publish and present at national conventions, other important things *accrue*. Organizations *will contact* you for consulting work and professional service. Your scholarly activities *will influence* your teaching.

For writers all: Get in the verb mindset. If you are not in that habit when you draft, then revise your writing with an eye toward eliminating weak verbs and replacing them with muscular ones. Once you start paying attention to verbs, you'll start to use strong verbs when you draft. Produce writing that lives by its verbs. Carry on an affair with active verbs. Flaunt it. Give readers something to talk about.

33

Weeding the Garden

It is with words as with sunbeams. The more they are condensed, the deeper they burn.

ROBERT SOUTHY

Waste is a bitterness. Wasted money. Wasted time. Wasted garden space. I like everything to count. I like functionality, things that pull their weight: programs, students, colleagues, words. I hate wasted words, except when I am drafting a piece. I try to be profligate then. The more words the better. When drafting, I'm seeking to generate ideas and meaning, so I'll accept just about any words that come along and follow them with more language to see where I am led. But when I'm crafting my authentic voice, I want language that's lean and pointed and clear. No waste. No beginnings that wander. No endings that meander. Not two words where one will work.

The best thing I've read about eliminating wasted words is the chapter titled "Clutter" in William Zinsser's *On Writing Well* (1998). If you, too, like your writing svelte, I recommend Zinsser. The five pages of "Clutter" will have you checking writing for empty adjectives, needless prepositions, ponderous euphemisms, unnecessary introductory words, and laborious phrases (like "at this point in time").

> Writing improves in direct ratio to the number of things we can keep out of it that shouldn't be there. "Up" in "free up" shouldn't be there. Examine every word you put on paper. You'll find a surprising number that don't serve any purpose. (13)

I am alert for clutter, so I am jolted when I read a sentence like this: "Teachers say students pick up [Spanish] quickly when they have little opportunity to revert back to English" (Mrozowski 2002, B2).

No need for *back*. *Revert* includes *back* in its semantic genes.

Cutting one word from a sentence might seem small, but one word here, one word there add up. "Every word omitted keeps another reader with you," writes Peter Elbow. "Every word retained saps strength from the others" (1973, 41).

I'm a gardener, so I know about strength-sapping excess. In my swimming-pool-converted-to-a-garden, tomatoes are the main crop. I pinch suckers that grow at vine junctures. I want fruitful bounty, not yards of vines. In mid-August I begin clipping blossoms that won't have time to transform into fruit that ripens. And if I don't keep weeds down, my garden isn't just unsightly. Weeds hurt the plants I'm cultivating. Weeds steal nutrients, water, sunlight, and garden space from them. To preserve and foster the growth of my vegetables, I weed the garden. To preserve and foster voice and meaning, I weed my writing. Students, too, should eliminate clutter in their writing, if they want readers to stay with them.

> As an undergraduate I became aware of my excessive use of *really* and *very*. I was including a lot of little words that did not change the meaning of what I was writing. Therefore, I had to become more precise and cut to the chase.
>
> *Stacy Larson, Graduate Student*

Excellent realization. (And I say cut 33 percent of the words from the last sentence by revising it to "I became precise and cut to the chase.").

In a brief, helpful article titled "Write Research to Be Read," Donald Murray writes,

> The writer should have no greater joy, perhaps, than pruning a piece of writing, cutting out every word that can be cut out, changing constructions so that they are clearer, simpler, shorter, making the abstract concrete, the general specific, the complex clear.
>
> Each writer will develop his own list of editorial enemies. Mine include quite, that, ings, would, the verb "to be," transitional phrases. This list will change as the writer changes. Of course, these are stylistic choices (and, of course, of course should be on my list) and, of course, there will be times when they are appropriate, but they tend to clutter my page. You will have to identify your own clutter and then eliminate it. (1982, 112)

Adverbial Hit Man

Adverbs are part of my clutter. Adverbs sneak into my writing. (The first draft of this sentence, for example, read, "Adverbs surreptitiously and all-too-easily work their way into my writing." *Sneak* outguns both adverbs.) I watch out for adverbs. They lure writers into laziness. Scattering adverbs about is easier than finding precise, active verbs. I bite a knuckle and swear a blood oath against adverbs. I am an adverbial hit man. When student teachers tell me they've done a thorough job teaching adverbs, I grimace. "Just what we don't want," I tell them, "kids learning to clutter their writing with adverbs." Adverbs can puff up writing, make it mealy-mouthed. Instead of producing direct, accurate writing, students waffle with adverbs.

"I'm sort of having difficulty with this assignment." (Be bold: "This assignment is difficult.")

"I am currently selling bicycles at the Bike Center." (Cut *am* and *currently*; make *selling sell*. Present tense tells us you are peddling bikes now.)

"The teacher was really tall." (How about "The teacher towered over the children"?)

"A very imposing woman filled the doorway." You can cut *very* just about every time it slips into your writing. "Poet Rolfe Humphries remarked that '*very* is the least *very* word in the language'" (Burroway 1992, 71).

Writers can often cut adverbs without harming meaning. A sentence is usually improved by the excision. Without the adverb, the verb is left to carry meaning, and verbs are up to the task when no adverbs are around to sap their strength.

Have students cut the adverbs in the following sentences and gauge whether meaning is adversely affected.

Mr. Mason shouted loudly for his son.
Katie viciously ripped off the Band-Aid®.
Bob swaggered cockily into the room.
Financially speaking, my money had just about run out.

Now, have students take out a piece of their own writing and circle all adverbs. Then ask themselves: Can the adverbs be eliminated? Will stronger, more accurate verbs make the adverbs unnecessary? Then act on the answers to the questions.

Respecting What You Work With

People who make things with passion and dedication love the tools and materials of their trade. My mother loved paint: squeezing it from tubes, smelling it, mixing it to achieve a color she wanted. She loved the feel of a brush in her fingers and the softness of camel hair tips. She loved the palette knife she sometimes painted with.

My sister is a cross-stitcher. She loves linen fabric, twenty-six-gauge needles, silk floss, hand-stitched needle cases, scissor fobs, delicate designs.

I love words: choosing them, manipulating them, considering them, arranging them. I love words so much that I cut them whenever I can. I cut them with great respect, since the word I cut has served me in getting thinking started, deepened, and sharpened. Here is a page from the prospectus I wrote for this book (see Figure 33–1). I had printed a copy and weeded it using a uni-ball® vision fine-point green pen to see how I might cut and clarify, leaving what was left stronger, crisper, clearer.

Authentic Voice:

Freedom, Discipline, Craft

```
This book is about developing voice ~~in our writing~~, particularly in our expository writing. Voice is the author's presence, ~~on the page,~~ the author's stamp of language, ~~and~~ perception, and thought. Sometimes that presence might be indiscernible, like a clean window pane providing ~~that provides~~ an unobstructed view. Or just the opposite might occur; ~~Sometimes~~ that presence might be impenetrable, like an unyielding, brick wall with ~~; there is~~ no moving beyond it no matter how hard you try. Sometimes that presence might be spirited, like a roaring fire~~place that calls attention to itself~~ warms a room and lures people closer.
```

Figure 33–1.

Out of ninety-five words in that paragraph, I cut eighteen of them but added five for clarity. That's a word reduction of 14 percent. I'm delighted in that. It's significant. Think how happy I would be if I dropped my weight from 200 pounds to 172.

Peter de Vries says, "When I see a paragraph shrinking under my eyes like a strip of bacon in a skillet, I know I'm on the right track" (quoted in Murray 1990, 187).

Weed the following sentence by a high school junior. Are there words you can cut? To preserve meaning, do you have to change the forms of any words or add words for clarity?

> Two middle-aged guys in ragged clothes that had mud on them were standing on my porch looking nervous and out of place.

Follow Zinsser's wise counsel, and you'll have lean, vigorous writing:

> Look for the clutter in your writing and prune it ruthlessly. Be grateful for everything you can throw away. Reexamine each sentence you put on paper. Is every word doing new work? Can any thought be expressed with more economy? Is anything pompous or pretentious or faddish? Are you hanging on to something useless just because you think it's beautiful?
>
> Simplify, simplify. (1998, 17)

It isn't logic alone that's necessary to cut our writing. It takes courage too. We have to be able to generate and nurture language on the one hand and eliminate it on the other. Sometimes that isn't easy. We become emotionally attached to what we say and how we say it.

Cut that word? That passage? That section?

Take my left eye instead.

Here is a poem that captures the dilemma:

Letting Go
That one word
That sacred word
That sparkling, dazzling
Inspired word—
How do I let it go?

The succulent
lush
dripping
juice of that word
which spreads its honey
across my heart—
How do I let it go?

Once it is dropped
onto the clean white napkin
of the page,

it sends
succulent
lush
dripping-sweet
fragrance
back to me.

I love that word
That gift-word
That totally perfect
                    unnecessary
                    extraneous
Word.

            If I cut it out,
                    I bleed.

—*Nancy Barker, High School Teacher*

34

Placement and Payoff

Where and when matter. Words, information, ideas gain or lose impact by where and when they appear in a sentence, in a paragraph, in an essay. If placement is wrong, an effect that should be dramatic is minimized, maybe ruined. Your voice peeps instead of punches. The end of a sentence or paragraph is a powerful spot for placing information. End with something strong, and readers receive a payoff.

Anne Lamott is a master at placing information in the right spot. In *Bird by Bird* (1994) she writes a scene in which she wonders what the wire-covered caps are called on champagne bottles. She does some telephone research to find out:

> I finally got through to the winery's receptionist and told her what I needed. She said she always just thought of it as the wire thing, too, so she transferred me to a two-thousand-year-old monk. Or at least this is how he sounded, faint, reedy, out of breath, like Noah after a brisk walk.
>
> And he was so glad I'd called. He actually said so, and he sounded like he was. I have secretly believed ever since that he had somehow stayed alive just long enough to be here for my phone call, and that after he answered my question, he hung up, smiled, and keeled over.
>
> "Ah," he said, when I told him what I was after. "That would be the wire hood." (149)

Lamott's information placement delivers multiple payoffs. In the last words of the second sentence, you meet a "two-thousand-year-old monk." In the next sentence, Lamott gives you two great adjectives (*faint* and *reedy*), then ends the sentence by comparing the monk to "Noah after a brisk walk." In the second paragraph she does not write, "I have secretly believed ever since that he keeled over after he took my phone call." No, "keeled over" gets the prime spot in the sentence—the final two words. The writing is so delightful and rewarding that we have forgotten why we entered the paragraph to begin with. Lamott hasn't. She pays off readers a final time with the answer to her question in the last six words. And note that she didn't write, "'Ah, that would be the wire hood,' he said, when I told him what I was after." Such a sentence would be perfectly grammatical, but the placement of information would steal the most powerful spot in the sentence from the payoff information. Placing "wire hood" in midsentence and giving "when I told him what I was after" the sentence ending would be like bringing out the warm-up band for one more number after the headliner had sung her signature song and left the stage with the audience roaring.

A student shows she is paying attention to placement and payoff when she writes me the following email message:

> I know you collect humorous spellcheck stories so here's a good one for you:
>
> I was writing about how Molly's mom gave me her silver ring when Molly died. The ring bears the amazing inscription, *Penses è moi*, which translates, "Think of me." My spellcheck had issues with "*Penses*." Its suggestion?
>
> "Penises."
>
> *Sara Boose, College Senior*

My wife and I have different ways of revealing information. Kathy is a registered nurse, has worked in an ER the past nine years. She is no nonsense and to the point. She values directness, clarity, speed, and precision. I value those things, too. But I'm also a storyteller. I'm a storyteller whether I'm writing to entertain, persuade, or explain. Storytellers concern themselves with timing, placement, and payoff. That concern seeps into my teaching too.

Following are two perceptive, effective pieces of writing. Note how each writer places important, surprising information at the end of the piece. The first example is the opening paragraph of a case study of a first-grade student written by his teacher:

> He just sits there. Skinny, bird-like frame, red glasses way too big for his tiny face, hands touching anything except his pencil, eyes focused on anything except his paper. I watch Barney and wonder what he is thinking. Is he wondering what the other kids are writing about? Is he wondering if I am going to notice him not working again? He slowly picks up his pencil—YES! Today will be a writing day for Barney! And then he sticks it up his nose with obvious approval from his classmates.
>
> *Kristen Curtiss, Teacher*

I love the way Kristen uses her beginning to engage readers in a miniportrait of Barney, capturing his physical appearance, his antsiness, and her anticipation and patience. Were this writing going one draft further, I'd suggest two things for the last line: that Kristen replace *it* with *pencil*, and that she reshape that last sentence so that the final words of it were "up his nose." That's the surprise. That's the payoff.

> Have students tinker with Kristen's final sentence so that pencil is mentioned again and the payoff is last.

Anna wrote a multigenre research paper about obsessive-compulsive disorder. Her paper is informative, surprising, and funny. At one point she includes this poem about a guy with a compulsion for fours:

I knew a girl once who dated a guy who did everything in fours.
Opened the car door for her. A real nice guy.
  On the fourth slam of the car door, she began to wonder.
They went to the mall to catch a movie. He claimed he kept
forgetting something.
  But on the fourth time through the sliding doors, he
remembered otherwise.
  Paid for four tickets to the movie.
Gave them to the couple behind them in line. A real nice guy.
He kissed her goodnight. Not once, not twice,
  But four times.
  He must have really liked her.
  He called four times the very next day.
When she dumped him once, he didn't know what to
    do with
          himself.

—*Anna Lettieri, College Freshman*

I've got some OCD myself, especially when it comes to writing. Since numbers—four and its variations—are so important in Anna's poem, I'd suggest rearranging the words of the last sentence so that *once* gained a more powerful position:

He didn't know what to do with himself
  when she dumped him once.

Writers use placement to establish a voice that delivers. Through repeated strategic placement of words and information, they gain readers' trust. Readers see that the writer can be counted on to guide them to surprise, payoff, and meaning.

Have each student bring in a joke that involves some narrative. After sharing them verbally, talk about the information that needs to be told first in order for the payoff to work. Have students practice placement and payoff by crafting their jokes in writing. (Be sure to demonstrate the joke telling, analysis, and writing before assigning students to find classroom-appropriate jokes.)

35

Great Lengths

What is the ideal sentence length?

"Long sentences. Only possible choice. Long sentences provide writers the space to stretch their thinking toward complexity of thought, offering readers depth, substance, rigorous explanations, and illuminating details all in one rhythmical unit of meaning that doesn't stop until readers have all the information they need."

"Long sentences best? As if! There is no contest when it comes to sentence length. Short sentences win every time. No doubt. Short sentences emphasize. Short sentences are comprehensible. Short sentences are pointed. They stick."

"Both long and short sentences are valuable to writers. But medium-length sentences provide the best opportunity for understanding. Medium-length sentences stay an even course, are not radical in either extreme. Medium-length sentences accomplish both complexity and comprehension."

Me? I like writing with sentences of varying lengths. I like writers to create sentences that enhance the meaning and music they're after. I like medium-length sentences that come at me with assertions. I like long sentences that are comprehensible, jargon free, and rhythmic, leading me confidently to pointed meaning. I like short sentences. Even fragments. Such brief sentence structures rivet my attention, compel my focus on a brief offering of words.

Teachers of young writers are rightly concerned about them gaining syntactic sophistication. Teachers want to see young writers learn to consolidate into one sentence information they have written in several sentences, so their writing isn't choppy. They want to see students learning to combine sentences too. Consolidating information and combining sentences are sophisticated skills to learn. We want students to be able to fashion long enough sentences to contain their thoughts. In fact, we want students to have the facility to embark upon long sentence structures that will help them generate thought while they are writing.

All too often, though, as writers develop and become more syntactically sophisticated, they turn their backs on the power of short sentences. They associate short sentences with immature, undeveloped communication. When used strategically, however, short sentences emphasize meaning, vary language rhythm, and provide definitive closure.

Middle school teacher Shelley Bowers read *Educating Esmé* and was stirred by Esmé's forthright, creative personality, her penchant for not hanging back, but rather stepping forward to make learning happen for children. In Shelley's written response to the book, she writes, "Esmé did not 'go with the flow' as most first year teachers do. She was the flow."

Her four-word sentence that plays off the cliché is emphatic. Shelley takes a stand. As a reader I am ready to follow Shelley in her essay as she discusses ways in which Esmé "was the flow," a dynamic presence in the classroom and the school.

Writing teachers frequently hear about times in students' lives when they realized they liked writing. One of my undergraduates writes about such a time. In the following paragraph Bonnie uses two four-word sentences to make positive assertions. The most important assertion she saves for the final sentence.

> For the last two years, I have focused on improving my writing. It was in Mary Fuller's advanced composition class that I became aware of how important it was for a writing teacher to be an avid writer. It was also in her class that I first heard the term "show, not tell." Ever since then, I've spent hours at my computer trying to improve this skill. The work paid off. I was getting A's on every written assignment I turned in and, more importantly, I had acquired a new identity. I was a writer.
>
> *Bonnie Nickles, College Junior*

I love the rhythmical variation Bonnie creates in the last four sentences. A fourteen-word sentence followed by a four-word payoff sentence. A twenty-word sentence with a brief adverbial hitch; for an instant you wonder what identity she is talking about. She lets you know what she's talking about in a brief, emphatic assertion that's crucial to the life she sees ahead of herself as a teacher.

Another "becoming teacher" uses short sentences and fragments for an opposite effect. Elizabeth uses them to set up a medium-length sentence that reveals her commitment and resolve.

> I walked home from class last Thursday with a lot on my mind. "What was I prepared to do as a teacher?" What if I became burned out? What if I began to dread teaching? How could I prevent it? Could I even prevent it? What if

burnout happens to teachers as a sort of wake up call? A million questions ran through my mind. I didn't have the answers for any of them. All I could think was "That won't happen to me." Something new happens every day in a classroom. There's always someone or something new to experience. How could that become boring? I didn't understand—and still don't. Kids are so interesting and so full of life; I don't see how their enthusiasm couldn't be contagious.

By the time I reached my house, I realized that I would never allow myself to become bored with teaching. If I begin to see myself falling into a rut, I am going to do something different. Play a game. Listen. Share. Ask for advice. Introduce something new. Read a book. Write a story. Rearrange my classroom. I will do anything to free myself from the downward slope of the rut.

Elizabeth Bowling, College Junior

Sometimes in our drafting, we try to pack too much information into one sentence. We have the linguistic skills to be complicated, so why not do it? The sentence becomes top-heavy and collapses of its own bumfuzzlement. We might need to employ shorter sentences in the revising stage to make our writing clearer and more accessible. Remember Zinsser's advice via Thoreau: Simplify, simplify. It makes me hearken to Milton White, my writing teacher of many years ago. "Say it simply," said Milton.

Here is an example of a paragraph that shows how I sometimes jam too much into one sentence:

> Sometimes writers do well to take a stand early in a piece of writing (i.e., write and then defend a thesis statement), but other times writers are better off unfolding a story or explaining something or posing a dilemma and discussing it in the following paragraphs. Top-down, urgently argued thesis-driven essays are not the only way to share our thinking and communicate our ideas.

My thinking is jumbled here, my language awkward, too many actions packed into the second half of that opening compound sentence. When I gained some distance from the writing and reread it, I realized that my final sentence would serve meaning better if it came after the first sentence. And the *unfolding, explaining, posing,* and *discussing*, I saw, would be more comprehensible if I broke the first sentence down into several shorter sentences. Instead of two sentences, I use five to communicate in the revised paragraph. Saying it simply, breaking down syntactic complexity can clarify voice.

Sometimes writers do well to take a stand early—write a thesis statement and defend or explain it. But top-down, urgently argued, thesis-driven essays are not the only way to share perceptions and communicate ideas. Sometimes writers are better off unfolding a story and revealing surprises to the reader. Sometimes they are better off posing a dilemma, then exploring and discussing it.

Ask students to take out a piece of their writing and examine it for sentence length. Does one sentence length predominate? This could indicate rhythmical sameness. Do some sentences need to be combined? Do some long sentences need to be broken into shorter ones for better comprehension? Find a place where a short sentence can be used for emphasis, as Bonnie Nickles did in writing about her identity as a writer.

When I reviewed my drafts to find examples of saying it simply and reducing sentence length, I found passages when I did the opposite, too. I often draft difficult writing in simple statements. I'm not thinking about the reader. I'm thinking about meaning. I'm trying to be direct and make a topic clear to myself. The drafting has little variety in sentence structure and few flourishes of my voice. At times like this I find myself revising to add nuance and lengthier sentences. Look at this draft of part of the final paragraph in Chapter 1:

> I've tried to create a voice so compelling that it might keep you awake some night longer than you intend. You can decide whether the voice succeeds. I've enjoyed the work of writing. And it has been work. I hope you enjoy reading it. May *Crafting Authentic Voice* quicken your voice and the voices of your students.

Through revision, that paragraph became this one, which includes a new sentence that's longer than any the paragraph originally contained:

> I've tried to create a voice so compelling that it might keep you awake some night longer than you intend. You can decide whether I've succeeded. I've enjoyed the work of writing. And it has been work, *no question about it*. *But it was the sweet work of creating—work that both empties and replenishes mind and spirit*. May *Crafting Authentic Voice* quicken your voice and the voices of your students.

What made me add the four-word sentence extension and the seventeen-word sentence? It was a felt need for elaboration. When I reread "And it has been work," I felt the need to emphasize that writing was indeed work, thus the addition of "no question about it." I also felt the need to elaborate about what that work of writing was like. I like what the revision added to the language rhythm of the passage. But I like even more what the long sentence pinned down about the work of creating that's both emptying and replenishing. It will resonate with anyone who writes.

This business of writing—of sentence length and sound, of verbs and adverbs, of creating pictures and hitting the senses, of getting rid of clutter—is never just about the words we use and how they look and sound on the page. Bound up with those language concerns is meaning. Meaning is the right bower. Meaning trumps everything. When we work with words, we must never forget about meaning.

Create writing in the full gush of thought and language. Trust the word rhythms that arise in you. Risk saying what might later appear wrong but will get you to what is right. Ride that flow as long as you can. Then step back. Reread for meaning. Anything too complicated for its own good? Try breaking down the complicated sentence into simpler, clearer ones. Does a point need to be elaborated in a longer sentence that admits more details and reasoning? Try creating such a sentence. Does a piece of information need the emphasis of a short sentence? Try it.

36

Get Your Pipe and Blow Doughnuts: The Speed of Metaphor

I stand at the dry-erase board in Stephanie Brider's second-grade classroom at Mason Heights Elementary School. On the carpet in front of me are twenty-four children, attentive to the visitor demonstrating how he chooses a topic and begins to write.

I decide to write about our schnauzers this morning, Murray and Minnie Mae, named after our dear friends in Durham, New Hampshire, Don and Minnie Mae Murray. I brainstorm what I know about our dogs, filling the board with bits and pieces of information. I'm talking aloud as I write and think. The children begin asking questions:

"What color are the dogs?"

"Do they bite?"

"Do they like to eat crackers? Our dog Mickey likes to eat crackers, but we can't feed him too many or he'll throw up because of the salt, mom says."

"Who's older, Murray or Minnie Mae?"

"Do they ever go inside?"

"Go?" I ask.

"You know, go, like to the potty? That's why our dog stays in a doghouse."

The interaction with the children makes me talk and think of more details, which I add to my list. When I feel full, I turn to open white space and begin a first sentence. I get five words down and something occurs to me. I turn to the children, "You all know what a schnauzer looks like?"

Tyler scrambles to his knees and blurts, "An old grandpa-lookin' dog!"

Nothing is faster than metaphor. A cheetah? A thoroughbred? A peregrine falcon? A rocket? Sunlight? None beats a metaphor. It's instantaneous. Eyes meet language, image flashes in brain. Suddenly, two things that really aren't, are.

A writer tells it like it isn't but is, and readers see something more vividly than they ever have before.

I awakened to metaphor in my mid-twenties when our daughter, Mariana, began talking, firing off figurative language like a gunslinger in Tombstone, Arizona.

She was two when we walked into a shopping mall, she for the first time. Once inside, she began hopping at my side, pointing to the middle of the mall, shouting, "Jumping water! Jumping water!"

I took to smoking a pipe as a young man, trying to look professorial, I suppose. One afternoon Mariana, not yet three, strolled up to me where I was reading and said, "Get your pipe and blow doughnuts."

She called cough drops *cough drips*, which made another kind of sense. The petals of one flower looked like eyelashes. On walks around the neighborhood, the "drifty-looking tree," you'll know, was a weeping willow. Snow fell in the kitchen when I shook a box of pancake mix to see how much was in it, and flour floated down upon my shirt.

Children are natural metaphor makers. They are like poets in that sense. Poets avoid the general and abstract and hunt detail and figurative language. James Britton maintained that children do this of necessity.

> Their ideas must take a concrete form of expression because they have not yet mastered the art of making and handling abstractions. A five-year-old boy in an infants' class once said, "Oh, yes, I know Geography. It's polar bears at the top and penguins at the bottom"! (1970, 155)

Metaphorical language is gold bouillon. It is concentrated, desirable, and does so much. Metaphorical language is economical: few words carry swift meaning. Metaphorical language traffics in images; it's the ultimate show don't tell. Metaphorical language can be sensory. It is nimble, playful, inventive, and arresting. Metaphorical language bridges that gap between fact and emotion, between vivid detail and abstract idea. I imagine those Universal horror movies of the 1930s: the setting is Dr. Frankenstein's laboratory: Fritz throws a switch, electricity jumps jagged from one electrode to another, and something comes alive in the lab. Metaphor is that fast.

I wrote in Part II, "Qualities of Voice," that some qualities of voice were perception, information, narrative, surprise, and humor. Metaphor can accomplish all of them in one synaptic jump. Metaphor heightens readers' delight.

One student explains his voice, tells how he loves rhythm and bounce in his writing. "My goal," writes David Kunkle, "is to have the reader groove, to be the Otis Redding of writing."

Another student, Tracy Ksiazak, laments that her personality does not get into much of her writing, but in her electronic writing, well, that's another story: "In my emails, my personality does more than take its quaveringly usual steps forward. It positively stands on a table and tap-dances. 'Look at me!' it shouts, rather than quietly playing the wallflower."

College freshman Sarah Yost tells me that she has been told so often that she could be good at writing that now writing makes her "flinch in anxiety." "Even in my journal," she writes, "my own private place to dance and play, every word is premeditated to such an extent that the final passage fails to reveal even a shadow of truth in my life. It's exhausting to rehearse each phrase. I crave an open-mike night instead of a primpted and choreographed show."

Another student, Jenny Bird, picks a bone with the contradictory dictums that her high school teachers laid down about writing: "My teachers twisted my writing around like a windsock caught in a storm."

When writers use metaphorical language, readers are more likely to make the leap from simply understanding to experiencing what the writing is about. See if metaphorical language lets you visualize and feel the exhilarating scene my Utah linguist friend writes about in this email message:

> Another thing I have which I didn't when I woke is the fresh memory (my shirt is still wet and cold) of dragging a plastic sheet over my "Kellogg's Breakfast" tomatoes while the hail pelted my head like bee stings. What a glorious, scary few minutes—the lightning and thunder arriving only a couple seconds apart and the sky black as coal smoke. A storm like that freshens everything, including your appreciation for just being alive. Only my family or my tomatoes could have made me brave it.
>
> *Will Pitkin, Logan, Utah*

The similes of bee stings and coal smoke are clear enough, but I also like the personification of lightning and thunder arriving separately at the party, both intent on doing some damage.

> Encourage students to make metaphors. Point them out in the literature you're reading. Hold metaphor share sessions. Place metaphors on the walls. Let students get wild and loose with metaphors. Show mixed metaphors. Laugh at them. Show how mixed metaphors sometimes work despite the mixing. Let students practice looking at one thing and seeing another. Talk about metaphors that were once fresh but have become clichés. Once we get metaphors flooding into our writing, we can always revise and tinker and tune.

Extended Metaphor

Once writers produce metaphors, we can see if meaning would benefit from extending those metaphors. Here is an email message I sent to Linda Miller-Cleary, a writing/teaching friend in Duluth, Minnesota:

On Mon, 18 Nov 2002, Tom Romano wrote:

I've been working this past week to get back in the writing groove. It's worse than laying brick. It is like getting ready to lay brick, hauling the bricks, mixing the mortar, assembling the right tools, all this to say that confidence in what I'm writing now is low and I ain't happy. Take care, Dr. Miller-Cleary. Tom

The next day Linda wrote back a buoying note and a surprising, delightful extension of my metaphor:

Yuch! It's amazing how that writing flow can be broken. It's almost like you have to start all over. Metaphors haven't left your arsenal though; great brick laying metaphor. Sometimes my mortar sits around too long and solidifies, and then I have to find some place to knock it out of the bucket and start all over with a fresh batch. Well, remember your words have great power with prospective teachers and keep that mortar moist. L.

That's two adults being playful, having fun with language, extending a metaphor, all the while with their eyes on the truth of what they think and feel: that sometimes writing is tedious, painstaking mindwork, frustrating, exhausting, and despairing.

By extending a metaphor a writer can explicitly reveal the implications of the metaphorical language. Look at the lead sentence of this Barbara Kingsolver essay, titled "In Case You Ever Want to Go Home Again":

> I have been gone from Kentucky a long time. Twenty years have done to my hill accent what the washing machine does to my jeans: taken out the color and starch, so gradually that I never marked the loss. (1995, 35)

We all know how the color of blue jeans fades. We all know the colorful speech and rhythms of dialects. They have definitive words, expressions, and pronunciations. Dialects can become less pronounced after years away from that dialect community.

When writers extend metaphors, readers see their creative and analytical minds working at once. Look at some of the ways my students have written metaphors and then extended them by choosing language appropriate to the comparison:

Lisa Ayers writes about her first day of band practice as a freshman in high school during Ohio's broiling, humid August: "By the end of my first day, I was like a wet dishrag. Limp and sweaty, I crawled to the car."

Another student read Carol Jago's *With Rigor for All* (2000) and was taken by the author's forthright language and exacting arguments:

> Jago's writing style does not beat around the bush but rather weed whacks right through it.
>
> *Susan Affeld, College Junior*

"Beat around the bush" is a tired expression that many call cliché. Susan, however, breathes life into it by choosing language that revs up the engine and roars forth like the author she praises.

In an earlier passage, Sarah Yost wrote about the anxiety she feels when writing. She longs to write unself-consciously, without the feeling that someone is looking over her shoulder, judging every language move she makes. She wants to trust the gush but finds it difficult:

> I want to lose all awareness of the fact that I am at that moment in the act of writing. I simply want to be there with my thoughts and my pen, watching their courtly dance. Instead, I find myself always cutting in, always insisting they were drawing too near or ignoring the other guests.
>
> *Sarah Yost, College Freshman*

I delight in seeing that young woman talk about her writing as a courtly dance between her thoughts and her pen, a dance that never develops rhythm because of her cutting and monitoring and pestering.

Extending a metaphor—choosing subject-appropriate language—reveals the writer's intellect and imagination. Metaphors are fulfilling for the writer to write and the reader to read. Consider this sentence that I wrote long ago:

> I have found exploratory, nonstop writing valuable in figuring out a knotty section of the story.

I look at that sentence now and think that I could do better with word choice to keep the metaphor consistent. What might be more appropriate than "figuring out" a section of a story that's knotty? Sorting out? Unraveling? Untying? Something else entirely? Pay attention to language. Bring your mind to bear on words you've written. You might be able to extend meaning with metaphorical language—subtle language pleasure for both you and your readers.

The Naming of Parts

I've spoken generally here of metaphorical or figurative language. I'll leave it to you to make distinctions like simile, personification, hyperbole, apostrophe, and so on. Never make the mistake, though, of just teaching these terms of figurative language so students can pick out examples of them on tests. Teaching students only to identify metaphorical language in literature does them a disservice.

Deeper, more useful teaching and learning gets students to *create* metaphorical language. It's not out of reach; they did it naturally as children. Figurative language spices writing with flavor and depth, and maybe, like adding saffron to risotto, some color, too.

The best comes when students naturally employ figurative language: the personification of that personality tap-dancing on a table, the simile of those bee-sting hailstones, the metaphor of that dog that looks like a white-bearded, bushy-browed grandfather, the hyperbole of writing that is as difficult as laying bricks.

37

Ingmar Bergman, Janis Joplin, and Howard Cosell: Allusions to Extend Meaning

The late sports journalist Howard Cosell ruined a word for me. During his sportscasts, Howard never *referred* to anyone or anything. He always *alluded*. There he would be on television in his hairpiece and pontificating voice alluding all over the airwaves.

"I was earlier alluding to, of course, Polish light heavyweight Zbiegniew Pietrzykowski, who was beaten soundly at the Rome Olympics in 1960 by the then Cassius Marcellus Clay, a callow youth in those days whose punching speed and footwork the world of pugilism had not seen the like of since the reign of middleweight champion Sugar Ray Robinson, whose name heralds an earlier era of boxing history when fighters were not wont to deride and belittle their opponents, but I digress."

I knew allusions. I was a friend of allusions. Cosell's references were no allusions.

Four years of lit-tra-chure courses at Miami University taught me that the only allusions that mattered were literary allusions—figures of speech making reference to a famous historical or literary figure or event. This also included biblical allusions that English-speaking authors were so fond of making. When I talked to my students about an author alluding to something, I didn't just mean that the author was referring to something. I used *allude* in the refined literary sense, like T. S. Eliot, by God, alluding all over the map in "The Wasteland"—so much alluding, in fact, that you spent more time reading Eliot's footnotes than the poem.

Allusions are kissin' cousins to metaphors. In fact, allusions are a kind of metaphorical language. In the preface to his first collection of short stories, *Welcome to the Monkey House*, Kurt Vonnegut writes this paragraph:

> My sister smoked too much. My father smoked too much. My mother smoked too much. I smoke too much. My brother used to smoke too much, and then he gave it up, which was a miracle on the order of the loaves and fishes. (1970, x)

As a child I wasn't long into Sunday school before I found out about the loaves and the fishes, Jesus Christ's culinary miracle that stretched five loaves of bread and two fishes into satisfying meals for the five thousand people gathered to hear him preach, the ultimate making do with leftovers. Bernard Vonnegut's accomplishment, the allusion tells me, in ridding himself of the pernicious addiction to nicotine was an eye-blinking miracle.

But let's talk literary elitism for a moment. I loathe it. And the reason I find it so loathsome is because I practiced it as a young teacher, disdaining the teenager reading *Hot Rod*, even though my own bookmark had been permanently fixed on page 288 of James Joyce's *Ulysses*. I shuddered at the ignorance of students who mixed up *affect* and *effect*, turned my nose up at anyone who read a translated version of *The Canterbury Tales* instead of reading it in Middle English.

I've left most of that literary elitism behind. That's what happens when you teach writing long enough—rooting for your students all the way—and couple that teaching with writing yourself and seeking to get that writing published. That's what happens when you learn about the genesis of errors, the logic that goes into making them, and the inevitable growth and development people experience when they engage in learning something in good faith.

I like inclusion, not exclusion. So I like allusions that are inclusive and don't leave people feeling stupid. I like it when writers make allusions that you don't necessarily have to know in order to understand the writers' meaning. But if you do understand, it's a bonus, a delight, a pleasurable revelation to find that some bit of knowledge you know but rarely use is not mere cerebral baggage.

In *Bird by Bird* Anne Lamott discusses looking for books to help her with a newborn son. She makes two allusions, one possibly more difficult to understand than the other:

> I couldn't find any books about single parenting when Sam was first born that were funny and sick and therefore true. There were some great books on child rearing, but none that made me laugh, and none that went into the dark side, the *Seventh-Seal*-with-Milky-bras part. They were all so nicey-nice and rational and suggested that surely if you did this or that, the colicky little darling would come around, pull himself or herself together, get a grip. And this simply wasn't true. Having a baby is like suddenly getting the world's worst roommate, like having Janis Joplin with a bad hangover and PMS come to stay with you. (1994, 188)

To appreciate the passage you don't have to know that *The Seventh Seal* is a dark Ingmar Bergman movie about a knight facing and accepting his own death. It's a bonus if you do. The full weight of bleak Swedish melancholy gets linked in your mind to Janis Joplin, bad hangovers, and PMS, a bizarre and hilarious combination. If you don't recognize the allusions, though, no problem. Lamott helps you understand "*Seventh-Seal*-with-Milky-bras part" by using it as an appositive for "the dark side." *The Seventh Seal*, we can guess, is not *Mary Poppins*. And even if the reader is not a rock aficionado or survivor of the 1960s—so who's Janis Joplin?—Lamott gives you "worst roommate," "bad hangover," and "PMS" to work with.

I have no examples of writing from students in which they made allusions. Or maybe I just haven't kept such papers. Making allusions—like making metaphors—takes a nudge in some of us to associate or to be bold and respect our thinking when one thing reminds us of something else in history, literature, the Bible, or contemporary culture. Allude and readers experience your voice as wide-ranging, inventive, and associative. It's a bonus.

38

Behold This Visage: How Speech Helps Writing

For years, teachers have admonished students when their writing became too colloquial, informal, or slang-ridden. "Writing isn't talk," we preached. We could make a big deal about this. Writing cannot be talk. Human speech is supported by facial expressions, eye contact, and gestures. Speech rises in volume and pitch to indicate emphasis. Writing has none of those supports. Words must work on the page by themselves. No facial expressions, eye contact, or gestures help written words communicate.

But I want to resist this long-standing admonition. When I analyze my own written voice, I find that I co-opt attributes of speech to craft my authentic voice.

How on earth, you ask, can I duplicate facial expression in writing? Here's how. Think of that seldom-used literary word *visage*. Just as I wear a certain look when I speak to listeners, I want my writing to wear a certain look when readers read it. I don't want the visage of the page to intimidate, put off, or alienate. The very look of my words on the page can do any of those things, if I don't take care. And then I risk losing readers. That's the worst.

In college I took a Renaissance English literature course from Professor David Becker, a genial, scholarly, bearded expert on all things Elizabethan. Dr. Becker was the first of my teachers to acknowledge publicly that there was pleasure in literature. He had us pick our favorite Shakespearian sonnets and read them aloud, simply to experience the joy and music of Will's language.

There was joy involved in this serious business of lit-tra-chure? I knew that, but none of my college professors before David Becker ever said it. Renaissance English wasn't all joy though. Some of the literature was tough going. When I encountered Thomas North's *Life of Julius Caesar* (c. 1570s), I was stopped cold. I couldn't find my way through, around, or over North's words. In 2,240 of them, North had paragraphed only twice. The excerpt spanned three pages, which meant that each page contained about 750 words of small print with no breaks.

Good grief! A wall of words, it was. An imposing block of letters. A tsunami of language that washed me away from the text. Writers can reduce the work of reading, if they pay attention to the visage of the page. Reading can be hard enough. Why make it harder by refusing to paragraph?

I don't often quit reading something. I'm compulsive that way. But when I turn a page and am faced with a solid block of unbroken print, I become distressed. I beetle my brows and bear down for difficult decoding, grumbling subconsciously about the writer not taking more care in presenting his ideas. So when I am in charge of how a page will look, I make lots of paragraphs. I rarely miss an opportunity to do so. A little dialog? I paragraph. An explanation getting too long? I paragraph. Need to emphasize something?

I *might* paragraph.

You can dramatize the effect of paragraphing by placing on the overhead a piece of writing that is unparagraphed, margin-to-margin print from top to bottom. Want to make the reading experience worse? Use boldface, ten-point type. The screen will be solid black. I'm getting a headache imagining how imposing that will look. The landscape is bleak. My blood pressure rises. My breathing is shallow and rapid. Now replace that overhead with another that features the same text that is this time divided into five or six paragraphs without the boldface and with twelve-point type. Here comes the sun. The blood pressure drops. I'm breathing easy and deep, ready to read.

Good cooks know what they are doing when they spend time attending to the presentation of a meal. Writers can take a lesson here. You have spent plenty of time digging deep and developing ideas, crafting the language to emphasize that meaning, maybe even making music out of words on paper. And then you're telling me you're going to disrespect all your efforts by simply slopping your words on the page? Think of how an unparagraphed page will look to the reader. And then think of how welcoming will be the effect of a new paragraph now and then, a bit of dialog, perhaps.

Sentence length also affects the visage of the page. If a sentence I draft gets too long, convoluted, and bumfuzzled, if I've tried to pack too much information into it, I break the sentence apart into shorter ones. When I've done such simplifying and clarifying, not only is the thought easier to comprehend, but the line is less imposing to readers. I want the visage of my writing to look like my facial expression when I confer with students: open, inviting, friendly.

What about voice inflection? That's a major factor in speaking. Vocal chords and breath control combine to vary tone of voice and provide emphasis where the speaker wants it. Exact words change meaning when I emphasize one word over others. Here is what I mean:

I didn't say Tammy hit the tree. (Shelley did.)
I *didn't* say Tammy hit the tree. (Not me.)
I didn't *say* Tammy hit the tree. (I thought it.)
I didn't say *Tammy* hit the tree. (I said Sandy hit it.)
I didn't say Tammy *hit* the tree. (Tammy rammed it.)
I didn't say Tammy hit *the* tree. (The prize peach tree is unscathed.)
I didn't say Tammy hit the *tree*. (Tammy hit the honeysuckle bush.)

Can I inflect words, phrases, and ideas in my writing? I think so. I can emphasize a point by casting it in a short sentence. I can emphasize words and ideas by strategic placement—often at the end of sentences, paragraphs, and chapters (see Chapter 34).

Look at these sentences from earlier in this chapter:

> Think of that seldom-used literary word, *visage*.
>
> I want the visage of my writing to look like my facial expression when I confer with students: open, inviting, friendly.

Writing cannot be talk. There are features of my own talk that I don't want in my writing, like digressions, stammers, stumbles, redundancies, mispronunciations, insincerity, little eye contact, mumbled words, filler words. But you've also heard effective talk. You've been convinced by it, you've been moved by it. You have spoken clearly and effectively yourself. When you are crafting your writing, don't abandon what you know about speaking well. Your ways with spoken words can add to the appeal of your written ones.

39

In the Beginning

Milton White urged us to send our stories to publications. He warned us, though, that the publishing world was ruthless. Milton would hold someone's paper and say, "This is what you're trying to get an editor to do:" then he'd turn the first page. "Editors know if they'll reject a story after reading one page, sometimes one paragraph."

The most important part of a piece of writing is the beginning: the first sentence, the first paragraph, the first page. Newspaper writers call the opening of a story the *lead*. Once readers are beyond the *lead*, of course, then other things matter more. But if the beginning doesn't work, nothing else matters.

That brilliant insight in paragraph four?

Wasted.

That convincing argument?

Squandered.

That powerful extended metaphor woven throughout the essay?

Fruitless.

All wasted, all squandered, all fruitless if the lead doesn't work.

Writers have crucial work to do in the beginning. They must arouse interest, propel readers forward, establish a voice that is trustworthy, reliable, accessible.

Bad first impressions can sometimes be overcome, but why risk having to do it? Start strong. Be smart, direct, and interesting.

Writer Paul O'Neil of *Life* magazine said, "Always grab the reader by the throat in the first paragraph, sink your thumbs into his windpipe in the second, and hold him against the wall until the tag line."

Maybe that directive is too violent for you. Maybe for you a better metaphor is to make the lead an irresistible seduction. No violence. No imperiousness. Just writing that is so appealing, so promising, so alluring that readers follow along helplessly. Give readers information in the first sentence that begins a hunger to know more. Hook them.

I say forget this business of starting an essay generally and ending the introductory paragraph with a thesis statement. Professional essayists rarely begin this way. "If you look for thesis statements in collections of essays," writes linguist Edgar Schuster, "you will regularly be disappointed" (2003, 136). Writers have a responsibility to be interesting immediately. They want readers to turn that page. Or if readers are required to read the writing—as we teachers are—students should want them upbeat, piqued with interest, and eager to learn.

Look at your favorite contemporary writers. How do they open their essays? Analyze their leads to discover their opening gambits. One of my favorite contemporary essay writers is Barbara Kingsolver. She is a master of lead writing. The following essays are contained in her first collection of essays, titled *High Tide in Tucson* (1995).

In "Making Peace" she employs humor and a literary allusion her educated audience will recognize: "When I left downtown Tucson to make my home in the desert, I went, like Thoreau, 'to live deliberately.' I think by this he meant he was tired of his neighbors" (23).

Kingsolver sometimes startles readers with hyperbole: "How Mr. Dewey Decimal Saved My Life" begins with "A librarian named Miss Truman Richey snatched me from the jaws of ruin, and it's too late now to thank her" (46). In "Life Without Go-Go Boots" her first sentence is simply, "Fashion wrecked my life" (54). "The Muscle Mystique" starts like this: "The baby-sitter surely thought I was having an affair" (80).

Kingsolver can tell a startling anecdote that surprises, delights, and has you oh-my-goodnessing to know more. In "The Household Zen" she begins,

> In Barbara Pym's novel *Excellent Woman*, published in 1952, there's a moment when our heroine pays a call on her new downstairs neighbor, a dubious kind of woman who wears trousers and is always dashing off to meetings of the Anthropological Society. When this woman answers the door, she shrugs without remorse at her unkempt apartment and declares, "I'm such a slut." (59)

Slut, we learn, didn't always have a sexual edge to its definition.

Kingsolver might begin another essay with a paradox to pique readers' interest, as she does in "The Not-So-Deadly Sin": "Write a nonfiction book, and be prepared for the legion of readers who are going to doubt your facts. But write a novel, and get ready for the world to assume every word is true" (257).

Kingsolver gets me turning that first page.

Leads matter. Strong leads are the first step in getting readers to forget about why they are reading and simply read to satisfy a voracious need to know, a need created by the writer.

Experiment with Lead Writing

Here is a piece I wrote quickly about my father and a character from my childhood:

> George Stoltz galled me, even though I liked him. My dad owned a bowling alley and George bowled in the Thursday night men's doubles league. He was thin and elegant and gentlemanly. Every Thursday night—even though this was a men's bowling league where plenty of beer was swilled and cigars were smoked—George wore a long-sleeved white shirt and a wide tie.
>
> "Hello, Thomas," he said to me each Thursday night when he came through the door.
>
> His bowling style was elegant, too. He took the bowling ball, took a position in the middle of the approach, set himself, then took two steps and lofted the ball. It banged on the alley and made its way slowly down the lane. He was a mediocre bowler, and that would have been fine, except that he was my dad's partner—my dad, who was a great bowler, 191 average, but he wasn't great enough to pull up George's mediocre game. They lost every week and were listed on the bottom of the standings on the chalkboard that hung above the counter for the public to see.
>
> That is why George galled me. My dad was better than last place. It wasn't enough that I knew it. I wanted to see it. But he was never on the winning doubles team, because of George Stoltz. Why couldn't Dad bowl with Uncle Ralph or Norm Burwell or Chuck Crawford—great bowlers all. Then he wouldn't have his name paired with George's on the chalkboard that featured the standings of all the leagues.
>
> "Why do you have to bowl with George?" I asked Dad.
>
> "I like bowling with George."
>
> "You always lose," I said.
>
> Dad slid his bowling ball into the battered black leather bowling bag that he'd bought in the 1930s.
>
> "I win every Thursday night," he said.
>
> "You lose! Look at the sheet! They beat you all three games!"
>
> Dad looked at the score sheet. "Those numbers don't begin to tell the whole story."

Interesting exploration for me to call forth George Stoltz from so many years ago. And I like what I drafted and smile, too, at where I *took took took* in the third paragraph and where I lose my head with *b* alliteration in the eighth. Just draft, right? Go with the language that volunteers itself. Don't be embarrassed or ashamed. Have faith in revision.

I stepped back from the writing, got some distance, then rapidly created five new leads for the sketch.

I tried creating a paradox:

> When I was a kid, my dad was one of the best bowlers in the men's doubles bowling league. And every week he lost.

I love dialog in just about anything I read, so I tried opening with conversation, moving the dialog I had generated up front to see how the sound of voices might draw readers' interest:

> "Why do you have to bowl with George?" I asked Dad.
>
> "I like bowling with George," he said as he slid his ball into the worn leather bowling bag he'd owned since the Depression.
>
> "You always lose!" I said. And that was the truth. The first night of league play Dad and George gained a firm grip on last place in the men's doubles league and held it unchallenged through early May.
>
> Dad zipped the bowling bag and hoisted it into his locker.
>
> "I win every Thursday night," he said.
>
> "You lose! Look at the sheet! They beat you all three games!"
>
> Dad looked at the score sheet. "Those numbers don't begin to tell the whole story."

(I like the humor I bump into with discussing their last-place status. I also gain control of the alliteration.)

For the next lead I turned my attention to George, tried characterizing him with detail, using sentence fragments and a metaphor for humor:

> George Stoltz didn't roll his bowling ball. He lofted it. All sixteen pounds. Three feet into the air. When it cracked on the boards of the alley, I imagined giant redwoods toppling in California.

I tried writing a blunt statement, saying something severe and connecting Dad with failure and George Stoltz:

> My dad was a failure and George Stoltz was the reason why. Never mind that Dad had immigrated to this country when he was nine, never finished fourth grade, and still ended up at thirty-five as the owner of a night club and bowling alleys, saved enough money to pay off the mortgage in three years, and bought stock in his children's names that paid for their college education.
>
> None of that mattered in my eyes. George Stoltz made my dad a failure because George Stoltz was a lousy bowler. He was my dad's partner in the men's doubles league.

(This beginning leads me to divulge more information about my father that I could use elsewhere in the sketch if I don't go with this lead.)

In the last lead I tried stating my point bluntly, laying out a thesis statement (note that this thesis statement didn't come until I had written a draft and created several leads, a lesson to teachers who demand that students formulate a thesis statement before they write a word):

> My dad was a dismal failure in the men's doubles bowling league and a sterling success at interpersonal relationships.

When I share this experiment with teachers and ask them which lead they prefer, I usually get votes for each one. I ask them to explain why they like a particular lead. They always have reasons, so we're able to consider taste and values and the work words are doing in our subjective eyes.

The important thing for me about writing alternative leads is uncovering new information about my topic. I also might find a more engaging beginning. When students take time to generate experimental leads with a mindset for risk and provocation, they, too, discover further information and alternative ways to begin. They realize the flexibility of their minds. They realize that some ways of beginning a piece of writing are more compelling than others. I want students to see that they are not stuck with the lead that volunteered itself when they started to write. That lead might be perfectly suited for pulling readers in. But it might not.

Ask students to draft a narrative of a strong memory. It is important that the writing is just a draft, that students haven't invested too much time in it. You draft a narrative, too. Then write five new leads to your piece, as I did here. Write fast with faith and fearlessness, getting down as much detail as you can muster.

Collect the narratives students wrote. In two or three days, pass them back. Show students the multiple leads you generated for your narrative. Let students discuss each, revealing what they like and why. Ask students to reread their pieces and then to create five or six new leads without forethought and judgment, just as you did. Remember, have students write fast and write only leads. No more. Ask them to risk and experiment. Try writing leads they doubt will work. Then discuss their experiments in small groups and large. Later, dig in to putting the writing together anew, possibly using one of the experimental leads and incorporating newly discovered information and ways with words.

Commencing to Begin or Beginning?

In revising poetry, William Stafford advises to look at the opening lines:

> Is the beginning just fixing to commence to begin? Can you take out some of the scaffolding you felt you needed when you were writing it? (1998, 140)

These are good questions for writers, regardless of the genre they are writing in. I once had a simultaneously sinking and exhilarating experience when a manuscript was returned to me along with a note announcing its acceptance. On the manuscript, the editor had xed out the first two paragraphs. I began reading the third paragraph and saw that the editor was right on the money. The first two paragraphs were scaffolding when I was "fixing to commence to begin."

Beginnings of anything can be difficult. Sometimes I get just the right sentence or just the right tack before I write a word, but usually I plow into my subject, so my leads always bear a second look. My goal when drafting is for the lead not to be an obstacle. I start wherever I can.

Unlikely Places

Writing in education has a reputation for being dry, jargon filled, and abstract. It doesn't have to be. When authors think about audience and care about the craft of writing, they create leads that seize readers' attention and trigger their curiosity. Here is the first paragraph of Chapter 1 in Frances Fowler's *Policy Studies for Educational Leaders* (2000):

> "Toto, I don't think we're in Kansas any more." A doctoral student who was taking an education policy course began one of her papers with this quotation from *The Wizard of Oz*. The student, principal of an elementary school in a large metropolitan area, had written a reflective essay about a trip that her class had taken to the state capital. This visit to the halls of power had left the students—all practicing school administrators—stunned. (1)

I applaud the doctoral student. I applaud Dr. Fowler. I read on, eager to learn the reason for the *stunning*.

Leads are crucial. It is your first chance to hook readers, to gather their goodwill, to pique their interest, to get them wanting to follow your lead. There isn't a genre of writing in which the lead matters little—at least there shouldn't be, not if writers are thinking about their audience.

40

And in the End

The ending of the introduction of Julia Cameron's *Right to Write* (1998) goes like this:

> I have a fantasy. It's the pearly gates. St. Peter has out his questionnaire, he asks me the Big Question, "What did you do that we should let you in?"
>
> "I convinced people they should write," I tell him. The great gates swing open. (xvii)

In *On Writing Well*, William Zinsser has this to say about endings:

> The positive reason for ending well is that a good last sentence—or last paragraph—is a joy in itself. It gives the reader a lift, and it lingers. (1998, 65)

Do you have favorite endings? I remember being sent to the old Alumni Library at Miami University to read two Hemingway stories. I climbed a narrow, winding stairway up into the stacks. Between bookshelves there wasn't much space. I found Hemingway's collected stories and sat down at a desk against the wall. I was alone, the only sounds a ventilation fan and my occasional page turning. When I finished the final line of "The Short Happy Life of Francis MaComber," I felt as though I'd been knocked on the seat of my pants. In the last pages of the story, MaComber finds courage. And when the wounded water buffalo bears down on him, just moments before his surprising death, MaComber thinks only of aiming his gun lower to bring down the bull.

As a young teacher one summer I read *The Grapes of Wrath*. I remember lying on a couch reading the ending, in which Rose-of-Sharon—who has miscarried a child—lets a starving man suckle at her breast. I looked up from the book and took a deep breath.

Endings are important no matter what the genre. You are leaving your readers. You won't have a chance to talk with them again. This is it. When I visited a lifelong friend several years ago, visited for the last time, he in the final weeks of cancer, I made sure that I told him I loved him, made sure that I told him how much better my life had been because of his presence in it. There was no second chance. He was leaving, and we both knew it. This ending had to count.

In Chapter 14 I criticized the five-paragraph you-know-what. Here I criticize the idea of a final paragraph in which writers tell readers what they said, sum up their positions, recapitulate the whole.

Are you kidding? After I've worked so hard to show scenes, elaborate ideas, clarify sentences, and craft my authentic voice, I'm going to leave the reader with redundancy? Not me. Not my students, either.

I can craft an ending to be powerful just as I can craft a voice to be authentic. I can end with a short sentence, I can echo the beginning, I can find a telling quotation, I can find a surprising story.

A Short, Final Sentence (or Fragment)

During the first class session of my literature methods course, I ask my students to think of the worst and best experiences they have had with literature. We share these stories and spur each other's thinking. I take a poll and always discover that about 50 percent of the best experiences with literature were related in some way to school. And the bad experiences with literature? About 90 percent of those were related to school. My students withstood those bad experiences. They ended up sitting in a class designed to help them become English teachers.

I ask students to think about George and Aimee, students who sat near the door when they were in high school, the best spot to make a quick getaway when the bell rang. George and Aimee, who were ever made to feel stupid because even when they read the literature assignment, they never got the meaning the teacher wanted them to get. George and Aimee, who were told what this and that symbolized as though the teacher had been inside the author's mind when she wrote. George and Aimee, whose experience with literature in high school taught them that it had nothing to do with their lives and people they knew.

I ask my students, "What are you prepared to do? What are you prepared to do so that George and Aimee will want to pick up a piece of literature on their own one day?"

In a one-page response to an article about literature circles, small, peer discussion groups in which students control the text they talk about and the way in which they talk, one of my students ends her writing with these lines:

> I think it is important that before being let loose in literature circles, students are taught in class how to read and interpret texts and how to relate prior

knowledge to their readings in order to make meaning for their lives. This will probably require a lot of modeling on the part of the teacher, but then, when kids get into lit circles and are allowed to use their skills independently, they will feel confident doing so. I know, I know . . . more time (a teacher's greatest enemy). But, as far as I'm concerned, it's time well spent.

So ask me again: "What am I prepared to do?"

Whatever it takes.

Sarah Wilson, College Junior

A Wonderfully Rhythmic Final Sentence

Pleasing rhythm is a strength all through a piece of writing. It's especially effective in a final sentence. In a brief, powerful essay, "On Charon's Wharf," Andre Dubus writes of the sacraments that soothe our passage, how ritual can remain a constant to remind us of our time on this earth together. He writes about how words sometimes fail us, sometimes entangle us and communicate what we really do not feel, but how ritual reminds us of our ever precious mortality. The Eucharist, he believes, the touch of tongue and lips on flesh and blood, makes God more than an idea and affirms the mysteries of love and mortality. In the last paragraph, Dubus reflects upon what he has said, provides echoes to what has come before, and in the last sentence uses language and rhythm to replicate the ultimate act of sacrament:

> It would be madness to try to live so intensely as lovers that every word and every gesture between us was a sacrament, a pure sign that our love exists despite and perhaps even because of our mortality. But we can do what the priest does, with his morning consecration before entering the routine of his day; what the communicant does in that instant of touch, that quick song of the flesh, before he goes to work. We can bring our human, distracted love into focus with an act that doesn't need words, an act which dramatizes for us what we are together. The act itself can be anything: five beaten and scrambled eggs, two glasses of wine, running beside each other in rhythm with the pace and breath of the beloved. They are all parts of that loveliest of all sacraments between man and woman, that passionate harmony of flesh whose breath and dance and murmur says: We are, we are, we are. . . . (1991, 82)

In that final paragraph Dubus mentions "beating and scrambling eggs," and the reader is reminded of the third paragraph of his essay when he describes making breakfast for the person he loves, the importance of the act of offering and receiving food together. Dubus has provided an echo to language and meaning earlier in his essay. We readers note the meaning and are fulfilled by revisiting the familiar. Endings that echo beginnings are pleasurable.

A Quotation as Final Sentence

Zinsser says that what usually works best for ending an article is a quotation (1998, 67). This holds true for a lot of the writing we do: personal essays, fiction, poetry, reports. That bit of voice we've gathered from print or speech can perfectly end a piece of writing. It can make the ending "implicitly emphatic." The writer does not explain or elaborate in the final paragraph. She simply uses a story or a quotation to end the piece with an unmistakable implicit point. In *Writing with Passion* (1995), in a section of the book about reading and literature, I render this anecdote and end it with a quotation that is assertive and ironic:

> In doing some work a few years ago at a wealthy suburban school, I was given a copy of their in-house publication filled with articles by teachers and administrators. I came upon an article by the head of the high school English Department, a driving argument detailing the reasons why classic literature must be taught in secondary school. The article was well written and readable. It began with an anecdote:
>
> As the author stood in the check-out line at the grocery store, the mother of one of his former students approached him and said, "Mr. Thebes, I want to thank you for making Charles read *Silas Marner*. If he hadn't gotten that experience in high school, he *never* would have had it."
>
> This was the author's point. If students don't "get" the classics in high school, they may never come to know them. His opening anecdote, however, didn't end there.
>
> The mother continued talking about her son, "That boy's been out of school four years now, and he hasn't read a book since!" (151–52)

Ask students to reevaluate their endings. Remind them that to end powerfully is to end with the reader fulfilled. In the final paragraph maybe students can echo the beginning of the essay or some strong image within it. Maybe they can create a final short sentence. Maybe they can tinker with the rhythm of that final sentence to carry readers away. Maybe they know a perfect quotation they can end with. They can arrange the language to make the last words count.

The End

In conclusion, let me reiterate: the ending is your last chance to speak with readers, your last chance to drive home your message and leave the reader with a final consideration. You may choose to be implicitly emphatic and use a story or quotation that communicates an unmistakable impression. You may choose to be explicitly emphatic and say something powerfully analytic, perhaps employing a short, sharp sentence or fragment or language that is rhythmic and accessible. Whichever you choose, if you wish to impress readers one last time, if you wish to leave them lingering over what you have written, you'll need to craft an effective ending.

I couldn't end this chapter with that ending, but I wanted to try it. Not as bad as I thought it might be, but not the ending I was hoping for. I'll try again:

The Real End

Writing about endings to pieces of writing has made me think about life. I've lived fifty-four years now, long enough to lose many people I love and know well. Many of those lives ended badly, some ended well.

My mother died several years ago at eighty-four. She enjoyed good health most of her life, but took three months to die of congestive heart failure. Near the end, in a nursing home, every three or four days fluid built up in her lungs and she struggled for each breath until an IV of Lasix did its work. Her struggle ended one morning when her worn heart gave out, not a friend or relative at her bedside.

My father died in an automobile crash that took him instantly at fifty-nine. But, oh, the horror I imagine of those last seconds when the lights of the drag-racing cars bore down on him.

Death surprised my brother at sixty-six. Although he had cancer, he was holding his own. He went into the hospital with breathing difficulty that was diagnosed as pneumonia. After a bronchoscopy he fell asleep, went into a coma, and shortly died. His wife was at his bedside, talking to him and holding his hand.

Fireman died at the World Trade Center while working desperately to save the lives of others.

Most people don't control their ends. Good. Bad. Desperate. Courageous. Noble. Ignoble. There are some things, though, in life we can control. One of them is writing. I'm not left to destiny, fate, or chaos there. After I've begun as strongly as I can, after I've developed my ideas and rendered detail, after I've crafted my voice, paying attention to what the language I choose is doing on the page, after all that, I can craft an ending too. I don't have to just run short of words. Don't have to just stop. I can leave my writing for a while. I can let my subconscious work on the impressions of what I have done, which is what I have done with this chapter, going swimming and letting water, rhythm, and unbidden thought do their work. This is what I've come up with. This is the best I can do now.

41

Working Together

I met Jan Reeder when I taught a summer writing course for Northeastern University on Martha's Vineyard. Jan teaches high school in Missouri and now holds a master's degree in writing from Northeastern. I keep giving her a "you oughta" about writing a book. She knows teaching, she knows writing, and she knows teenagers. She writes about them with detail, voice, and insight. In the following piece Jan melds prose and poetry and demonstrates one way of beginning and ending well.

Forever

How I tire of love stories, love poems, love this and love that. Teaching writing makes it the nature of the beast to drown in the repetition of how much these girls and even these boys fall in love love love and how nothing else matters and how no one else has ever treated them so good and no one else is so beautiful or so handsome and they know in their hearts that they will be together forever. And then I must make myself remember. . . .

1971 Mercer County Fair

One of those big inflatable things that you pay to go
inside and jump around on. My friend and impending
college roommate Cheryl and I see the Holden twins. We
have our usual good-natured argument about which of
the boys is the cutest as we watch them smoking their
Kool cigarettes which they have done since
they were seven.
They're so ornery that they're sexy.
They drive (taking turns) a '67 Malibu which can
outrun every other car in town in the quarter mile
north of town.
ooohhh

John pushes his chin-length hair out of his eyes for
the tenth time and makes a running-tackle jump at me,
knocking me to the plastic. How cool.
An hour later I'm in that Malibu and stay in it for
three years, sometimes driving when John loses his
license for beer or pot possession.
How cool.
But he loves me and wants me and no one else
No one has ever treated me so good and no one else is
as handsome as he is and I know that we'll be together
forever. . . .

—Jan Reeder, High School Teacher

Part V

Voice and Identity

Antipasto
Huck, Holden, and Talya

Talya was in the final class I taught at Utah State University—Literature for Adolescents. She was Israeli and had been living in Logan, Utah, for several years while her parents completed advanced degrees. Talya spoke English clearly and deliberately with a distinct accent. Her vowel sounds differed from the Iowan flatness that American television newscasts so love. The pitch of her voice often rose at the end of sentences as though she were asking a question. Although Talya said little in large-group discussions, she never failed to contribute in other ways. She completed all the readings, worked well in small groups, and wrote papers with surprising and interesting assertions.

When we read *The Devil's Arithmetic* (1988), Jane Yolen's story of a modern New Rochelle, New York, adolescent Jewish girl and the Holocaust in Europe, Talya agreed to teach our class the rituals of the Seder dinner, the Jewish holiday celebrating Passover. We needed teaching. I was heathen and most of the students were Latter-Day Saints. Talya respectfully covered her head with a yarmulke and laid a prayer shawl over her shoulder. She brought out a special serving board with depressions to hold bits of food: parsley, horseradish, hard-boiled egg, matzo, lamb's shank, and charoset. In the middle was a bowl of saltwater to dip the parsley into. Talya explained what each food symbolized. She was a patient, low-key teacher. We listened, asked questions, then tasted charoset from the big batch I'd made with directions from a Jewish folklorist colleague.

The first novel we read that quarter was J. D. Salinger's *The Catcher in the Rye*, not written for adolescents, yet when I taught high school, it never failed to reach the teenagers who read it, both male and female. It was not uncommon for me to hear a student say, "This is the best book I've ever read," or, heartbreakingly yet triumphantly, "This is the first book I ever finished."

The Catcher in the Rye wasn't so popular with most of my USU students. They didn't care for ol' Holden's speech or his topics of discussion. "Why does he have to swear so much?" "All he does is lie." "Doesn't he think about anything besides sex?"

The day we came to class with the novel read and one-pagers in hand, class discussion was strained and halting. I sensed students holding back, not wanting to hurt my feelings, since I had chosen this book for our first reading. Discussion was polite and uninspiring. The students' one-pagers later revealed that the novel appeared to many of them as an attack on their principles of religion, morality, and family life. Talya's one-pager didn't reveal those sentiments, but she had said nothing during discussion.

After class, I was emotionally drained and pedagogically defeated. Feistiness was building inside me, though. Salinger's novel of adolescent disillusionment told in Holden's distinctive voice had spoken to many of my former high school students. It had spoken to me at various stages in my life. My present students—most studying to be English teachers—were going to encounter adolescents who, like Holden, were alienated, sarcastic, self-conscious, confused, misguided, and essentially decent. I had to do better by the novel. I had to do better by my students.

I decided to delay moving on and instead take one more crack at Holden, Pency Prep, Phoebe, and New York City circa 1947. To prepare for the next class, I went to another adolescent boy in literature. I tracked down the scene in *Adventures of Huckleberry Finn* when Huck debates himself about whether to notify Miss Watson about Jim, the friend and runaway slave whom he has been traveling with down the Mississippi River and who has recently been captured in Arkansas.

I led off the next class by reading the germane passage from the novel, ending with Huck's decision not to turn in Jim, which he knows is "wrong" and will doom his soul. Here is Huck's memorable voice, complete with uneducated locutions, cultural speech habits, and dramatic irony:

> The more I studied about this, the more my conscience went to grinding me, and the more wicked and low-down and ornery I got to feeling. And at last, when it hit me all of a sudden that here was the plain hand of Providence slapping me in the face and letting me know my wickedness was being watched all the time from up there in heaven, whilst I was stealing a poor old woman's nigger that hadn't ever done me no harm, and now was showing me there's One that's always on the lookout, and ain't agoing to allow no such miserable doings to go only just so fur and no further. . . . (Twain [1884] 2001, 268–69)

Huck tries to pray, but the words won't come, and he knows that the words won't come because his heart "warn't right" (269). He can't bring himself to betray his friend. In fact, he's made up his mind to free Jim from his current bondage. "'All right, then,' says Huck, 'I'll go to hell'" (271).

I was hell-bent, too, flying in the face of the dominant culture, orchestrating one more discussion to win the hearts and minds of my students.

"Despite what Huck says about his heart," I said to the class, "what do you think? Is Huck's heart sound?"

Most of the students had read *Adventures of Huckleberry Finn*. They understood this boy who knew right from wrong on big issues, despite his lying, smoking, and hooky from church. After brief discussion, the class agreed, Huck's heart was sound.

"How about Holden?" I asked. "Is his heart sound?"

Before they could answer, I went on: "Forget his cussing and lying. Forget his obsession with sex, which is not unusual for a sixteen-year-old boy. Look at his heart, the moral decisions he makes, how he acts, the motives behind those actions. Look at what he cares about. Is Holden's heart sound?"

Discussion ignited. I pressed for specific details from the novel to support generalizations. We talked about Holden's response to the obscene word written on the wall at Phoebe's school, the two nuns on the train, Holden's crass roommate, Stradlater, Mr. Antolini's petting, the scene in the hotel room with the prostitute, Holden's brothers, D. B. and Allie. More voices than the one-pagers had revealed two days earlier found good in Holden, felt sympathy for this boy who lived such a different, irreverent life from theirs. Plenty of other students, though, still were unmoved. Spirited debate continued.

Near the end of the period a hand rose from the seat in the back of the room by the door: Talya.

"I think Holden's heart is sound," she said, her voice rising right up to the ceiling.

"Say more, Talya."

"Look at when Holden's roommate goes out with his old girlfriend. When he came back from the date, Holden could have said, 'Did you fock her?' But no, instead he asked if she still kept all her kings in the back row when she played checkers."

Class was pretty much over after that. I felt better as a teacher. Specific discussion and debate had given Holden a fairer chance to take hold of the students' moral imagination. I couldn't ask for more. Talya's words—her one contribution that day—remain with me. She spoke when many in class were against her. Everyone was surprised by what she said, including me. But I was something else, too. I was grateful for Talya's careful, determined voice, for her courageous, perceptive identity.

42

The Moves in One Piece

Assignment: Write an essay that analyzes one or several pieces of your writing to uncover qualities of your written voice. What characterizes the way your words appear on paper? What is it you like to do with language to communicate your ideas? Don't write in abstractions or unsupported generalizations. Get down to specific information about sentences, phrases, and words.

Writing such an essay is revealing to students. The writing makes them examine their writing process and end product. They'll discover things that they do and become aware of some things they usually ignore. Sharing what they learn with their classmates will widen and deepen understanding about voice.

Many of the student quotations throughout this book came from such voice papers. After writing, we talk semantics, syntax, punctuation, parts of speech, metaphorical language—many of the things I've written about in previous chapters. Students begin to make explicit to themselves what they do in their writing and why they do it. Sometimes they find that there are no good reasons for what they do. Students become more conscious of writing craft. I hope the talk and my explicit teaching nudges them to expand their repertoire of writing moves.

Following is what one such voice paper might look like. I provide a piece of my writing that appeared in *Writing with Passion* (1995), then follow it with an analysis of my authentic voice.

> Sometimes my passionate writing voice has gotten me into trouble—like the time I published my first piece in *English Journal*. I had come home from school one unsettling day and furiously written several pages in my journal about the emotional roller coaster I had ridden. I wrote madly in both senses

of the word. Just hours before, an administrator at the county vocational school had moved to censor our creative arts anthology.

"Either delete all four-letter words and these two stories," he said, "or we won't print the magazine."

I was proud enough of the students' work and artistic integrity that I stood up to the administrator's soft-spoken, fascist ideas of control. I refused to alter the anthology, gathered the negatives that had been shot by the graphic arts students, and walked out of his office.

My principal helped me find Mr. Bruck, community member and printer by trade, a gentle man whose bright, witty daughter Vicky—my former student—was dying of cancer. In the living room I spread the negatives on the floor and discussed with Mr. Bruck what needed to be done. All the while Vicky dozed feverishly on the couch. By working nights and one weekend, Mr. Bruck rescued our publication.

A few months later I shaped my inflamed journal entry into a case history of the incident, including both the attempted censorship and the subsequent triumph. I sent "Censorship and the Student Voice" to *English Journal.* Editor Stephen Tchudi accepted it.

Months later when the article appeared, I was giddy with pride at being published in a national journal. I shared the article with my colleagues. The next day, amid my euphoria, I was summoned by my superintendent. The meeting featured considerable browbeating and was not about the deathless quality of my prose. (22–23)

My Analysis

Maybe the most authentic qualities of the vignette—the characteristics most natural and spontaneous to my personality—are its playfulness and sense of humor. I like to kid, enjoy laughing, love irony. Humor, playfulness, and irony emerge naturally when I write. And I work to enhance that tone as I revise my writing. I can't imagine keeping something I enjoy so much in life out of the me that appears on the page. Writing is important to me, and I spend a significant part of my life doing it.

When I say in the vignette that I wrote *madly*, I intend the double meaning. I was crazed like some Poe character; I was also angry. Now that I'm many years removed from the superintendent's browbeating that afternoon, I know, too, that my teacher-readers might smile wryly at the final line because they most likely know the experience of landing in hot water with an administrator over an issue of language.

The Death of Adverbs

I count 3 of them in this vignette of 299 words, a mere 1 percent. I need them all. There are always opportunities to be adverbial, but I passed on them. I could have written that the county administrator had "wrongly moved" to censor the magazine. I can trust readers to know my stance, and I must allow them room to make up their own minds about the rightness or wrongness of the administrator's decision. I could have written that I had been "peremptorily summoned" by the superintendent, but that word would have drained energy from *summoned*. In the right context—in this context—*summon* connotes *peremptory*. I left *furiously* and *madly*; I needed them to describe the way I was writing in my journal. I needed *feverishly* to describe the way Vicky was dozing.

Verbs of Muscle

I abide by Mary Oliver's dictum to use "verbs of muscle" (1995, 89). Verbs are important to my authentic voice. Much of my tinkering and reseeing is finding the right verb, replacing a weak verb with a stronger one. In the vignette I *wrote, refused, gathered*, and *walked*. Vicky *dozed*. Mr. Bruck *rescued*. Stephen Tchudi *accepted*. The one passive verb construction I use—*was summoned*—is appropriate since I was the victim of the superintendent's high-handedness.

Tension

Tension in writing is a powerful draw. Tension piques my interest in life and in writing. Tension rivets attention. Stand in line at a checkout counter and see how much more interesting the wait is when a customer ahead of you argues with the cashier (in an earlier draft I had written "gets into a disagreement with the cashier" but cut the wordiness for *argues*, the no-nonsense verb of muscle). Tension moves readers closer to the edge of their seats. Tension makes readers tune out the world and concentrate deeply on their reading. Tension propels readers forward and long for release.

I include tension in my writing a number of ways. Through character conflict, for example: In the vignette, an administrator blocks publication of the magazine. He and I are toe-to-toe. We want different, conflicting things. Readers want to know how this confrontation works out. That kind of tension is obvious. A more subtle tension can be created by mystery. The mystery of the "unsettling day" and "emotional roller coaster" introduced in the second sentence I explain in the fourth. In the third paragraph I characterize the administrator's manner with two adjectives: *soft-spoken* and *fascist*. How can that be? These adjectives seem to be from opposite camps. Put them together and you have an oxymoron. In tension with each other, the adjectives are all the more prominent, all the more dangerous.

There is further tension present in the information about Vicky. I hated what happened to that dear girl. I taught her in classes over three years. She was such a bright light with an ironic, rewarding writing voice, a passion for the Marx Brothers, a quick wit of her own, and a Veronica Lake haircut one year. I want readers to taste some of the pain I felt at her circumstance. I want to surprise them horribly by the news of Vicky's illness, just as I had been stricken by it seventeen years earlier, so first I write that Vicky was "bright" and "witty" and only after that let readers know she was dying of cancer.

Other Voices

Only one other voice in this vignette besides mine, but it is an important one. The county administrator's stance is the major tension in the sketch. I want to punch it. Relating or telling or summarizing his words won't do. I want the drama of what happened. I want readers to better imagine his unyielding presence, understand that the issue was black and white in his mind, and, above all, I want readers to hear and see his ultimatum, "Either delete . . . or we won't print."

Inflection Through Placement

I'm careful where I place words so that emphasis and meaning fall where I want them. I don't write, "Mr. Bruck rescued our publication by working nights and one weekend." I want to emphasize Mr. Bruck's stout deed for fifty-two adolescent writers and artists, so I tell when he worked and end the sentence with "rescued our publication." That's the payoff. That's the act that foils the administrator. And when I let readers know that Vicky "was dying of cancer," I do so in the final four words of a sentence.

Rhythm

I'm attentive to the cadence of writing because I know that rhythm and controlled changes in rhythm appeal to readers. In the third paragraph I consolidate action in one sentence of parallel structure with verbs and verb phrases. I like the assertiveness of *refused, gathered*, and *walked*. When the administrator speaks, notice that I concern myself with rhythm there, too. I place the dialog tag—*he said*—amid the quotation, not at the end. I want to end the sentence with important information, not the utilitarian *he said*. But I also like how the dialog tag within the quotation creates a rhythm that rises, pauses at its apex (creating a tad of tension), then descends to the administrator's threat. With *he said* at the end,

I would lose balance in the sentence and also miss the opportunity to end it with the administrator's threatening words.

Surprise

I love delightful surprise in writing and in life. Surprise is especially satisfying when it is meaningful and the writing builds toward it. Look what happens in the vignette: the county administrator has been foiled. The magazine has been printed. I've written about the experience and been published. One triumph after another. Then the last line of the vignette reveals how my superintendent viewed my *English Journal* publication: "The meeting featured considerable browbeating and was not about the deathless quality of my prose." I try to find language and imagery that communicate unmistakable meaning. When I prepare readers with significant detail, I trust them to understand the unsaid. I tell readers what my meeting was not about, and because of everything that's come before, they will know what it was about. I can understate an ending. Instead of a raucous exclamation point, I can use a quiet period. I can be implicitly emphatic.

Diction

I emphasize meaning—add inflection—by choosing the right word. Despite my bias against adverbs, *feverishly* is precisely the word to communicate Vicky's fitful dozing. *Summoned* is perfect for how the superintendent requested my presence. And in that final sentence, *deathless* contrasts beautifully with *browbeating*. Browbeating is base and thuggish; deathless is triumphant and eternal. Often I get the right word when I'm drafting. But just as often, I don't. Without revision, *deathless* doesn't come. The word did not volunteer itself in the gush of drafting. *Deathless* was earned as my playful, ironic sensibility interacted with language and meaning during my second and third looks at the writing.

Punctuated Voice

Punctuation is my friend. Punctuation helps me communicate. Periods stop my sentences and keep them in control. Commas separate independent clauses in compound sentences that might get confusing without them. Commas let readers know when someone is being addressed by name so they don't encounter an alarming sentence such as "I ate Grandma." Commas keep appositives and asides separate from the body of a sentence, let readers take a breath after long introductory language, and keep items in a series from jamming into each other. Semicolons enable me to put two sentences together that are closely related (though I must admit that I have taken of late to splicing short, related sentences together with a comma). Exclamation points help me show shouting and/or excitement (I'm spare with these, though, and rarely use them outside of dialog). Dashes—*two* hyphens, not one, in typed papers—can serve as commas in appositional phrases and can also direct readers' attention forward to another sentence or a list of items. And sometimes I like to use a colon to make readers come to a full stop and direct their attention to a list or a word or an idea.

When I taught Super 8 filmmaking to high school students years ago, I told them that depth of field was their friend. Depth of field is the area in front of the camera that is in focus. The major technical problem in students' films was blurry images. Depth of field varied with the speed of the film and the distance of the lens setting. If students paid attention to both, they could use depth of field to their advantage. Same with punctuation marks in writing. They are not something to get right or wrong. Punctuation is to help writers communicate. Punctuation can enhance authentic voice.

There's one punctuation mark I have an uneasy relationship with: the question mark. I often forget to place it at the end of a sentence, even though it is clear that the sentence is a question. And maybe that is why I forget to use it. Still, I'm usually a man of convention and use question marks in my writing most of the time.

Have students analyze their writing voices. The act will heighten their sensitivity to language. They'll begin to think about how they think. They'll begin to question why they do what they do in writing.

the teacher
Why do I forget question marks.
I am notorious for it.
My students scoff at me.
"How can you teach English when
you don't punctuate proper?"
I don't teach you anyway, I think,
just lead you like a scout master
and hope you'll dip your hand
into the brook—cold like no
tap water you've ever felt,
let you marvel, a little frightened,
at a snake, mouth agape,
before it darts between rocks,
an image you'll carry for years,
spur you to anger when I won't
stop to let you rest,
even hope you catch poison ivy,
and, as we race up the hill,

urge you on when
you leave me behind,
gasping,
a seeming spear
wedged between my ribs.

Of the absent question mark, I say,
"An innocent, harmless error,"
And those of you who aren't smug
point out that I should
extend to you
the same courteous understanding.
I uncap my canteen,
drop to the grass, and,
before I take a long swig,
say, "Why not"

—*Tom Romano* (1982, 89)

43

A Small Work I Have to Do

Two English professors took vehement exception when they asked me what the most important thing was in a first-year college writing course and I answered voice. One professor was a technical writer. The other a grammarian. Both were competent writers, precise, exacting, logical. Both valued elegant expression. Both were deeply knowledgeable about language. And both thought that voice was one of the last things a writer developed.

I'm inclined to agree with them now. But I don't think that voice is something you finally turn to when you have everything else in writing under control. Voice is something you attend to all through your development as a writer. Voice is something I talk to writers about regardless of their ages: second graders gathered on the carpet, graduate students sitting around a seminar table. Putting yourself into your words helps make writing pleasurable to read and pleasurable to create. That's you there in the words, my friends. You are responsible for how you appear. Your words are part of your identity.

Several years ago my wife noticed that one month she received no statement from the bank where we had established a home equity line of credit. When she called the bank, an employee in the lending department told Kathy that there had probably been a mix-up with an account number close to ours. Twenty minutes later the employee called back and told Kathy—with a pronounced degree of righteousness—that the reason we had not received a statement was because our address had been changed by a letter written by Thomas Romano.

"I can tell you," said Kathy, "my husband wrote no such letter, and once more, he never signs his name *Thomas*."

The employee begged to differ. In her hand, she said, she held the letter Thomas wrote that had been faxed to her.

"Then you fax it to us," said Kathy.

The text of the letter read,

REQUEST FOR CHANGE OF ADDRESS

This is to inform you of my address change. I would appreciate it, if all necessary document can be send to my new address.

Thanks for yours co-operation.

Sincerly yours

Thomas S. Romano

The author had my social security number, my bank account number, my date of birth, and my present address.We called the bank and told them that the letter was fraudulent, that we had not changed our address in the last five years. We were surprised to learn that the burden was on us to prove we had not moved. The faxed change-of-address letter apparently carried a lot of weight. We were told to write a letter verifying that we hadn't changed address and to—can you guess?—fax it to the bank. We did immediately.

The next day the bank released $18,600 to the identity thief based upon another faxed letter:

Dear sir/ma

I will like a wire transfer to be made from my account no XXXX-XXXX-XXXX-XXXX to the following account:

Name of beneficiary : XXXX

Account number: XXXX

Routing nuber: XXXX

Name of the bank: XXXX

Address of the bank: XXXX

Amount: $ 18,600.00

My social security number is XXX-XX-XXXX and my date of birth is XX/XX/XXXX

Your urgent response will be highly appreciated.

Yours sincerely

Three days after that, the bank released another sum of money to yet another beneficiary with another account number. This letter began the same way, asked for $19,200.00, and ended with this sentence: "This is needed for a small work i have to do in Hollywood, California and your urgent response will be highly apprecited."

We lost no money. The bank was the loser, and its loss was attributable to slipshod lending practices and maybe a bit of arrogance.

I was fascinated by the role of voice in the fiasco. This was a big bank in a large city that had solicited our business. The bank employees in the lending department didn't know me from Adam. They were processing paper, punching keys, emptying "in" trays and filling "out" trays. I had no identity to them beyond the numbers pertinent to my line of credit. In the small town where I live, though, where I am known to the credit union employees, I wonder if the voice of the letters coming over the fax machine—even with their minimal text—would have red-flagged the requests for address change and loans, would have prompted phone calls before the release of $37,800.00.

I confess: the spelling errors could very well have been mine, but what about the voice of the letter writer? "[A]ll necessary document can be send to my new address"? "This is needed for a small work i have to do"? "Thanks for yours co-operation"? Is that the voice of a writing teacher, a college professor?

Uh-uh. Not Tom. Not me.

I've worked hard over the years to forge an identity in my writing. It's the small work I have spent my life doing, and although I'm Tom, not Thomas, the *I* is always capitalized.

44

Utmost Essence

As a writer, I'm a work in progress.

JENNIFER HERDEMAN, College Junior

When I was sixteen years old, I liked wearing a rhetorical three-piece suit. My teacher complimented such garb. As she taught me to write essays, she encouraged me to wear a tie with a proper Windsor knot, twirl a gold-handled cane, and carry a pocket watch and fob. I recently found a high school essay of mine, one I'd toiled over, revising and polishing until I got the words the way I wanted them. The essay was resplendent with usage errors, misspelled words, grammatical blunders, an unintentional sentence fragment, and a voice I cultivated earnestly. Here is how I dressed as a high school junior:

> In *The Scarlet Letter* Hawthorne used many symbolisms. The symbolism of the utmost essence, aside from the letter itself, is probably Pearl. This devilish little imp is the immediate product of sin, and her character corresponds to it very well. As she does represent sin, she stands as a constant reminder to Hester. Throughout the book she is forever at the childs mercy. If not by Pearl's very actions, then by the cutting words emitted by her sharp little tongue.
>
> She also takes advantage of every chance to show her defiance to Hester's authority. The only time the child shows any love or affection toward her mother is when she wants something or when her wild curiosity persists her in the pursuit to acquire a bit of knowledge.
>
> Pearl's soul is not burdened by the inscrutable letter as her mothers is. Therefor she flits around in her birdlike manner laughing and smiling gaily. Pearl is the symbol of a lilt and carefree spirit in contrast to her mother's somber and entombed repose.

It's no wonder that in college I got a C in first-year composition but an A on a paper in which I was charged to emulate the style of Henry James. The abundant surface errors in the essay are a good reminder to me—I who became an English teacher, earned a Ph.D., and write for publication. The reminder is to be patient with my students and not become disdainful of their lack of skills as I help them learn the conventions of writing. I'm pretty sure that "devilish little imp," "immediate product of sin," and "inscrutable letter" came from the teacher's lectures and the novel itself. But "her mother's somber and entombed repose" and "persists her in the pursuit"? That's me. That's sixteen-year-old Tom emulating the voices of nineteenth century writers and drunk to the gills with language.

In Barbara Kingsolver's *High Tide in Tucson* (1995), she describes an indelible moment with her young daughter:

> When a camera takes aim at my daughter, I reach out and scrape the peanut butter off her chin. "I can't help it," I tell her, "it's one of those mother things." It's more than that. It's human, to want the world to see us as we think we ought to be seen. (36)

The moment in front of the camera is a metaphor for me. I am mother; my writing is daughter. Scraping peanut butter off the chin means more to me than correcting surface errors. I want the world to see me in a certain way through my writing. I felt this way at sixteen, too. Correct all the grammar and usage errors of my Hawthorne essay and you still are left with an adolescent boy who wants himself seen a certain way.

My teacher worked hard and had us writing plenty, more than most teachers did, I believe, in the mid-1960s. She wanted us to expand our vocabularies, break away from teenage slang, and learn to enter educated discourse communities in college. I have a dozen papers similar to that one about the "symbolisms" in *The Scarlet Letter*. You sometimes hear professional writers talking about the writing they produced as adolescents. They assure listeners that they no longer write such drivel. "Mercifully," you might hear them put it, "my sophomoric gushing was destroyed long ago."

Shame on them.

I cherish my youthful writing. I cherish the me I was and the me I was trying to become. This writing business is ultimately about writing that works for an audience. But for anyone learning to write and for the teachers guiding them, writing is about growth and development, evolution and change. Don't forget that.

One of my students wrote these wise words:

> Authentic voices in writing are our best attempts at creating the voice we think will let the world see us as we want to be seen. We want to appear more

clever, humorous, intelligent, witty, insightful, and talented than we really are. But at the same time, in creating this voice, we in effect become more clever, humorous, intelligent, witty, insightful, and talented than we really are. I believe that people can really grow through thoughtful and reflective writing. I also think that writing can help people to learn things about themselves they might not have otherwise thought to question or explore. In this way, writing and creating "authentic voice" is a form of self-discovery.

Laura Strandberg, College Junior

One of the great things about writing is that by doing it, we can construct a persona. We can craft an authentic voice. There is so much in our lives we cannot control. We can, however, control our writing. The usual thinking is that who we are makes for our authentic voice. We want students' personalities to emerge in their writing. But I think it works the other way, too. In our writing we can forge a personality. When we tinker with words, when we shift, cut, change, and arrange them, when we appeal to readers' senses, place words and ideas strategically, invent strong beginnings and resonating endings, when we attend to the rhythm and music of language, it isn't the writing only that we craft. We craft an identity, one that no one can steal. When our verbs and diction change, so does our thinking—it stretches and deepens. Over the years, writing has enabled me to become. The me I create on the page has evolved considerably since I began writing in seventh grade. That written persona has in turn shaped the living, breathing me.

I want students to sound their barbaric yawps, and I want to make sure I silence no students' songs, even inadvertently. But I want students to craft their songs, too, to shape the authentic voice of the singer who sings them. Students have intellect and heart; I want them to bring that intellect and heart to bear on language. I'll show students how I do this, how *they* might do this, how they might knock readers on the seat of their pants or make them melt with sympathy and understanding. I'll coax and encourage, nudge and push, cajole and require students to work with their words beyond first spontaneous gush, shaping their language, surprising themselves with further thinking. What's at stake, I believe, is their very identity.

Works Cited

Ackerman, Diane. 1990. A *Natural History of the Senses*. New York: Vintage Books.

Bowden, Darsie. 1999. *The Mythology of Voice*. Portsmouth, NH: Boynton/Cook.

Bradbury, Ray. 1966. "How to Keep and Feed a Muse." In *On Writing by Writers*, edited by William W. West, 39–47. Boston: Ginn and Co.

Brewer, Ken. 2003. *Sum of Accidents: New and Selected Poems*. Salt Lake City: City Art Books.

Britton, James. 1970. *Language and Learning*. Harmondsworth, Middlesex, England: Penguin Books.

Burroway, Janet. 1992. *Writing Fiction: A Guide to Narrative Craft*. 3d ed. New York: HarperCollins.

Cameron, Julia. 1998. *The Right to Write*. New York: Jeremy P. Tarcher/Putnam.

Cisneros, Sandra. 1991. *The House on Mango Street*. New York: Vintage Books.

Codell, Esmé Raji. 1999. *Educating Esmé: Diary of a Teacher's First Year*. Chapel Hill, NC: Algonquin Books.

De Palma, Brian, dir. 1986. *The Untouchables*. Paramount Pictures.

Dickinson, Emily. 1890. *The Complete Poems of Emily Dickinson*, edited by Thomas H. Johnson, 710. Boston: Little, Brown and Company.

Dubus, Andre. 1991. *Broken Vessels: Essays by Andre Dubus*. Boston: David R. Godine.

Dunning, Stephen, and William Stafford. 1992. *Getting the Knack: 20 Poetry Writing Exercises*. Urbana, IL: National Council of Teachers of English.

Elbow, Peter. 1973. *Writing Without Teachers*. New York: Oxford University Press.

———. 1981. *Writing with Power: Techniques for Mastering the Writing Process*. New York: Oxford University Press.

———. 2003. "Three Mysteries at the Heart of Writing." In *Composition Studies in the New Millenium: Rereading the Past, Rewriting the Future*, edited by Lynn Bloom, Don Daiker, and Edward White, 10–27. Carbondale, IL: Southern Illinois University Press.

Erardi, John. 1996. "Woodward vs. Withrow." *The Cincinnati Enquirer*, 10 February. final edition/East: A1 and A6.

Fletcher, Ralph. 1993. *What a Writer Needs*. Portsmouth, NH: Heinemann.

Fowler, Frances C. 2000. *Policy Studies for Educational Leaders: An Introduction*. Upper Saddle River, NJ: Merrill/Prentice Hall.

Fowler, Joy. 2001. *Redheaded Angel*. Unpublished.

Gaughan, John. 2001. *Reinventing English: Teaching in the Contact Zone*. Portsmouth, NH: Boynton/Cook.

Gibson, Walker. 1969. *Persona: A Style Study for Readers and Writers*. New York: Random House.

Gildner, Gary. 1984. *Blue Like the Heavens: New and Selected Poems*. Pittsburgh: University of Pittsburgh Press.

Gopnik, Adam. 2000. "Essay: The Voice of Small-Town America." Sunday *New York Times* Review of Books. *New York Times*, 3 December: 44 and 46.

Graves, Donald. 1983. *Writing: Teachers and Children at Work*. Portsmouth, NH: Heinemann.

Hoffman, Gary. 1986. *Writeful*. Huntington Beach, CA: Verve Press.

Huddle, David. 1991. *The Writing Habit: Essays*. Salt Lake City: Peregrine Smith Books.

Jago, Carol. 2000. *With Rigor for All: Teaching the Classics to Contemporary Students*. Portsmouth, NH: Boynton/Cook.

Jimenez, Francisco. 1997. *The Circuit: Stories from the Life of a Migrant Child*. Albuquerque: University of New Mexico Press.

Kesey, Ken. 1962. *One Flew Over the Cuckoo's Nest*. New York: Viking Press.

Kingsolver, Barbara. 1995. *High Tide in Tucson*. New York: HarperCollins.

———. 2002. *Small Wonder*. New York: HarperCollins.

Knoblauch, C. H., and Lil Brannon. 1984. *Rhetorical Traditions and the Teaching of Writing*. Upper Montclair, NJ: Boynton/Cook.

Lamott, Anne. 1994. *Bird by Bird: Some Instructions on Writing and Life*. New York: Pantheon Books.

Macrorie, Ken. 1976. *Writing to Be Read*. Rev. 2d ed. Rochelle Park, NJ: Hayden Book Company.

———. 1984. *Writing to Be Read*. Rev. 3d ed. Upper Montclair, NJ: Boynton/Cook.

Melville, Herman. [1851] 1964. *Moby Dick*. New York: Holt, Rinehart and Winston.

Michaels, Judith Rowe. 2001. *Dancing with Words: Helping Students Love Language Through Authentic Vocabulary Instruction*. Urbana, IL: National Council of Teachers of English.

Moffett, James. 1983. "On Essaying." In *Fforum: Essays on Theory and Practice in the Teaching of Writing,* edited by Patricia L. Stock, 170–73. Upper Montclair, NJ: Boynton/Cook.

Morales, Aurora Levins, and Rosario Morales. 1986. *Getting Home Alive*. Ithaca, NY: Firebrand Books.

Moyers, Bill. 1999. *Fooling with Words: A Celebration of Poets and Their Craft*. New York: William Morrow and Co.

Mrozowski, Jennifer. 2002. "Students Bypass Original Language." *Cincinnati Enquirer,* 30 November: B1–B2.

Murray, Donald M. 1982. *Learning by Teaching: Selected Articles on Writing and Teaching*. Portsmouth, NH: Boynton/Cook.

———. 1998. *The Craft of Revision*. 3d ed. New York: Harcourt Brace College Publishers.

———. 1990. *Shoptalk: Learning to Write with Writers*. Portsmouth, NH: Boynton/Cook.

———. 2002. "One Writer's Notes on Voice." Email communication with author.

Nasdijj. 2000. *The Blood Runs Like a River Through My Dreams*. Boston: Houghton Mifflin Co.

Nathan, Ruth, et al. 1988. *Classroom Strategies That Work: An Elementary Teacher's Guide to Process Writing*. Portsmouth, NH: Heinemann.

Oliver, Mary. 1995. *Blue Pastures*. New York: Harcourt Brace.

Payne, Lucile Vaughan. 1970. *The Lively Art of Writing*. Rev. ed. Chicago: Follett Educational Corp.

Pirie, Bruce. 1997. *Reshaping High School English*. Urbana, IL: National Council of Teachers of English.

Pollan, Michael. 2001. *The Botany of Desire: A Plant's-Eye View of the World*. New York: Random House.

Probst, Robert. 1991. "Five Kinds of Literary Knowing." In *Literature Instruction: A Focus on Student Response*, edited by Judith Langer, 54–77. Urbana, IL: National Council of Teachers of English.

Ray, Katie Wood. 1999. *Wondrous Words: Writers and Writing in the Elementary Classroom*. Urbana, IL: National Council of Teachers of English.

Robinson, Edward G., with Leonard Spigelgass. 1973. *All My Yesterdays: An Autobiography*. New York: Hawthorn Books.

Romagnoli, Margaret, and G. Franco Romagnoli. 1974. *The Romagnolis' Table*. Boston: Little, Brown and Co.

Romano, Tom. 1982. "The Teacher." *English Journal* 71 (3): 89.

———. 1987. *Clearing the Way: Working with Teenage Writers*. Portsmouth, NH: Heinemann.

———. 1990. "The Day School Gives Out." *English Journal* 79 (Nov.): 90.

———. 1995. *Writing with Passion: Life Stories, Multiple Genres*. Portsmouth, NH: Boynton/Cook.

———. 1998. "Relationships with Literature." *English Education* 30 (1): 5–18.

———. 2003. "The Danger of Countenance." *English Journal* 92 (July): 26–30.

Rose, Mike. 1989. *Lives on the Boundary: The Struggles and Achievements of America's Underprepared*. New York: Free Press.

Rosenbaum, Ron. 1996. "In Praise of Dangerous Women." *Esquire* 125 (3): 102–11.

Salinger, J. D. 1964. *The Catcher in the Rye*. New York: Bantam Books. (Originally published by Little, Brown, and Co., 1951.)

Sanborn, Jean Donovan. 1994. "The Essay Dies in the Academy, Circa 1900." In *Pedagogy in the Age of Politics: Writing and Reading (in) the Academy*, edited by Patricia Sullivan and Donna J. Qualley, 121–138. Urbana, IL: National Council of Teachers of English.

Sanders, Scott Russell. 1999. *The Country of Language*. Minneapolis: Milkweed Editions.

Schuster, Edgar. 2003. *Breaking the Rules: Liberating Writers Through Innovative Grammar Instruction*. Portsmouth, NH: Heinemann.

Smith, Jeff. 1993. *The Frugal Gourmet Cooks Italian*. New York: William Morrow and Co.

Sommers, Nancy. 1993. "I Stand Here Writing." *College English* 55 (4): 420–28.

Stafford, William. 1986. *You Must Revise Your Life*. Ann Arbor, MI: University of Michigan Press.

———. 1998. *Crossing Unmarked Snow; Further Views on the Writer's Vocation*. Ann Arbor, MI: University of Michigan Press.

Strong, William. 2001. *Coaching Writing: The Power of Guided Practice*. Portsmouth, NH: Boynton/Cook.

Twain, Mark. [1884] 2001. *Adventures of Huckleberry Finn*. Illustrated by E. W. Kemble and John Harley. Los Angeles: University of California Press.

Vonnegut, Kurt. 1970. *Welcome to the Monkey House*. New York: Dell Publishing Co.

Wallace, Robert. 1982. *Writing Poems*. Boston: Little, Brown, and Co.

Weathers, Winston. 1980. *An Alternate Style: Options in Composition*. Rochelle Park, NJ: Hayden Book Co. Distributed by Heinemann, Portsmouth, NH. OP

Whitman, Walt. [1855] 1981. *Leaves of Grass*. Franklin Center, PA: Franklin Library.

Williams, William Carlos. [1938] 1951. *The Collected Earlier Poems of William Carlos Williams*. Norfolk, CT: New Directions Books.

Wolfe, Tom. 1968. *The Electric Kool-Aid Acid Test*. New York: Bantam.

Yolen, Jane. 1988. *The Devil's Arithmetic*. New York: Puffin Books.

Zinsser, William. 1998. *On Writing Well: The Classic Guide to Writing Nonfiction*. 6th ed.—rev. and updated. New York: HarperPerennial.

Acknowledgments

Twenty years after I took his classes at Miami University, Milton White told me I was one of the most "loyal" of his former students. I tried to be. Milton's writing and teaching have had a lasting impact on my life. Whatever I am, I am composed of much, made of many. I will try here to be loyal in my gratitude to those who've had a hand in making *Crafting Authentic Voice*.

For thirty-three years now I've been sustained in this profession by the writing of my students. That used to be fifteen- to eighteen-year-olds. Now, most of my students are about twenty and studying to become integrated language arts teachers, as Ohio is calling English teachers now. I also teach a great many teachers each year who are seeking further professional development. The writing of these undergraduates and teachers has taught me things I didn't know. They have surprised me with candor and insight. They have entertained me with absorbing stories. They have made me laugh.

Over the years, I have saved interesting writing from students—poems, stories, essays, multigenre papers, notes. The first day of a class, I ask students to write on a three-by-five-inch card the name, address, and phone number of someone who loves them and is likely to stay put. One day I might find myself calling that loved one's number in an effort to track down a student who has moved on, maybe even changed her name. My thanks to those parents, relatives, and friends who have led me to the loved ones who once wrote in my class. Sometimes when I've sought to contact a former student twenty years have passed, sometimes just a few months. The former student might be teaching English somewhere, but just as likely might be doing something else, like teaching sign language and raising four children or defending indicted sailors as a navy lieutenant.

Here are some other folks who helped me hunt down students for permission to publish their work. Indispensable were they all: Nikki Fuson, Mindy Ganz, Marcia Brown, Retta Hurlbert, Sarah Rockwell, Heather Smith, Aimee Bendel, Linda Cunningham, Lynda Hamblin, Bill Strong, Anne Shifrer, Karen Denzler, and at Miami University's Alumni Addresses Office, Cindy Keller and Paula Ayers. I especially thank the dogged efforts of Stephanie Musselman Huff, who knows how to leave it alone and let it heal.

I've also been sustained in teaching by writing: journal entries, articles, letters, poems, stories, sketches, quick-writes in class, books. All that creation with words has given me great pleasure. The writing often enabled me to solidify a memory of teaching and learning. I've had many teachers who kept me writing: Helen Romano (no relation) at Malvern High School in the mid-1960s, Larry Rockefeller, who taught me freshman English and American literature at Miami when he was a graduate student (the first teacher who rewarded me for taking a risk), the late David Frazier at Miami University, who directed me to Hemingway's stories and opened my writing world.

It is impossible to overestimate the influence of Milton White on my writing and teaching. At Miami University from 1968 to 1971 I elected Milton's writing courses four times. I couldn't get enough. Milton understood growth and development in the most unlikely writing students. Milton taught, Milton inspired, Milton took students' writing and showed it to editors. I learned to write better in his classes; I also learned to teach by watching him. See if you can find Milton White's novels in libraries: *A Yale Man*; *Cry Down the Lonely Night*; and *Listen, the Red-Eyed Vireo*. You'll enjoy these gentle, poignant fictions and see a real artisan with language at work.

I wrote up a storm, too, in classes with Don Murray and Don Graves at the University of New Hampshire, two stalwarts in my life. What an experience it was to learn with them, and then to maintain friendship with them over the years. Who'd 'a believed?

Places are crucial. They shape us and shelter us. All hail to these writing places: Starbucks on Dempster in Evanston, Illinois; the apartment at Whitmyre Hall on the campus of Indiana University of Pennsylvania (11/01–2/02); the Twin Palms Hotel, Tempe, Arizona (2/28/03); the Caffe Ibis in Logan, Utah; the dining room table of Bill and Carol Strong; seat 30D on Delta Flight 510 from Salt Lake City to Cincinnati (10/22/02); my second-floor home office overlooking West Bull Run in Oxford, where summer heat and humidity turned to colored leaves, then blowing snow in the worst winter we'd had in years (and I got to use my snowblower eight times), where brown-bellied squirrels gnawed walnuts and where deer crossed the lawn into the trees; and, maybe the most gratifying place, the Olympic-sized swimming pool at Miami University's Recreation Center, where ideas got expanded, decisions got made, reasoning got sounder, and chapters got shuffled—all this unbidden amid the rhythm of stroke, kick, and breath.

I thank Linda Rief and Maureen Barbieri. As editors of *Voices from the Middle,* they invited me to write an article for the Spring 1996 issue. "An article about what?" I asked. "Anything," they said, "just so we have it in two weeks."

And that open invitation got me thinking about Vicki Scott the previous summer at UNH. Vicki gave me a wonderful raspberry seed that made me squirm and fret when she remarked upon the authentic voice of *Writing with Passion* (1995). The raspberry seed wouldn't dislodge for months, so I knew precisely what the lead would be to the article.

I thank Bill Varner, now with Stenhouse Publishers, but my editor at Heinemann for *Blending Genre, Altering Style* (2000). When that book was in production, I began to talk with Bill about writing a book about voice. "No one better to do it," said Bill. I don't know about that, Bill, but it sure helped to tell me. You are a friend to writers.

I thank Miami University for granting me a yearlong faculty improvement leave to write. Particularly I thank my department chair, Jim Shiveley; my dean, Barbara Schirmer; and Miami's provost, Ronald Crutcher. Lisa Portwood, Kristy Adams, and Linda Dennett are crack secretaries in the Department of Teacher Education and ever helpful to me. Peter Pedroni, professor of Italian, provided timely information and Emily Pate, my graduate assistant, completed much appreciated research and clerical work.

I thank readers who granted me their intellects and points of view. Sometimes they read bits and pieces of the manuscript; sometimes they read the whole thing: John Gaughan, Bill Strong, Lisa Luedeke, Anne Wood, Brittany Ballard, and Chad Pergram.

I thank Tom Newkirk of the University of New Hampshire and Tim Donovan of Northeastern University, who invite me to teach in the summer at Durham and Martha's Vineyard. In those places, I've enjoyed friendship and professional stimulation—also great seafood.

The good people at Heinemann, my publisher since 1987, have my loyalty and gratitude: Editorial Director, Leigh Peake, publishing wizard who knows just when a drink is in order; production editor, Lynne Reed, copy editor, Elizabeth Tripp, and cover designer, Judy Arisman. My biggest thanks go to Lisa Luedeke, my editor on this project. Lisa has brains, taste, and presence, and skillfully mixes a palatable cocktail of praise, response, and push.

Lastly, I thank two women who keep me on my toes and make this life all the sweeter: Mariana Romano, who teaches at Evanston Township High School in Illinois. Mariana engages me in conversation about teaching and reading and writing. Recently, she demonstrated how to make risotto with calamari so the rice is creamy. I've cooked it right ever since. The second woman is Kathy Romano, my spouse, lover, and friend since 1970 and a registered nurse par excellence. If you came into the ER at McCullough-Hyde Hospital in Oxford, Ohio, you'd feel safe and comforted with Kathy tending your hurts. It's amazing how much savvy, efficiency, and diagnostic skill is packed into such a little woman. Kathy is also adept at spoiling our schnauzers—Minnie Mae and Murray. She is a breast cancer warrior and a hot-flash expert. She can arrange just about anything; I'm glad she arranged to love me.